I WANT
MAGIC

http://ulpress.org
University of Louisiana at Lafayette Press
P.O. Box 43558
Lafayette, LA 70504-3558

Printed on acid-free paper in the United States
Library of Congress Cataloging-in-Publication Data

Names: Cannon, C. W. (Charles W.), author.
Title: I want magic : essays on New Orleans, the South, and race / C.W.
 Cannon.
Other titles: Essays on New Orleans, the South, and race
Description: Lafayette, LA : University of Louisiana at Lafayette Press,
 2022. | Includes bibliographical references.
Identifiers: LCCN 2022002091 | ISBN 9781946160867 (paper)
Subjects: LCSH: New Orleans (La.)--Social life and customs. |
 Exceptionalism--Louisiana--New Orleans. | New Orleans (La.)--Social
 conditions. | New Orleans (La.)--Race relations. | New Orleans (La.)--In
 popular culture.
Classification: LCC F379.N55 C26 2022 | DDC 976.3/35--dc23/
eng/20220207
LC record available at https://lccn.loc.gov/2022002091

I WANT MAGIC

Essays on New Orleans, the South, and Race

C.W. Cannon

Foreword by Jed Horne

2022
UNIVERSITY OF LOUISIANA AT LAFAYETTE PRESS

Also by C.W. Cannon

Soul Resin

Katrina Means Cleansing

French Quarter Beautification Project

Sleepytime Down South

TABLE OF CONTENTS

PART I

NEW ORLEANS FROM A NATIVE PERSPECTIVE

PART II

AMERICANISM VS. EXCEPTIONALISM

PART III
NEW ORLEANS AND RACE

FOREWORD

BY JED HORNE

The photographer Ansel Adams called it Zone Five, that point of perfect visual balance. For Adams it lay midway between pure black and pure white. For C.W. Cannon it's the midpoint between his abiding love for his hometown and his richly entertaining skill at excoriating all that's wrong with New Orleans and those who would save us from ourselves.

There's a second dialectic in play in these essays: Cannon is pulled in different directions by his bemused delight in fancy-pants academic lingo and the vernacular in which we more typically speak, laugh, curse, and carry on.

As the opinion-page editor at a post-Katrina news website called *The Lens*, it was my privilege and great pleasure to occasionally arm-wrestle with C.W. over precisely where Zone Five lay in any particular essay.

He clearly is unashamed of his facility with the fancy language of academia, where he earns his keep. He relishes—and so do I—his ability to both exploit its useful precision and sometimes mock its pretentiousness.

It's the full-spectrum range of C.W.'s language and the topics he chooses that makes him great fun to read. He mixes insights out of sociology, history, and literature with turns of phrase that rise up off the streets, like jazz from a second line parade passing through a Creole neighborhood.

In any given moment, his framework of reference may include the Marxist French philosopher Pierre Bourdieu and the likes of Chicken Man, the Voodou practitioner who for many years sold talismans, potions, and fetishes from a tiny storefront in the French Quarter. And while he's at it, you're going to see ideas as fresh as this morning's beignets placed in the context of the city's great writers and thinkers.

He chats with nineteenth-century authors—George Washington Cable, Lafcadio Hearn, Grace King—as though he were sitting with them on stools in a bar; and look who just walked in to join the conversation: William Burroughs and Jack Kerouac and other more recent fans of the city. He'll pull non-New Orleanians like Norman Mailer and Henry David Thoreau into the mix. Or that ridiculous journalist from Cleveland who told the world that there were aspects of Carnival that could be considered racist and classist. (Who knew!?)

But whether he's defending the city against the ignorance of outsiders or savaging resident wannabes trying to go "super-native," what always comes through is C.W.'s affection for his hometown, his sense that it's a special place under constant threat.

He was reared in the downriver district where he lives to this day, the Marigny, walked to grade school at McDonogh 15 in the French Quarter, made groceries with his mother at Schwegmann's, before the original store, at St. Claude and Elysian Fields, got bought out and went upscale.

Cannon sees the topics of current discourse and dispute from every side. But just when you think he might be reaching out his arms to embrace you and your own routinely liberal or conservative point of view, he lets out a devilish laugh and rips the rug out from under you. Lefties will relish his evisceration of Lost Causists and outright racists on the right. Just as surely, the right wing will snort along in happy derision at the quick work Cannon makes of the kale-munching trendies now driving up prices for real estate (as well as kale) in "rediscovered" urban neighborhoods. Best not laugh too loud, boys and girls, because C.W.'s blade cuts both ways and he's coming after you next.

Like the city itself, a town where Black Mardi Gras krewes parade in blackface alongside white revelers wearing grass skirts and leopard-skin Zulu vests, Cannon is more likely to scorn political correctness than yield politely to its dictates. That said, he is as relentless in his disgust with bigotry and its lingering toxicity as he is disdainful of the armchair critics of New Orleans— usually but not always outsiders—who aren't alert enough to acknowledge the progress the city has made in overcoming the uglier aspects of the South's traditional social compact.

In reading through Cannon's essays, you become aware of twined themes—a recurring bipolarity. He casts the culture—and fate—of New Orleans as an endless tug-of-war between the "exceptionalists" and the "Americanists."

The exceptionalists—and Cannon is more or less one of them—savor and value all that is quirky and venerable and often infuriating in New Orleans way of doing things (well or badly).

The Americanists heave sighs of exasperation over the folkways of the city they profess to love, the city they would like to give over more completely to the bland pleasures of consumerism and the easy profitability that comes when chain stores take over the retail sector. It means the death of the economy that once put a mom-and-pop store on every street corner and dispensed po' boys and locally roasted coffee instead of Starbucks and Big

Macs. It's the corporate juggernaut that makes virtually every other city in America peas in a pod.

In the bars and clubs where the city comes alive at night, the dichotomy pits the old-time hipsters against the Johnny-come-latelies. It pits the actual residents of a very public city—a city of working-class rituals and street celebration, of parades and pick-up brass bands—against tourism interests unable to comprehend that the Disneyfication of New Orleans has a way of hugging to death the very traditions the travel brochures ballyhoo and the tour buses pause to gawk at.

Among Americanists are the chamber of commerce types who in the 1960s advocated—incredibly!—for running an elevated expressway across the French Quarter in the mistaken belief that it would lubricate access to the faltering downtown department stores (whose destruction it hastened by facilitating even easier access to suburban shopping malls with acres of parking).

Among the Americanists, though they would loudly deny it, are the gentrifyers and "urban homesteaders" who have swept in from the suburbs or, since Katrina, from Boston or New York or Seattle, thinking that in Bywater they've found the next Greenwich Village. In a decade, they have made the old neighborhoods so trendy that they're too expensive to live in. The upshot: soaring taxes and the impulse to list the house on Airbnb to meet expenses— which only drives real estate prices and taxes higher. Now, hand them a hankie as these same folks shed a tear for the blue-collar whites, Blacks, and Latinos they have driven out—the very people who gave the area the "authentic" allure that drew the hipsters and the wannabes in the first place.

Among the exceptionalists, paradoxically, are those who have made a religion of the city's much-vaunted music scene, deploring the threat of "noise ordinances" without quite grasping why sleep-deprived neighborhood folk worry that Bourbon Street is going to spread all the way down St. Claude Avenue to the Industrial Canal.

Cannon slaloms deftly among these polar divisions in the city's culture, frequently coming to contrarian positions on issues where you might think you could predict his stance. He loves the eccentrics and eccentricities of his hometown while remaining vigilant against the tendency to fetishize a short list of the city's "exceptional" qualities: the public drinking, teenagers with tubas and washboards in Jackson Square, our tendency to blame a subtropic sun for our slothful embrace of life's slower rhythms here in the "Big Easy"—"the City that Care Forgot."

In the aggregate, these essays are a crash course in cutting-edge urbanology. They teach us how to think about the relationship between culture and class, between revival and gentrification, between progress and preservation, between the city's greatest asset—its Black culture, its music, and cuisine—and the appropriation and cultish valorization of that culture by whites competing to seem more comfortable with and knowledgeable about it than thou. In short, if the urban experience is of interest to you, Cannon teaches you how to think.

In one of these essays, he introduced me to a French word I hadn't thought about forever: *métissage*. It's that mix of infusions that both powers the ceaseless evolution of any living culture and guarantees that, with a little luck, what Cannon so loves about New Orleans will be here for a long time to come. Call it hybrid vigor. It's the midpoint between black and white. Call it Zone Five.

Jed Horne was for many years the city editor of the Times-Picayune *and a recipient, with others on his staff, of a Pulitzer Prize for coverage of Hurricane Katrina. In semi-retirement, he has written books about New Orleans and served as a founding editor of* The Lens.

INTRODUCTION

Almost fifteen years separate the regional disaster of Hurricane Katrina and the global disaster of COVID-19. While Katrina shone a spotlight on New Orleans that caused locals as well as distant onlookers to reassess their understanding of the place, COVID-19 underlines the ways in which New Orleans falls off the map of national consciousness in crises that affect the country, and world, as a whole. As of March 18, 2020, New Orleans was the second-most infected city per capita in the country, after Seattle. Its economic vulnerability ranked third in the United States, after Las Vegas and Orlando.[1] Yet, for whatever reason, it didn't rank anywhere near those numbers in national news coverage of the crisis. New Orleanians react in different ways to this routine marginalization in the broader national context. Some wish to be de-otherized and recognized as an average—and legitimate—American city, though not a very large one. Others embrace the liberating possibilities of the pervasive othering of New Orleans in the national imagination.

Features of my own particular New Orleans upbringing have placed me in the latter camp, as the essays in this collection undoubtedly make clear. I see the tension between celebrating our cultural distinctiveness and bemoaning our American illegitimacy as the tension between New Orleans exceptionalist and New Orleans Americanist ideologies. Many people, especially since Hurricane Katrina, have critiqued New Orleans exceptionalist ideology,[2] but my view is that most do so without factoring in the broader context of Americanist ideology or seeing how New Orleans exceptionalism can be a salutary counterweight to Americanist cultural hegemony. The tension between these ideological poles is explored in different ways, and applied to different events and issues, in many of the essays in this collection.

The New Orleans I grew up in was awash in New Orleans exceptionalist attitudes, though I would not recognize them as such until years later. From first to sixth grade, I attended an experimental public school in the French Quarter, McDonogh 15. My mom lived on Frenchmen Street by Washington Square and my dad lived further down, on Piety Street in Bywater. In the 1970s, these neighborhoods attracted artists and left-leaning intellectuals like my parents. Like them, many of our neighbors were southerners—Black and white—who found in New Orleans an oasis of political progressivism and personal freedom without having to leave the South. Many neighbors were gay, but there were also still large families (Black and white) with deep roots in the six–nine wards. The social, artistic, and intellectual milieu of the downtown riverfront neighborhoods in that time instilled me with a sense of neighborly responsibility, an openness to hedonism, an appreciation of social diversity and personal self-determination, and an abiding respect and admiration for art and artists. I believed in Nietzsche's aphorism decades before I first read it: "Behind a remarkable scholar one often finds a mediocre person, and often behind a mediocre artist—a very remarkable person."[3] I like how this aphorism pushes back against the capitalist puritanical definition of artist as one who produces and sells art, emphasizing instead that aesthetic consciousness can enable a meaningful life even if the artist's product is "mediocre." The point is that the aesthetic life has value in itself, quite apart from the quality, much less salability, of what the artist produces. I've always prized the way that New Orleans invites all, not just successful professionals, to embrace beauty, creativity, and sensual fulfillment in their daily lives. From childhood I remember fondly one such neighborly invitation to creative practice: the New Orleans Poetry Forum, founded in 1972 by local poet and longtime Bywater resident Lee Meitzen Grue. My father was a participant, and it was surely a great solace for him after Brennan's Restaurant fired him for trying to organize a union in 1973.

New Orleans came of age in the Romantic era, and remains in the sway of Romantic aesthetics—decadent, gothic, magical. There's a tendency among progressive intellectuals in the United States today to distrust the Romantic imagination, to dismiss its musings as nothing but mystification of material conditions. The impulse to reject myth and romance is at best Apollonian, at worst puritanical. The link between revolution and Romanticism was always clear on the European continent, at least in the era before historical materialism, and Caryn Cossé Bell has shown how French Romantic revolutionary thought and practice impacted Afro-Creole resistance in early American New Orleans, too.[4] Without doubt, George Washington Cable, and before him Ludwig von Reizenstein, put Romantic literary devices (magic, spectacle, sentimentality) to politically progressive purposes. The prototypical artist of Kate Chopin's *The Awakening*, Mlle. Reisz, defines the artist in definitively revolutionary-Romantic terms: "the artist must possess the courageous soul. . . . The brave soul. The soul that dares and defies."[5]

My elementary school, attended also by Lee Grue's children, nurtured artistic inclinations, progressive politics, and the sense of New Orleans as an exceptional place, perhaps in part because of the high number of families who had migrated to the city to embrace and preserve what they deemed to be its unique characteristics. I now know that every generation has witnessed its own influx of New Orleans exceptionalists and that their dreams of New Orleans have indeed shaped the city itself, as well as the dreams of future locals and Americans of what New Orleans should be and stand for. At McDonogh 15, the kids of bohemian migrants engaged and exchanged with the kids of local political actors in a way that challenged the common stereotype of apolitical bohemian artists.

Personally, I found art before politics, but the art led me to the politics. Like many a character in New Orleans literature before me, I've always strived to live an aesthetic life. *A Streetcar Named Desire*'s Blanche DuBois is punished for it, but probably her other character traits (and her lack of money) are what doom her. *The Awakening*'s Edna Pontellier strives for it, though her courage fails her. Tom Dent's Joe Brown is denied his inalienable right to dream because of his race, and thus is driven to the form of social suicide named by the play's title, *Ritual Murder*. Even Ignatius Reilly, of John Kennedy Toole's *A Confederacy of Dunces*, is more of an artist than an ideologue, since his philosophy is really a fantasy enabling him to seek his own "promesse du Bonheur," in the phrasing of Stendahl.[6] The figure of the dashing Byronic rebel railing against the herd animals of complacent middle-class America is what motivates Ignatius more than the particulars of the philosophy he wears as a badge of his deeply felt difference. Though it would pain him to hear the characterization, he is a hopeless Romantic.

I'm far from the first New Orleanian to stress elements of local difference as strengths rather than weaknesses. The tug-of-war between NOLA exceptionalist and Americanist attitudes is as old as the Louisiana Purchase, though of course the terrain of the debate has shifted often. I felt the NOLA exceptionalist impulse very early, shortly after leaving the city for the first time after high school, when exposure to other American communities caused aspects of New Orleanian difference to stand out in greater relief. My years of study have only deepened the impulse and provided tools for its articulation. In other words, I feel like my intellectual growth over the years hasn't changed my mind as much as it's offered me reasons for why I feel and think as I do. Just as Marx helped me understand and voice my visceral rage at the handful of jerks who lord it over the rest of us, as Nietzsche clarified for me my innate love of freedom, beauty, pleasure, and performance, so also a long list of New

Orleans writers has shaped the empowering myth of the city that I embrace in my imaginative life (which I continue to value more highly than a good American probably should).

My reading of a couple of centuries of New Orleans writers let me know, first and foremost, that the debate over New Orleanian difference, or otherness, is centuries old, and not a result of more recent developments like Katrina, or gentrification, or the rise of the tourist industry. On the other hand, each of these events and trends must, in New Orleans, enunciate arguments that frame the debate in the terms of New Orleans exceptionalist rhetoric. That's good news to me, principally because my faith in American exceptionalism is so thin, and I see New Orleans exceptionalism as a rare challenge to the gospel of American capitalist "progress." Architectural preservation laws, to pick just one example, place an aesthetic obstacle before the goal of maximum profit at the expense of all else. Older folks these days recall the "Second Battle of New Orleans," when French Quarter preservationists blocked plans to build a riverfront expressway through the Quarter in the 1960s. But that generation was building on a tradition to preserve the Quarter—as a monument to both beauty and difference—that was already firmly in place. Writers like Lyle Saxon worked to get laws passed protecting the aesthetic appearance of the Quarter in the 1920s. And back in 1895, a similar movement blocked the destruction of the Cabildo and Presbytère, icons of a distinct past. Today the tourist industry is thankful for the preservationist instincts of earlier times, but money was not the reason the first preservationists took their stand. They did it for beauty, and for what they saw as aesthetic difference from the rest of the country. The New Orleans Artists' Association, petitioning to save the Cabildo and Presbytère in 1895, "declared that it was (their) pleasure . . . to foster a love of the picturesque and artistic among the people of New Orleans, and . . . their duty to guard these precious monuments."[7]

I also continue to see healthful benefits in the prioritization of leisure, community, or spirituality over hard work and social striving. As these examples of alternative values suggest, New Orleans can serve as a "Latin" counterweight to the Anglo-Saxon puritan model of value that so often defines "American" values: rugged individualism, hard work, and capital accumulation as a sign of virtue.

It's necessary to put words like "American" and "Latin" in quotation marks because the relationship between commonly held perceptions and factual history is so tenuous. There is no permanently established and universal "American" value system or way of life. Duh. But Americanist rhetoric, testified to in a long list of utterances over the centuries (about the "American way," "American values," etc.) does privilege certain virtues over others. The same can be said for New Orleans (exceptionalist) values, and it is important for those of us who have the gut inclination in that direction to familiarize ourselves with that textual history. The notion of New Orleans as a "Latin" alternative to Anglo-Saxon American value systems begins with the dawn of New Orleans as an American city, when Creole New Orleanians, white and Black, strove to maintain an element of French ("Latin") culture in the face of Americanist assimilation. Some sought to enlist New Orleans in the cause of the international Pan-Latin movement's resistance to a perceived Anglo-Saxon and Teutonic world conquest.[8] Nineteenth-century journalist Lafcadio Hearn's role in promoting New Orleans as a "Latin" alternative to "Anglo-Saxon" America is also well-known.[9]

New Orleans gives us a great opportunity to study how value systems evolve over generations, and my own intellectual genealogy is a case in point. Before I was already a fully grown adult, I knew absolutely nothing about the debates over Anglo-Saxon vs. Latin values in the nineteenth century. Yet, somehow, I ended up with a value system celebrating beauty, leisure, spirituality, and community over hard work, capital accumulation, and social value attained through social mobility. What somehow happened in New Orleans was a gradual transfer of "Creole," "Latin" values from a hundred years ago to the bohemian communities of New Orleans's downtown riverfront wards, where they lay waiting for young, impressionable me to adopt.

Another common mythical trope of New Orleans is the city's vaunted "decadence." The popular image of a "decadent" New Orleans offends many New Orleanians, but the representation is not all false—depending on what "decadence" means. Robert Azzarello has written about "decadence" in New Orleans literature, a theme that can be traced from the earliest to the most recent imaginative literature set in the city. He draws on an 1884 French novel, *À rebours* by J. K. Huysmans, to outline basic principles of "decadence" as an artistic movement: "reveling in inadequacy, debility, failure and weakness . . . a bipolar if not schizoid relation to modernity; an obsession with artistic refinement at the expense of rational judgement [*sic*]; a seemingly careless indifference to the world that is in fact carefully scripted and consciously performed [and] a fixation on artificiality and ornamentation over substance."[10]

My first thought upon reading these words was how well they seemed to describe my own novel, *French Quarter Beautification Project*, first drafted by a youthful me in the 1980s. That a New Orleans writer unversed at the time in literary theory or New Orleans literary history would produce a work so indicative of a certain aesthetic mode would seem to be evidence that "decadence," in the developed sense put forth by Azzarello, must be in the cultural water of the city. Anne Rice's vampires would undoubtedly agree. To put it in less metaphorical terms, such inexplicable convergence of style and focus seems to validate Raymond Williams's understanding of "collective" or "trans-individual" subjects, and therefore authors. According to this idea, authors give voice not so much to their own idiosyncratic visions of the world as they confirm widely shared aesthetic and social attitudes germane to their time and social milieu.[11] To put it more simply, the ideas that I share in the essays in this collection are only nominally my own. In fact, they represent the views of many other people who experience the same time, place, and social habitat that I do.

My second thought upon reading Azzarello's classic definition of decadence was that it was too uncharitable. It seems to present a valorization of art, sensual experience, style, and suspicion of modern capitalist "progress" in ungenerous terms, as an inability to recognize reality, an inability to act, and a rejection of community. In other words, it appears to define decadence from a puritanical perspective. It's true that a favorite saying among my high school friends was, "reality is for people who can't handle drugs." But, of course, the experience of people on drugs is also "reality," though it's different from the reality experienced by people who are not under the effects of this or that specific drug. People are empowered with a degree of agency in how they experience the world, and the choices they make to fashion their experience of reality does not make their experience non-reality.

Confusion about the meaning of decadence lies within the word itself and within the long contradictory history of the term since Théophile Gautier summoned it to define the aesthetic of Charles Baudelaire's poetry in 1868. Azzarello draws on the theory of Matei Călinescu, who does not agree with the traditional assumption that decadence involves a turning away from, if not resistance, to the modern faith in economic and technological progress. Călinescu asserts that "progress is decadence and decadence is progress."[12] Azzarello sees evidence of this conflation of decadence with progress in the morally reprehensible plunder of natural resources to satisfy the comforts of people who live now. But this involves a different register of the term, quite distinct from its denotation of people who choose to live for art and sensual fulfillment rather than for political, social, and economic power.

The most generous way of understanding decadence is to see it as a function of fatalism, which is to say as a recognition and acceptance (even if grudging) of insurmountable obstacles. In this regard, it's more a sign of a mature civilization than of a declining one.[13] The nineteenth-century notion of decadence is also without doubt a rejection of puritanical shame and repression, and as such is an affirmation, not negation of life.

I also need to step down out of the Olympian mists of academic discourse long enough to note that the "decadents" of contemporary New Orleans are, like the first modern "decadents" in nineteenth-century France, urban bohemians—who often have trouble making the rent—not the bourgeois capitalist magnates who preside over the pillage of nature to enrich themselves and grow their already obscene level of power over the rest of us. The original decadents were explicitly anti-bourgeois, and we can rest assured that New Orleans bohemians today vote for that smattering of candidates who seek to ameliorate the damages to nature and society that bourgeois capitalists have wrought.

Azzarello refers to the Beat poets as mid-twentieth-century "decadents," which allows us to piece together the genealogy of the prevailing boho world that shaped my consciousness as a boy in the French Quarter, Marigny, and Bywater. The original generation of *décadents* spawned bohemians, of which "hip" is an American iteration. The appropriation of hip resulted in today's consumerist "hipster," but such incorporation, Raymond Williams tells us, is widespread in the way late capitalist societies evolve without fundamentally changing the classic capitalist division of wealth and labor. To apply Williams's terminology, decadents and their descendants are—then always quickly *were*—"emergent cultural formations," which the effective dominant culture must incorporate. In the process of hegemonic incorporation, the cultural formation in question is "reinterpreted, diluted, or put into forms which support or at least do not contradict other elements within the effective dominant culture."[14]

Thankfully, the downtown riverfront wards of New Orleans have long been a magnet for America's latest "alternative cultural formations," who always seek themselves to incorporate older native forms of expressing alterity, in a way that I find amenable and charming. The colonization of hip by the hipster is a sign that the decadent urban bohemian is today either a fading demographic or a subject-position changing in a way that's difficult to recognize in real time. The reason may be, again in Williams's terms, that urban bohemia was always more of an alternative cultural formation than on oppositional one. In colloquial terms: more apt to sell out. Since the early twentieth century, when Mabel Dodge's Greenwich Village salons brought together "lyrical left" poets and anarchist revolutionaries, the committed political Left has had an uneasy relationship with the hip artist set, though they often rub shoulders in the same communities. Trotsky rails against them in *Literature and Revolution*: "[He] did not go to the factories and to the mills, but he made a lot of noise in cafes, he banged his fist upon music stands, he put on a yellow blouse, he painted his cheeks and threatened vaguely with his fist."[15]

Left-leaning migrants to New Orleans often represent more of a dropout instinct, out of a pessimistic or fatalistic apprehension of the possibility of real change and the short span of a precious and unrepeatable individual life. Literary antecedents include Voltaire's *Candide* (brilliantly rewritten for our times by New Orleans author Bill Lavender[16]) and Huck Finn, invoked in New Orleans poet Everette Maddox's decadent hymn to the transcendence of staying drunk in New Orleans, "Flowing on the Bench."[17] With the hard Right gaining ground in the United States, maybe the old model of dropping out and living a meaningful life on the fringes may be too great a privilege for basically ethical people to indulge.

But there's a more positive way to see it, too. Maybe that rejection of the broader community implicit in the earliest definitions of *décadent* (as a cultural formation), and genetically discernible in later iterations, is the fading feature. This may be the reason that I have trouble recalling downtown boho artist types in my lifetime who have not also been politically engaged.

In New Orleans, the forefront of political engagement has always necessitated anti-racist thought and action. The "soul that dares and defies," in New Orleans, as all over the United States, must also dare to defy racism. As the essays in this collection show, I'm impatient to move beyond the stage of simply acknowledging the victims of racism and into an era where the heroes of the resistance get more press (Jean St. Malo, the 1811 Uprising, Comité des Citoyens, etc.). This, again, is because of the specific conditions of my own upbringing. Because my parents were engaged in the Civil Rights struggle and because I grew up in integrated environments and attended New Orleans public schools (after desegregation), there was never a time that I was not aware of the history of racism and its depredations. I often read today that the severity of racist oppression is "not taught in schools," for example, but that was certainly not the case for me. I've had to learn over the years that my upbringing is far from the norm of most white people in America, including here in New Orleans, where so many white families fled Orleans Parish public schools (for more segregated private or suburban public schools) during the same years that I attended them. As a white person, however, I try to limit my discussions to what Black people and culture mean to me and to other white people—rather than lecture Black people about what they should think. We live in a time of acute racial discomfort because, as the

Trump era has reminded us, white supremacy just refuses to die, despite the fact that many people of all races have been joining together to fight for racial equality for generations. The distrust arising from the persistence of racism in America causes many white people to throw up their hands and not say anything about race at all, for fear of being branded a racist. The cowardly urge to avoid the issue just empowers the most racist among us. White people need to say something, be honest, and worry less about being called a racist than about continuing the struggle to overcome the legacy of horror that our white ancestors left us with.

I also don't think that discussions of race should be ghettoized into special classes, books, or essays devoted to just that subject. Everything I've written in this introduction so far, before bringing up the specific angle of race, applies, I hope, to New Orleanians of all racial backgrounds. Consider, for example, the role of decadence as a cultural style. The irony is that the sense of cultural decline causing nineteenth-century decadents to flee into art and the endless recesses of the unconscious was in many ways reversed, the culture invigorated, when colonialism yielded its unforeseen benefit: the gradual integration of non-European forms, paradigms, and people into the mainstream of a culture that had previously been created and consumed by white people. New Orleans is ground zero, of course, for the culturally productive (and socially painful) encounter between European and African civilizations. Ishmael Reed flips the dated European understanding of decadence on its head in his 1972 novel, *Mumbo Jumbo*, which tells the story of an "anti-plague" gripping the country, causing infected persons to get funky and reject the characteristic separation of body and soul that has defined Western (white) spirituality. "Some plagues caused the body to waste away; Jes Grew enlivened the host. . . . Some plagues arise from decomposing animals, but Jes Grew is electric as life."[18] The pandemic takes hold first in New Orleans, then spreads across the country, resembling the dissemination of jazz and hoodoo. The greatest possible irony is the way in which Reed's assault on the legacies of Platonic idealism (including Christianity) fulfills the mission Nietzsche ascribed to his *Übermensch*—a revaluing of the earthly life as the site of the most spiritual, highest aspiration of human endeavor, an end to the flagellation of the body in ritual demonstration of spiritual worth. Nietzsche was perhaps a bit less casually racist than most of his contemporaries (in regard to Jewish people, anyway), but it would certainly come as a shock to him that Africa held the answer to the problem of European modernity all along.

The problem, which is really a plus, for white New Orleanians, is that so much of the culture we celebrate as New Orleanians, and so much of its liberating potential, has roots in Africa. New Orleans is America's gateway to Africa, and white people born here were also born at this same gateway (unless their families did everything possible to avoid looking at it). Living in America's most African city is obviously a problem for white racists, but it also poses discomfort for white people who attempt to atone for their own or their ancestors' racism by performing a false degree of extreme deference to Black culture, which they usually voice as not wanting to "colonize" or "appropriate." This fear is common among white liberals who have not spent much time around Black people. A verdict of unethical cultural appropriation relies on two conditions: failure to acknowledge or failure to compensate Black cultural producers. My message to white people is to embrace multiracial political coalitions, accept Black leadership, punish practitioners of racist deeds and rhetoric, demand reparations for past crimes against your Black neighbors (even if it means a piece of your taxes), and embrace with pride and joy those aspects of your culture that have Black roots.

Racial angst too often contributes, along with misunderstanding of economic forces, to wholesale rejection of cultures that have been the site of racial struggle. New Orleans's miscegenated culture is the child of strife, but still beautiful, and still better for its mixed roots. New Orleans has been the site of racial oppression as well as the site of resistance against racial oppression—and also a place where people found a way to find meaning, to experience love, and to create, in spite of the social structures that sought to use and crush them. My strategy therefore is not to reject myths of the past altogether, but to refashion a mythology of New Orleans that serves the ethics embraced by the overwhelmingly anti-racist political will of the city today. The poetry of Brenda Marie Osbey, particularly her restoration of Black folk heroes like Juan San Malo, Mother Catherine Seals, and the Seven Sisters of New Orleans, is a great blueprint for how to do that.[19] The Paper Monuments Project (papermonuments.org) is a more community-oriented approach, bringing together local citizens to mount temporary art installations that raise to productive mythical prominence figures like nineteenth-century rebel maroon Bras-Coupé, and events like the 1970 "Desire Standoff" between the local Black Panther chapter and a racist state government and local police force. We need to view our cultural inheritance as a strength, and we have a long line of Black and white ancestors who made art and resisted racism at the same time.

In other words, living for art need not eschew basic political responsibility, and maybe it's a puritanical suspicion of art and artists—and people who like to party—that they are irresponsible, unable to put the self-absorption down long enough to engage in concert with others to improve society for all. The New Orleans community I grew up in offered a model of politically progressive action, including anti-racism, queer activism, feminism, and environmentalism, that also recognized and embraced the human need for sensual and aesthetic fulfillment. I like the old anarchist slogan, popularized by the International Workers of the World a hundred years ago: Bread and Roses. The challenge for cultural politics and the politics of culture in today's New Orleans is to continue to refuse the Americanist puritanical illusion that the bread would be ours if only we gave up our native love of roses.

PART I
New Orleans from a Native Perspective

Pretty Lively for a Dying City
2007

Goodbye, 2007. And good riddance. But will you really be gone? After we've had our Réveillon suppers and passed out, will we wake up to a new day?

Katrina, many supposed, would be far-ranging enough in destruction to wipe history clean so that New Orleans could finally reinvent itself along lines regarded as healthier by Yankee values of thrift, hard work, and suspicion of sentimentality (evidenced as much in Mississippi and Texas as up north).

Yet Katrina simply deposited another rich and stubborn layer of past atop an already deep trove of (to use the dismissive American term for history) "baggage." In other words, the storm only anchored New Orleans more firmly—not only in history, but in a history haunted by death.

The New Orleanian approach to the past, and to death, is (to put it mildly) unorthodox in America. Outgoing state poet laureate Brenda Marie Osbey has written eloquently on the subject: "Wear the memory of the dead plainly / speak of the dead as though you thought they might hear / live among your dead, whom you have every right to love."[1]

Many dry-eyed American optimists regard such an attitude toward death as unhealthy. Yet one could see it in opposite terms as well.

For example, New Orleanians are routinely disparaged as "delusional" or "in denial," especially when it comes to the region's physical future. The tone of the July 2007 issue of *National Geographic* is an apt example, as was Ben C. Toledano's nasty bit of petty vitriol last summer in *Commentary*, which he cutely termed an "autopsy."[2]

A transplant friend of mine, who still struggles with her choice to stay here, tried to put her finger on that nagging sense that New Orleans isn't a place to build a future. She said she just wasn't sure the city would even be here in a hundred years or so.

Instead of citing coastal restoration hopes or pointing to the miracles of Dutch flood control, I just flat-out agreed with her. Yes. Of course. The city, in time, will be under the ocean, Atlantis. So will you, darling, so will you. In time, the sun will supernova and the Earth will be destroyed. In time the

1

universe will expand into a dark cold place and the phenomenon of life will be no more. Do you really want to go there?

Maybe a little strategic delusion and denial is the height of rationality. Do you really think that glitzy new condo complex in some exurban boomtown is going to be there forever? Ask a homeowner with negative equity in South Florida or Phoenix. At least when we dress up like kings and queens on Mardi Gras, we don't think we really are kings and queens. Far from being irrational, New Orleanian frivolity in the face of death and decay is actually built on a sober apprehension of reality.

In comparison with other major American cities, New Orleans has been in economic decline for 150 years. Isn't it interesting that all the cherished cultural gifts the city has placed at the feet of the world have arisen during this period of supposed decline? We've been pretty lively for a dying city. Maybe "going down slow" isn't so bad.

After all that dying, we're still here, and, physically, we resemble our youthful self more than any other American city. We've stayed beautiful without plastic surgery, a feat that requires grace, wisdom, and, probably, economic underdevelopment. Though they might not admit it, other Americans love us for that.

So I'll stay until I'm neck deep—at least then I can still sing. Then I'll think about moving to a pseudo-New Orleans in some brand-new development somewhere, where death doesn't exist.

A Living Carnival Takes All Comers
2012

It's Carnival time. Time to celebrate our local culture, or upend it? Ah, the paradox of Carnival. Who's the real king of Carnival, Rex or 'tit Rex, and which is the pretender? What exactly is the nature of this elusive being called "Carnival spirit," anyway?

Carnival has changed so much over the years, decades, centuries, and, possibly, millennia, that it becomes hard to distinguish between what's a new Carnival practice versus what is simply a resurrected one. In the most basic sense, all people's experience of Carnival is authentic for them, and the concept of the Carnival spirit is broad and inclusive enough to allow for many interpretations. But this is only one reason that the reference to the old-line Uptown krewes as originators of "Mardi Gras as we know it" always bothered me, and the recent legal flap of Rex versus 'tit Rex reminded me why.[1]

When a group of Uptowners decided to imitate the Carnival practice of Mobile, Alabama, in 1857 (by staging the first Comus parade), they weren't inventing Carnival. They were adding a tradition imported from Mobile to an already vigorous local set of Carnival traditions. These traditions included more participatory, more informal, and perhaps more promiscuous festivities on the streets of the Quarter, like Downtown Carnival today (upper Bourbon excepted—or maybe not). Indeed, the social purpose of the Uptown route parading tradition was to standardize, control, and express who the bosses of the city were in a striking visual spectacle. Which is to say that the old-line krewe model may not actually contain enough make-believe to qualify as "Carnivalesque."

The complication is that it's not simply "culture" we're talking about here, but "Carnival culture," a far more problematic concept. Because the cultural concept of Carnival is to turn against, invert, or critique the broader culture in which it is enveloped. The bottom rail on top, the village fool in burlap (or blue tarp) finery. The issue of more general cultural authenticity aside, the Zulu king in his lard-can crown was always more Carnivalistically authentic than Comus, Rex, et al., in their faux jewels. The same distinction goes for humble shoebox floats, drawn by people (the practice of the toddling 'tit Rex krewe), versus tractor-pulled ones with people paying big bucks for the ticket.

Not that stemming a too anarchic free-for-all of Carnival madness is necessarily a bad idea. The crown for taking Carnival to the edge last year goes to the Krewe of Eris, whose namesake, Greek goddess of discord, announces well the terrain of Carnival cross-purposes it stakes out. Pre-Comus Mardi Gras also included random acts of aggression, like dumping persons deemed to be wallflowers with bags of flour or lime. The whole idea of Carnival, from its earliest manifestations in classical antiquity, poses a problem for social order. Conventions of social interaction ("be nice") and a big chunk of the city budget join forces to hold back the more dangerous of Carnival's disruptive impulses, with varying degrees of success.

Like a social storm, Carnival has aspects of both inevitability and unpredictability.

The funniest thing about Carnival arguments is how quick they are to devolve into authenticity appeals, aka "More New Orleanian than thou." This is especially strange, since Carnival with no one who was not from here would look nothing like Carnival "as we know it." So, the tourists, and even the shouting Christian demonstrators, also "belong." Everybody's Carnival is real. The key to a living Carnival is to keep inventing and taking all comers. For my kids, the Krewe of Les Enfants du Nod, wending its way through the Marigny for its ninth season this year, will seem every bit as foundational as Rex, Comus, and the more anonymous revelers that came before.

Arguments about the cultural implications of Carnival remind us that maybe the unique thing about New Orleans isn't so much its "distinctive culture," as the obsession to think about it so much and turn it to rhetorical purposes.

Carnival is our celebration of doing just this. (Just don't jump on anybody's car.)

Is NOLA Hip and Is That Cool? 2012

Congratulations, New Orleanians! The April 2012 *Travel + Leisure* magazine has voted you the fourth hippest city in America![1] If only we could pin down what "hip" is supposed to mean, we could feel even prouder. There is, of course, a great deal of confusion about what "hip" is, and the definition also appears to have changed a great deal over the decades. New Orleans is not a recently hip city, either, but easily qualifies as one of America's original hipster capitals—depending, again, on the definition. The *Utne Reader* ranked us as hipper than the others back in the 1990s,[2] and, in the era before magazines got into the hipitude-ranking business, there were other indicators. Norman Mailer's attempt to define hip (not very sympathetically) in his 1957 essay entitled "The White Negro" put New Orleans on the short list with New York, Los Angeles, San Francisco, Chicago, Paris, and Mexico City.[3] Earlier, Tennessee Williams famously dubbed New Orleans "the last frontier of Bohemia."[4]

However, the conclusive indices for these earlier thinkers and *Travel + Leisure* seem widely divergent. The *Travel + Leisure* article begins with this impressionistic stab at a definition: "They sport vintage bowling shoes and the latest tech gear—but they also know the best places to eat and drink." Thus, the once venerably countercultural, sometimes oppositional concept of hip has morphed completely into smart consumerism with a fashion sense (and a fairly conformist one at that, if everyone's wearing bowling shoes).

I take the issue personally because my neighborhood, Faubourg Marigny, is cited by the magazine as the best habitat for hipster-spotting, and because I'm sentimental about the concept of hip and would like to preserve it against its corporate co-opters. Many hip thinkers have been ready to dispose of the term for a long time. Tom Frank wrote an obituary for hip in his 1997 book, *The Conquest of Cool.* His argument was that "hip consumerism" had so totally repackaged the more truly politically and culturally iconoclastic foundations of hip that there was no going back.[5] *Travel + Leisure*'s reduction of hip to "indie boutiques" and "bar scene" (including the expensive and socially homogeneous Mimi's in the Marigny) matches Frank's thesis perfectly.

Happily, New Orleans is more truly hip, according to older definitions, than *Travel + Leisure* realizes. One of the earliest discussions of hip (then "hep") can be found in Mezz Mezzrow's 1946 jazz autobiography *Really the Blues.*[6] Mezz was an urban Chicago white boy who fell in love with New Orleans jazz, working with Sidney Bechet, Louis Armstrong, Leon Roppolo, and others, as they branched out from New Orleans in the early 1920s. The potent combination of jazz and marijuana (introduced to Mezz by New Orleans clarinetist Leon "Rap" Roppolo) form these first senses of "hep." Over the next several decades, "hip" would connote openness to drug experimentation and affinity for Black culture (see postscript below). These are the aspects focused on in Mailer's "White Negro" essay, as the title suggests.

An additional feature, from Henry Miller's Parisian exploits to the American travels of Beat generation writers like William S. Burroughs and Jack Kerouac (each of whom put in obligatory stints in New Orleans), was a lifestyle on the economic fringes of society. This is the "drop out" idea immortalized in 1960s sloganeering and in more sophisticated terms like Herbert Marcuse's "great refusal," discussed in his 1964 philosophical bestseller, *One-Dimensional Man.*[7] One wanted to avoid complicity—economic and political—with a society thought to be inherently corrupt. Henry David Thoreau argues a similar point in his iconic "Civil Disobedience" lecture, first printed in 1849, but Mailer dubs the tendency to institutional non-participation an "existentialist" response to a morally indefensible society. Amiri Baraka, in his 1963 *Blues People*—where New Orleans also figures prominently—grounds the related concept of "cool" in its original Afro-American manifestation: "to be *cool* was . . . to be calm, even unimpressed, by what horror the world might daily propose. . . . In a world that is basically irrational, the most legitimate relationship to it is non-participation."[8]

Fashion has always been a part of hip, but hip fashion today hardly resembles earlier iterations. Dressing up in flamboyantly iconoclastic outfits has been a feature of hip from flower power to punk rock mohawks, but "hip" fashion today suggests a trendsetting, normative function, the furthest thing from "alternative" in any true meaning of that word.

Throughout my childhood, we shopped at the Goodwill Store on Piety and Burgundy. At first, I didn't care. Then, I hated it (junior high years). And then, suddenly, it was hip. I was lucky to be part of the thrift store craze of the early 1980s, when I was, yes, a painfully hip NOLA teen. We were hip in the earlier senses of the term because our clothes were bought for pennies and were donated hand-me-downs. There was nothing the fashion industry could offer us, nothing we wanted to buy from them. But at some point thrift store fashion became "vintage," and this, too, is a great indicator of the corporate co-opting of a once explicitly anti-corporate movement.

Raymond Williams calls it the *incorporation* by the "effective dominant culture" of an *emergent* and *alternative* cultural formation. Williams says that the emergent alternative practice, once incorporated, is "reinterpreted, diluted, or put into forms which support or at least do not contradict other elements within the effective dominant culture."[9] The fashion aesthetic of cheap used clothes was thus transformed into pricey "vintage" clothes. Evidence of the transformation is the "hipster doofus" character on *Seinfeld*, Kramer. No surprise that "indie boutiques" with stiff price tags is one of the defining categories in *Travel + Leisure*'s measurement of hip in our time.

If the standards of hip are a willful retreat from national social and economic ambition, a live-and-let-live attitude, affinity for Black culture (see postscript), preference for alternative daily lifestyles, and alternative, self-directed fashion sense (bordering on costume), New Orleans has been more of a definer of American hip than a fourth-place expression of it. Of *Travel + Leisure*'s top ten cities, only New Orleans and number nine, Philadelphia, have sizable Black populations. Affordability is not a ranking category at all, as many of the top ten cities (like number one, Seattle, and number three, San Francisco) make abundantly clear. If you cut the more consumerist (and consumerist aesthetic) categories, like "attractive/athletic" people, we rank much higher.

For truly hip categories, we rate markedly higher. For "diversity," we rank number two, behind only New York (which, amazingly, doesn't even make *Travel + Leisure*'s top ten). There's one category, though, that best sums up the alternative cultural formation that true hip represents: "offbeat" people. Despite the vagueness of the adjective, *Travel + Leisure* voters got that one right: We're number one.

Postscript
(from *The Lens* comment section, May 2014)

I notice that this piece from a couple of years ago is trending again, so I wanted to take the opportunity to clarify an important point that's not well made in the essay. Some commenters have reacted critically to the criterion of traditional hipitude that I referred to as "affinity for Black culture." Yes, as phrased, this is certainly overly general, vague, and misleading. I should have been more clear that the American hip concept originates in Black culture, and that white hipsters of the earlier generations were enamored of a particular segment of Black culture and sought to emulate it. Hip is (was) basically

American bohemianism with a distinctively African American expressive element. Does this mean, as one commenter put it, that there can't be a Black hipster? Quite the contrary, it means that the original hipster is Black and that white hip is born out of an effort to embrace and adopt Black urban style and attitude, including the critique of the broader (racist) society.[10]

But that was a long time ago, yes. The Be-Bop and Beat generations of the 1940s and '50s encountered and merged with new models of hip coming from the West Coast, and then from Britain, all of which added other concerns (including eco-ideologies) to the complex of preoccupations, habits, and expressive traditions that had defined hip before. My point was that New Orleans's place in the hip pantheon is deeply rooted in the older urban hip paradigm circling around Black urban culture (particularly music) and the ways in which non-Black people embrace and interact with that culture. This is somewhat obvious, since New Orleans is ground zero for African/European cultural exchange in the United States. You could even see those white New Orleanians who sought out the secretive St. John's Eve voodoo celebrations on the lakefront in the late nineteenth century as proto-hipsters in this sense, not to mention the early jazz cats (white and Black) who become prophets of hip in the early twentieth century. At any rate, the current usage of "hipster," with the *de rigueur* mention of Brooklyn (or Portland), skinny jeans, expensive hi-tech gadgets, food neuroses, etc., bears little resemblance to the older idea of hip as an alternative ideology as well as lifestyle.

Go-Cups, Roosters, and NOLA Identity
2013

The ways in which New Orleans changes and resists change, and the reasons why, continue to fascinate. This process is even more contested in the downriver working-class wards, especially now, for a variety of reasons. One distinctive feature here is the ideology of New Orleans exceptionalism that permeates our debates about change, whether brought about by government, business interests, or by influx of new residents. The presence and rhetorical force of this exceptionalist spirit is in itself exceptional in comparison with most other American cities, especially given our relatively small population. Arguments, perhaps even hysteria, about the fight to preserve our unique cultural character have arisen on a couple of issues in 2013, but have been conspicuously absent on the one city council action of the year so far to actually enact a sweeping change on an economic and aesthetic aspect of New Orleans life as old as the city itself—and it's not go-cups.

I noticed the social media rumble about a city ban on go-cups last week and was as outraged as the next guy. But then I noticed that reasonable reporting in the *Times-Picayune, Gambit*, the *Advocate*, WWL, WDSU, and every other "traditional" news outlet showed that there wasn't even a molehill to the mountain piling up in cyberspace. Far from a contemplated citywide go-cup ban, it turns out that the fuss was about just two bars in the entire city. Why did such a non-issue strike such a real nerve? Or was it even a real nerve, rather than a "virtual" one inflated by a handful of bloggers and tweeters? The anatomy of a rumor in this case demonstrates the way internet-savvy new arrivals are able to seize and define the terms of debate, especially concerning the newly dubbed "St. Claude Corridor." One of the culprits drumming up the fairy dustup was a misleading petition on Neighborland.com, that newly imported watchdog for building a virtual New Orleans that can compete with the real one.

And why such chest-thumping from the newbies over the humble go-cup? The go-cup in itself is just litter waiting to happen, or, if disposed of "properly," more nonbiodegradable mass for the landfill. The more responsible method would be for people to take their reusable Mardi Gras cups around and refill them. But it's what the go-cup represents that matters: in a general sense, the city's famously liberal drinking laws; in a more specific sense, the freedom to consume alcohol on the public ways.

While the spirit of the former and the letter of the latter should be preserved in perpetuity, the level of freak-out over a relatively minor and arcane issue affecting only a couple of addresses shows that a doctrinaire mentality is taking shape, one often connected with identity politics. As soon as essential and reductive identity markers are in place, the loudest shouters can enhance their identity status by affirming the dogma. In this case, people who may not have lived very long in New Orleans can demonstrate commitment to New Orleanian identity by defining it narrowly and pledging allegiance. It's right and good that the dogma includes public drinking, since that is, in my view, one of those only-place-in-America qualities that people like me feel should be preserved as a beacon of alternative values to the boring other places that actually run the country. But if the range of aspects defining New Orleanian uniqueness is too narrow, then we fall into the trap of a vulgar exceptionalism, which cheapens the whole project.

We could group the go-cup scare under the same heading as two real city enforcement stories of 2013: the noise ordinance debate and the rooster ban. Each is an example of the city attempting to exert order on the human mass living under its jurisdiction through stricter code enforcement. The balance of the city enforcement grip on the chaos of a few hundred thousand separate individual wills has often been tricky in New Orleans, to phrase the matter delicately.

In the case of the ongoing revision of the city noise ordinance, which impinges directly on live music performances, a recognition of continuity with past practices provides necessary perspective. The raid on the St. Roch Tavern for unlicensed live music in spring will remind older residents of the raid on Tremé's Little People's Place fifteen years ago, which resulted in Davis Rogan's song named after the venue, the anthem for all live music lovers angry with what they view as capricious enforcement. But as Alex Rawls reasonably pointed out in April, this is as much a labor issue as it is cultural.[1] When a place is unpredictably raided and shut down, as happened at the St. Roch Tavern, musicians lose income.

On the other side of the debate are neighbors who fear waking up one day to find that the corner by their house has become Bourbon Street. While the reductively defined "pro-music" camp dishes out bromides about "destroying New Orleans culture," neighborhood residents also have valid fears. I felt this fear myself a couple of years ago when my own city council representative floated an idea for a curfew for young people beginning at 8:00 p.m. and including not only the French Quarter but the Marigny Triangle. The area was described as an "adult district," where children really don't belong.[2]

The fear that St. Claude is being sucked into a Frenchmen Street vortex was dramatized by comments on a WDSU story that ran August 8. Some parents of kids enrolled at the new KIPP school at the old Colton building were apparently upset at a theater poster down the street depicting a topless woman. A man interviewed by reporter Casey Ferrand said of the shiny new Colton school renovation, "At first, everybody thought they were just building condos, but then we found out it was a school, and we all thought that was weird just because of what is in this area."[3]

But the conflict of families and schools versus theaters, bars, and music clubs is a false dilemma, and, yes, there's an exceptionalist argument for that. There's a principle of exceptional New Orleans authenticity that overrides plastic cups and a laissez-faire attitude toward hedonistic lifestyles. It's the idea of *métissage*. In the most literal sense, it refers to racial and, by extension, social and cultural mixing—the proverbial "Gumbo Pot" of New Orleans cultural identity. On another level, it can mean a radical living and growing together of groups and practices that are separated in other places.

Parents of school-age children need to realize that part of the fabric of downtown New Orleans is an edgy bohemian and sexually tolerant aesthetic, and it's been that way for a very long time, for generations. But, more importantly, it means that newcomers who are drawn primarily by a greater level of freedom to party should not make the mistake of thinking that area families have the same squeamish aversion to more adult-oriented activities in their midst that they may remember from the average American suburban upbringing they're fleeing by coming here in the first place.

At any rate, for older residents like me, the opening of two new schools on St. Claude Avenue—KIPP and the neighborhood-grown Homer Plessy down the street—are far more key for preserving neighborhood authenticity than another high-priced craft cocktail boutique in Bywater that doesn't get to have go-cups.

So, I'm happy about the salutary influx of schoolkids to counter the twenty-something boom in the old neighborhood, but I'm sad about the loss to the neighborhood's aesthetic and sound fabric represented by the city council's most uncontroversial exertion of its authority this year: the rooster ban.

When I was a child in the 800 block of Frenchmen Street, the area was not known as a live music destination. But every morning was greeted by the crowing of cocks. The same was true of my dad's neighborhood on Piety

Street a few blocks down. For all those years I lived away from New Orleans, I always knew I was home when I heard the morning crowing that was never far away in Marigny and Bywater neighborhoods. As in many cities in the developing world, the practice of chicken raising in New Orleans blurred the typical American boundaries between urban and rural, thus contributing in another way to a sense of *métissage*.

Gambit Weekly did a story on the ban July 30 but, predictably, it treated urban chicken cultivation as a growing national trend rather than as a continuing practice of local culture.[4] The only mention of local culture was cock-fighting, thus tarring roosters the same way pit bulls get tarred by their own victimization. Viewed in a national light, the ban on roosters adheres to best practices put in place by communities faced with a new trend. Viewed from New Orleans's downtown working-class wards, however, it's a draconian measure that excises what had been a distinctive feature of local culture. Yet an imaginary threat to plastic cups elicited a greater outcry than this truly culture-changing new law. Because of newbies' reductive understanding of distinctively local culture (music and partying), they are unable to see our roosters as anything but a sign of a national trend. The only national trend going on is the banning of roosters because transplants are not used to being around them. While complaining about change, they are doing the changing.

Despite often polemical rhetoric, New Orleans isn't about to seriously restrict live music venues—if anything, the current conflict on that issue is a response to a vast expansion, not contraction, of local live music over the past couple of decades. But if the urban rooster really does vanish from the sound and visual tapestry of our neighborhoods, we will be one step closer to the average American burg. Not that there's anything wrong with that—but people who claim an interest in preserving what's different about life here should broaden the scope of their critique beyond the sacred right to party.

Faking Relevance at the French Market
2013

It's hard to think of an iconic New Orleans location that courts authenticity as ardently as the French Market does, and whose efforts result so strikingly in the opposite effect. That's why I was concerned to learn about the French Market Corporation's latest push to improve the place. New director Jon Smith is apparently dismayed by the quality of many of the goods sold in the flea market area. In his words: "Quite frankly there's a lot of garbage. A lot of people there aren't necessarily artisans."[1] He claims to have a "grand vision" for the market and looks forward to the attrition of those vendors who don't fit in with it.

The curious thing about his comments is how surprised he sounds. Did he just take a look around after they hired him? An art market isn't the same thing as a flea market, and would certainly be a departure from anything that's ever been in the space between old Gallatin Street and the river before. Smith also says he would like to see the return of groceries to the market, and so would I, but French Market Vendors Association secretary Heidi Diekelman has wisely pointed out how out of touch with the neighborhood's current needs such a plan would be.[2] If Smith is bothered because the market is purely a tourist attraction, not grounded in the kind of society that created and sustained it for 200 years, he's too late to fix the problem. Indeed, it's not a problem the French Market can really address, because it's about the surrounding area more than the market itself.

Perhaps the most famous historical account of the French Market is Lafcadio Hearn's sketch first printed in an 1885 guide to the city.[3] It's fun to compare today's French Market with Hearn's account, and even more fun to observe how today's designers invoke the market's past in an effort to establish authenticity.

The physical structures have been renovated a number of times, including in the 1930s, 1970s, and just a couple of years ago. After the newest renovation (of the sheds), a terracotta bas-relief was installed where Gov. Nichols Street meets North Peters. It serves perfectly as a symbol of what the French Market has become. As if taken from a mold of Pompeii lava, it depicts the market as a grocery for local people a hundred years ago. But the scene is far less hectic, crowded, and, frankly, filthy than Hearn's record suggests it was.

This cleaned up Hollywood past is reflected also in the mural in Dutch Alley, about a block from Café du Monde, that shows famous people smiling in a sunny environment, without the mess—human and otherwise—that surely crowded their ankles. The reminders of bygone glory also hang from the roofs of the sheds, a series of photographs and sketches from earlier days. If only they had been augmented with Smell-O-Vision. Anyone who has been to a functioning open-air market in the developing world knows that the ripe aromas would turn off the average American tourist, or, indeed, a newly minted French Quarter condo owner.

Back in the 1980s, the tendency toward reification was first signaled with bronze statues of a shopper with basket and butcher with steak in Dutch Alley—icons of sanitized consumerism not remotely true to the reality of the old Halle des Boucheries and the meat that used to stink up the place.

The most interesting new architectural addition is the fountain at the corner of Gov. Nicholls Street. I'm not sure if it replaces a fountain that had been there a century ago, but it's no longer attached to the purpose of a public fountain at a market: to provide animals with drinking water and humans with a place to wash themselves. Bereft of its purpose, the fountain is now purely decorative. And that certainly speaks also to the role of the French Market as a whole, cleaner and more purposeless than at any point in its history.

Jon Smith's "grand vision" can't really do anything about that. The space has changed as the neighborhood has changed. After describing the filth and diverse human mass of the market, Hearn's account follows a vendor's family to their quarters nearby. He then gives us a detailed portrait of a French Quarter courtyard in 1885—an unsanitary slum overcrowded with indigent immigrants. The vast and much-larger population of the French Quarter at that time is what gave it the character Hearn ascribes to it—polyglot and variegated, in terms of income level as well as race, ethnicity, and geographical origin.

During my childhood in the 1970s, the market was certainly less crowded and less polyglot than a hundred years earlier, but a substantial farmer's market remained. The 1984 Clint Eastwood movie *Tightrope* offers an unassuming view of it in 1984. We often bought our produce there. A special treat was a peeled bit of sugarcane stalk to chew on. But the Quarter was different then, too. There were still poor people in it and plenty of Black families as well as Italian and white Creole families. The flea market was a common destination for bored kids on a weekend afternoon.

In fact, there was a lot more of what Jon Smith terms "garbage" then than there is now. Besides literal garbage (the stinking organic kind), there were cheap sunglasses, shot glasses, plastic flags, figurines of drunks leaning on Bourbon Street lampposts, and other little souvenir trinkets that kids as well as tourists love, just because of their affordability. At that time, there were many more resale booths, with typical rummage sale items—old plates, glassware, etc. There were booths hawking old magazines, too, an inventory that included *Playboy* and *Penthouse*. (Not sure if that would fly anymore.) One booth I know wouldn't be approved today: the army surplus guy, who proffered daggers, bayonets, swords, and, as I recall, guns (though they may not have been operable). There were resale clothes racks too. Clearly there were people in the neighborhood, not just tourists, who benefited from such a product line within walking distance of their homes. No longer, though.

I can't recall a time when "artisans" were majority tenants of the flea market. Banishing fleas in favor of art will make the market cleaner and less crowded, but it will also erase a last claim to authenticity—if authenticity means continuity with a past tradition. The "garbage" Jon Smith refers to is actually the last link to a shabbier but more locally patronized market. It also represents a form of diversity that should be cherished rather than resisted. The cheap and the trashy rubbing shoulders with the elite and expensive used to be the allure of the Quarter. Gradual elimination of one side of that equation has already resulted in a bland "boutique" neighborhood that might as well charge an admission fee. Today's market already has art booths, some rarer, more expensive imported crafts, and handcrafted clothing and jewelry. These offerings exist alongside the cheap plastic crap. And that's fine. It leads to greater diversity of customers as well as vendors.

A lot of the "garbage" that offends Smith is the cheap stuff folks can actually afford, be they tourists or locals without much money, including a kid looking to drop a few bucks on a birthday present—sunglasses, key rings, phone protectors, wallets—for Mom or Dad. If it's all original art, starting at, say, $50 for a small lithograph, that substantially limits not only the number of people but the kinds of people who will patronize the place. And then there are the vendors, who represent a rare continuity with Lafcadio Hearn's French Market. While the customers are not as polyglot or diverse as they were in Hearn's day, the vendors are. Because of the affordable rates for stalls, the mix of nations represented at the flea market resembles the new immigrant mix of the United States in general, which isn't as visible anywhere else in today's New Orleans.

Once again, the issue comes down to affordability. Jon Smith says the French Quarter "at its core is a neighborhood where people live and work,"[4] but his use of the term "people" is far too general. If the people in the neighborhood are mostly part-time residents or people without families who rarely cook at home, will they want the daily grocery and houseware items the market used to offer?

Today's average French Quarter resident has a lot more cash than the person(s) occupying the same residence thirty years ago. It may be that newer French Quarter residents would, in fact, be more likely to patronize a French Market with more elite products and fewer vendors. They can always hang a photo from 2013 to show the vibrancy of the era before Smith's "grand vision" forced out the motley of immigrants hawking cheap goods, both used and imported. Like the Vieux Carré itself, it has the sound of history already. And I already miss it.

Why NOLA Hates Starbucks
2013

While the proposed Habana Outpost, a New York-based casual dining franchise, is drawing fire from neighbors on one end of the French Quarter, an older nemesis has moved in at the other end. On the way to drop the kids at school in the morning, I routinely pass the shiny, spanking-new Starbucks on the corner of St. Charles and Canal, with the oversized sign, as if rubbing it in the face of those New Orleanians who view Starbucks as an affront to local cultural identity. I doubt folks felt that way about the Russell Stover candy shop that occupied the corner in the late twentieth century.

Few national chains evoke feelings of disdain from exceptionalist New Orleanians like Starbucks does. The Walmart on Tchoupitoulas stirred up a firestorm of opposition, but that had a lot to do with the scale of the project, which isn't a factor for a corner coffee shop with no parking lot. Nobody grumbles about a new Costco, AutoZone, or Foot Locker, so it's not really a matter of automatically resisting national chain businesses of any type. Even a new McDonald's or Subway sandwiches doesn't rankle in the same way, so it's not even really about an onus on national franchises that serve food and beverages. The Habana Outpost fight has shades of locals-only sentiment, but, since it only has one other location—in Brooklyn—concerns of scale, noise, and parking seem to be the driving arguments against it.[1]

I think there's a sense that coffee, and the places that serve it, are especially beloved symbols of local identity. Exacerbating the anxiety of facing national competition in a field of such ancient and deeply held personal attachment is the symbolism of Starbucks itself: As a Goliath of international business, it represents exactly what New Orleans exceptionalists loathe and what Americanist New Orleanians long for. For exceptionalists, it threatens to wipe the last hold-out of an alternative, smaller-scale, and more locally managed way of life off the map. For local Americanists, it represents membership in a national community—"America"—that has often regarded New Orleans as a dubious investment.

I suppose everyone knows that coffee and coffee shops have been integral to New Orleans daily life since before Rose Nicaud, a free Afro-Creole woman, opened her French Market coffee stand in the antebellum era. George Washington Cable's 1880 saga of New Orleans at the time of the Louisiana Purchase, *The Grandissimes*, describes a "frugal" breakfast that nonetheless features "coffee, that subject of just pride in Creole cookery."[2] In Kate Chopin's 1899 novel, *The Awakening*, major characters run into each other at an out-of-the-way place—run by an Afro-Creole woman named Catiche—that they appreciate for its "good coffee."[3] Tennessee Williams, in the few words establishing the scene in *A Streetcar Named Desire*, notes the "faint redolences of bananas and coffee" coming from riverfront warehouses.[4] As a Marigny resident, I'm pleased that the same smell continues to bless the neighborhood today, just as it did in my childhood.

There's actually a more recent work of New Orleans literature about hating on Starbucks specifically: Barret O'Brien's *Midnight in the Marigny*, which I recall seeing at Southern Rep in 2000. The stage play depicts a plot to sabotage a new Starbucks before it can open. And in the introduction to the popular post-Katrina anthology, *Do You Know What It Means to Miss New Orleans?*, David Rutledge opined, "If there is a Starbucks in the French Quarter, something has been lost."[5]

The coffeehouse scene immediately before the Starbucks era was just as thriving as the nineteenth-century scene reportedly was. When Ben Franklin High School students in my day wanted to skip class, the original PJ's on Maple Street, with its spacious and shady backyard, was a preferred destination. Back in my neighborhood, we loved La Marquise on Chartres—for its French Roast and French pastry (where Restaurant Sylvain is now). Croissant D'or, in the old French Quarter Brocato's on Ursuline, was another favorite (it's still there). In the evenings we opted for the eminently bohemian Until Waiting Fills, in an old garage on the corner of St. Philip and Chartres. The Uptown boho choice was Borsodi's on Freret, or Penny Post on Danneel (now the Neutral Ground Coffeehouse). A later generation will remember Kaldi's on Decatur, which, like PJ's, offered a variety of roasts by the cup or pound.

Starbucks has done a great service to the United States in general by putting semi-decent coffee in places that never had it before. But that obviously doesn't apply to us. They've also done a grave disservice to American coffee by promoting and standardizing a taste that I, personally, find comparable to asphalt. The scorch they subject their poor beans to is beyond "dark roast"—it does violence to the flavor and actually gives it less body to balance off the hit your stomach takes when it gets there.

Just as with many a Pacific Northwest ultra-hopped microbrew beer, the point of the beverage isn't so much sensual enjoyment as proving oneself worthy. Starbucks is proud to be a "lifestyle" brand. It's not really about the coffee. Brands like Starbucks make Marx's notion of "commodity fetishism" easily understood by any eighth-grader. The idea is that the commodity is valued not for its use-value (what it actually does) but for the social signification conferred in the exchange—humanized commodities and dehumanized "consumers." Marx writes that commodities have a "mystical character," that every product, no matter the physical form, becomes a "a social hieroglyphic . . . for to stamp an object of utility as a value, is just as much a social product as language."[6] A century later, corporations would perfect this psychic alchemy into the emotional magic of "branding. "Starbucks, with its old world cultural pretensions (Italian words instead of "medium" and "large"), sells culture—that is, the idea of culture—to people who view culture as a stepping-stone of social mobility. It's a classy bit of urban, international cosmopolitanism in a safe, clean, predictable, and homogeneous environment (in other words, everything urban cosmopolitanism isn't).

The good news is that Starbucks doesn't seem to be much of a threat to local, independently owned coffeehouses. The Seattle invasion burned through New York like a brush fire, but I guess Chock Full O'Nuts wasn't a satisfying alternative. We have two local large franchise chains here as well as smaller chains (of two to three shops) and lots of totally independent options. This is because few new residents of New Orleans, and few tourists, feel the itch for Starbucks's products—either the coffee or the pseudo-identity conferred on the buyer.

A *New York Times* travel section article on New Orleans by a new resident specifically praised the absence of Starbucks franchises as part of the "intoxicating, tradition-steeped charm"[7] that is the fetish of our brand as a city in general. The new residents' go-to site for remaking the city in their image is Neighborland.com, and it does have a call for a new Starbucks in Mid-City, but only two people have signed on since 2011.[8]

Pierre Bourdieu writes that taste is really a matter of placing oneself in the social hierarchy. He speaks of the "sense of distinction" that many people seek to imbue themselves with in their personal taste choices.[9] The idea is that some people make choices that will set them apart from an imagined mass of people without taste. Starbucks offers this allure—of being classier than the guy who gets his coffee from McDonald's (even though McCafé tastes better). But the sheer size and omnipresence of Starbucks limits its ability to confer a more refined exceptionality on the buyer.

The new residents of New Orleans's downtown wards are far more sophisticated than the Starbucks crowd in their efforts to set themselves apart.
Some of the newest establishments in the Marigny-Bywater area are proud to
offer not Starbucks but elite roasts from Portland. Pair with a hoppy microbrew beer, perhaps a craft distilled spirit, and a tapita with a rare vegetable
and animal organ, and you and your buddies are truly in a class unto your-
selves. The choice of New Orleans as a place of residence is part of the game,
too, since, until recently, it was a "well-kept secret." Thus, the exceptionality
of New Orleans expands the exceptionality of the highly cultivated hipster.

The tenacity with which many New Orleanians defend the uniqueness of
their city is attractive to seekers of personal distinction, as well, even though
they may not fully understand the terms and history of local exceptionalism.
The problem is that coffee roasted in Portland or Boulder and flown in is totally divorced from the local historical and cultural contexts of coffee in New
Orleans. The result is a culture that's unique to a growing handful of great
American cities, but not necessarily unique to here. Also, I want to smell that
roasting coffee wafting from the river like Tennessee Williams and generations before him did, and coffee that's not roasted here doesn't accomplish
that special aesthetic effect.

Because of its visibility and international cachet, Starbucks poses a greater
challenge to preserving New Orleans as a different-tasting and different-look-
ing place than the new hipster haunts of the latest bohemia to occupy the
downtown wards. I have no doubt that Barret O'Brien's script for *Midnight in
the Marigny* would be reenacted today in the event some unsuspecting person
proposed a Starbucks on St. Claude,[10] and the newest downtown transplants
would no doubt be on the front lines.

I'm grateful for the new residents' general commitment to difference
from mainstream American norms (whatever their personal motivations),
because it contributes to the ongoing mission of presenting New Orleans as
a place that offers an alternative value system to the uncritical, unthoughtful consumerism that characterizes so much of the rest of the United States.
Having fewer Starbucks per square mile than other cities continues to be a
worthy symbol of that alternative frame of mind.

The Golden Age of Carnival Is Now
2014

Nowhere do we see more clearly the symbiotic relationship between the idea of New Orleans and the material realities of life here than in Carnival. The holiday is special not only because we still do it (unlike most of the world) but because we analyze ourselves in the process.

Yes, making money off tourists is a major motivation, too, but locals have always insisted that there's a deeper, more spiritual purpose at work. The city doesn't sponsor Carnival as much as it seeks to manage it, contain it, and, yes, insure some revenue as a lagniappe. The city's role in what locals perceive as an organic social phenomenon is often bitterly contested.

This year's Carnival ordinance affecting parade-route practices is nowhere near as contentious as the 1991–92 fight over desegregation of once powerful and racially exclusive krewes. Yet both city interventions are in keeping with the socially healthful benefits that I and many of us detect in Carnival.

You may have heard people refer to a "golden age" of Carnival in the late nineteenth century, when "If Ever I Cease to Love" was composed. Don't believe them. The golden age of Carnival is now, and the dawn of this new golden age came about right around when they finally buried the corpse of the supposedly golden Carnival of a hundred years ago. That necessary development was the Carnival desegregation ordinance, passed by the city council in 1991, revised the following year, and struck down by federal courts in the following years. Despite its legal failure, its intent was basically realized: to ban from city streets krewes who refused to open their memberships to all races, thus forcing from the streets the very krewes who had originated the krewe system and defined the reigning institutional practice of Mardi Gras in New Orleans for a century.

Of course, these organizations (notably Comus, Proteus, and Momus) were not only elitist but patently racist, and, yes, the parades who filled the vacuum—like Orpheus, Krewe d'Etat, and everybody's current favorite, Muses—offer a far richer spectacle than the tired older parades could, despite the superior float design of the old-line krewes at their best. More significantly, the conception of Carnival in the hands of the Uptown old-line krewes was an aberration in the vast lineage of Carnival history. Carnival is ancient, many centuries older than New Orleans itself, and its practice has been in constant evolution.

Looked at from a certain angle, we might see a contraction of Carnival in our time rather than a flowering. When I was a kid, I used to enjoy walking to the corner of Piety and St. Claude to catch the Okeanos parade. The Krewe of Carrollton rolled in Carrollton and the Krewe of Mid-City rolled in Mid-City. Now, of course, all of these krewes have been sucked into the Uptown parade route, where they are joined every year by other krewes abandoning their old neighborhood routes—this year the Westbank's Alla is the latest krewe from the provinces to stroll down St. Charles Avenue. Endymion hangs on as the only Orleans Parish parade to shun the Uptown route.

But then, that depends on how you define "parade." The model of tractor-drawn floats tossing throws, interspersed with high school marching bands, equestrians, and perhaps Shriners in little cars, is one vision of a Carnival parade, but there wouldn't be much cause for golden age claims if that's all there was to it. That Mardi Gras has diminished, yes, but a more exciting, more participatory, and more *Carnivalesque* Mardi Gras has bloomed in the vacuum. Furthermore, taking the long view of the history of Carnival, with its antecedents in the ancient world, how foundational is the practice of the modern, top-down, mechanized street parade, anyway?

Russian literary critic Mikhail Bakhtin, in a book about folk culture influences on the great Renaissance French writer Rabelais, outlined a theory of Carnival practice based on ancient and medieval Carnival traditions. It's remarkable to witness how the "Carnivalesque" spirit he details lives on so palpably on the other side of the world, decades after his death and centuries after the practices he analyzed so astutely. A few of the key attributes Bakhtin ascribes to Carnival are a satirical impulse of a bawdy kind that he calls "grotesque realism," the inversion of normal prevailing social hierarchies, and mass participation.[1]

In light of principles like these, it's a no-brainer that the latest city ordinance[2] supports, rather than inhibits, the ancient foundations of Carnival tradition. Even here in New Orleans, one of the prevailing social strictures upended by Carnival time has been segregation in public settings. Blocking off and segregating swaths of the public space for members-only parties doesn't jibe with the Carnivalesque injunction to cast off social distinctions and rub shoulders with strangers for a brief spell. Setting up private facilities like port-a-lets and denying access to strangers or broke people is the norm forty-six weeks of the year, try something different for the other couple of weeks. So, the city council's very restrained measure will certainly do no harm to the still unfolding Carnival golden age we're privileged to witness, but it also covers only a tiny aspect of the possibilities of Carnival experience today, which has become more broadly participatory than ever.

For one thing, a proliferation of smaller parading organizations that march with the large night parades has expanded the opportunity for affordable participation by a greater number of adults. It's true that fraternal organizations have had this access in the past, but today's adult marching clubs are far more performative. Since the Pussyfooters took to the streets in 2001, they've been joined by other adult women dance troupes like the Bearded Oysters, the Cameltoe Steppers, and, in 2011, one without an anatomically suggestive name, the Sirens. New additions keep coming, like the NOLA Chorus Girl project, who will hit the streets for the first time in the entry-level Pygmalion parade on February 22 this year. The 610 Stompers famously opened the dance troupe genre to all male clubs, too. Amateur musical societies like the Ninth Ward Marching Band and the Noicisian Coalition add their colors as well, so that the big street parade of our time is far more diverse in its offerings and boasts also that infatuated energy that comes from amateur cultural participation, the genius of Carnival in the first place.

But the gorgeous splashy extravaganza of the super krewes are just one of many ways to do Carnival. Krewe du Vieux gets a lot closer to the spirit expressed by Bakhtin. They're very decentralized, formed by seventeen sub-krewes. The krewe captains vote on a theme, but then each of the seventeen sub-krewes handles their own theme delivery (in float design, costume, handmade throws, and even print texts).

This is democratized aesthetics, highly appropriate for the people's holiday. Since they're a walking parade, they're at eye-level with spectators, and they parade on the narrow streets of the Quarter and Marigny, so the contact between participant and spectator is more egalitarian, if not downright intimate at times. The irreverent obscenity of Krewe du Vieux's performance is as old as Carnival's earliest incarnations, even though Uptown Carnival practice broke from that tradition back in the morally hypocritical 1800s. Bakhtin calls the emphasis on baser bodily urges and functions the "material bodily principle," and Krewe de Vieux dishes out steaming bowlfuls of it.

Bakhtin sees bodily degradation as a predicate for transcending the merely lewd, a liberation from imprisoning hypocrisies of ideology, the bull#@$* we have to contend with all the rest of the year. Krew de Vieux is quite conscious of itself not only as an insurrection, but also as a resurrection, an effort to recover from the anti-Carnivalesque aspects of the nineteenth-century Uptown

Mardi Gras model. Their mission statement is explicit about this intention: "We believe in exposing the world to the true nature of Mardi Gras—and in exposing ourselves to the world." Since Katrina, Krewe du Vieux has been joined by several other downtown parading clubs—'tit Rəx, Chewbacchus, Red Beans—all of which follow the Krewe de Vieux model far more than the Uptown one, especially by keeping dues affordable.

But the ultimate expression of the Carnivalesque instinct in our time is what happens Downtown on Mardi Gras day. Here the line between spectator and performer is almost totally erased as thousands converge in the streets in a utopian vision of mass civic participation. And on this day—if only for a day—we also witness New Orleans's idealized sense of itself come down to earth to shape the city's social reality.

Many of the most enthusiastic and freshly creative participants in the Downtown Fat Tuesday are transplants drawn to the city by the idea of New Orleans more than by direct connections to its preexisting social world. On Mardi Gras day, they join native-born residents to perform this idea of New Orleans in elaborate ways, making clear the utopian kernel of New Orleans exceptionalist ideology: an abandoned colony of misfits and outcasts turning lemons into spiked lemonade. The more biting the satirical edge, the crasser the transgression of genteel proprieties, the greater the punch.

Senseless beauty is also a great value in itself, transgressive because of its brazen occupation of such a large swath of a city, if only for a day. Public theater with an amateur cast of thousands, clustering and breaking apart at different points—Frenchmen and Chartres, Royal and Kerlerec, the Cathedral, the Moonwalk.

One of the greatest artworks I've ever seen was a guy by the corner of Royal and Esplanade wearing only a bath towel. His hair was messed up and he had shaving cream on half his face and a disposable razor in his hand. He just stood and shivered and eyed the crowd nervously, as if he'd just inexplicably been transported from another universe.

Chicago Tribune jazz critic Howard Reich has praised New Orleans's contribution to American culture generally as the promotion of a "freewheeling, anti-elitist, come-one-come-all prototype for making art."[3] Though he wasn't referring to Carnival specifically, nothing fulfills that vision more than Downtown on Fat Tuesday.

Those who rue the relative dearth of local private contributions to institutional mainstream art organizations often cite the drain on people's funds caused by Carnival spending. But making our own art, music, and theater, utterly without professional credentials and on a scale no other city does, is nothing to be ashamed of.

Sadly, many locals, for generations, have carefully avoided the Creole districts on Mardi Gras day. It was once out of social and cultural intolerance (fear of Blacks, fear of freaks). Now it's often because of misguided and static notions of authenticity, as if their own New Orleans experience is the only legitimate one. They have no idea what they're missing, but its ancient name is Carnival.

Frenchmen Street and
the *Nouvelle* New Orleans
2014

One of the most striking examples of the balance between continuity and change in New Orleans has been the meteoric evolution of Frenchmen Street over the past thirty years. In 1984, two music clubs were emerging as hot new venues in the 500 and 600 blocks. The Faubourg, at 626 Frenchmen (soon renamed Snug Harbor), offered straight-ahead and experimental jazz—from Ellis Marsalis to Astral Project. At 532 Frenchmen, the Dream Palace, with its psychedelic décor and galactic ceiling mural, catered to the rock crowd, most notably through now legendary Saturday night Radiators gigs for the "fishhead" fans.

What brought Frenchmen Street to critical mass as the live music mecca it is today probably was the liquor license Adé Salgado got in the late '80s as he converted his coffeehouse into a club called *Café Brasil*. The shuttered space now sits like a ghostly guardian of legend amid the cultural explosion it helped to set off.

A nocturnal stroll down Frenchmen Street forty years ago was a quiet and lonely excursion, even on a Saturday night. LaBorde's Printers, the Swiss Confectionery, the Diamond Grid Battery auto shop—all would be shuttered for the night. Today? Rip van Winkle would find himself in an alien world indeed. The birth of what we imagine today when people say "Frenchmen Street" is evidence of how rapidly change can happen and, more interestingly, how change is portrayed, in New Orleans. The very first platitude it shatters is the old one about a New Orleans supposedly "resistant to change."

The notion that New Orleans "resists change" is rooted in Americanist rhetoric, to cast the city unfavorably in comparison with go-getter American boomtowns like Chicago or Houston. The "resistant to change" rap is laid on us when we don't uncritically accept the latest national trend, be it a riverfront expressway, high-rise waterfront housing, or placing sharper limits on the rights of African Americans in the first decades after the USA purchased Louisiana in 1803. One political option is cast as "progress" (usually in an economic sense), while the other—reluctance to tear down old houses, for example, or to adopt American-style racism in the nineteenth century—as evidence of our "backwardness." But we need to understand the relationship between history and rhetoric, meaning we have to understand how rhetoric shapes our perception of history.

A list of historical facts built around the narrative that New Orleans is "resistant to change" will highlight certain events at the expense of others. We might do well to remember the incident Frenchmen Street's name commemorates. The five Frenchmen executed at the foot of the street in 1769 had instigated the first anti-colonial revolution in the Americas, eight years before the thirteen colonies came up with the Declaration of Independence. In Louisiana, the enemy was the Spanish crown, not the Court of St. James, but the goal was the same—a loosening, if not severing, of the bonds of colonial control, in the name of free trade.

Slave insurgents weren't any more successful, but that didn't keep them from dogged acts of resistance throughout the antebellum era, including the German Coast Uprising in 1811, the largest slave revolt in US history. After the Civil War, multi-racial delegates meeting at New Orleans drafted the most radically far-reaching of all Reconstruction state constitutions and elected Black men to statewide office. If you weren't familiar with this history of revolutionary struggle, it may be because the master narrative of the region's history buries such facts. The idea of a New Orleans "resistant to change" obscures our ability to recognize a very different narrative of New Orleans, as constantly and radically in a state of change, not only socially but politically.

New Orleanian skepticism toward "progress," as defined in most of America, can't be reduced to "resistance to change," but it is one of the city's special assets. New Orleans exceptionalism, the will to see in New Orleans an alternative to American hegemonic values, is a critical counterweight to the affirmative arguments of American exceptionalism, which focus very much on profitable business climate at the expense of all other considerations.

The Frenchmen Street boom is also evidence of how exceptionalist rhetoric is applied, ironically, to explain (and defend) instances of sweeping change of a particularly American cast—such as the hypergentrification that has swept the old Creole districts since Katrina.

The economic rationale is deemed insufficient to justify change in New Orleans, and that's a unique aspect of local political culture that we should all be proud of. Changes, if they're going to be welcomed, need to be reconciled with notions of local identity—not just whether something is "good business" or "the American way," or "best practices," or whatever.

So, Frenchmen Street proudly asserts itself as an expression of a uniquely and deeply New Orleanian spirit, a utopian evocation of an ineradicable New Orleanian ethos, with appreciation of live music as its cornerstone. The most recent Frenchmen club, Bamboula's, makes the will to embody this ideal explicit, with its eponymous reference to the historic Congo Square song and dance genre. The relocation to Frenchmen of the Louisiana Music Factory record store is further testament to the street's status as the city's music mecca. The HBO series *Tremé* might just as well have been named "Marigny" for its many Frenchmen Street scenes.

Frenchmen Street, on just about any night of the week, is a loud and proud symbol of New Orleans's reinvention of itself as a holy city for live music and the culture surrounding it (including cocktails, food, fashion statements, etc.). But then, many American cities, especially in our region, boast "nightlife" districts with abundant live music.

What makes Frenchmen Street a more exciting total experience than similar thoroughfares in Nashville, Memphis, or Austin, is the same thing Bourbon Street has going for it: public drinking. It turns a street rife with music clubs into a unified festival experience that takes root in the public space and thus defines an entire area—and its residents—rather than just being a handful of dots on a map. Every other attribute is secondary but still meaningful.

Frenchmen Street offers a wide range of music styles, many rendered with great talent, most for free or cheap (better for consumers than musicians). Frenchmen Street goes late, but so does the party in other urban music districts—though, again, our liberal alcohol laws, allowing for bars that never close, give us the edge if a never-ending party is the yardstick.

What's more unique is how Frenchmen starts early. Early gigs broaden the pool of performers as well as audiences, and steer the appreciation of live music (and drinking) away from the limiting category of "nightlife" and into the unashamed normalcy of daylight. Again, the way all of this activity spills into and occupies the public space depends upon the nuts-and-bolts legal glue (public consumption and legalized loitering) that makes the magic—and the music—possible.

If Frenchmen Street is the temple complex of New Orleans music, more than ever that makes it a temple to New Orleans itself. The city has been famously musical for centuries, a reputation that hinges on the abundance of live music venues, street music, patronage, and participation. Previous loci have included Congo Square, the old French Opera House, Storyville, South Rampart Street, or Milneburg in the early jazz era. But never before has devotion to an extensive culture of live music been as central, as foundational, to New Orleanian identity as it is today.

This can be seen as an offshoot of a growing "touristic" culture, where locals begin to perceive and experience their hometown in the same way tourists do. Or it can be thought of as the consummation of practices long since baked into the city's culture, and well-suited for assimilation by New Orleanians seeking to preserve a sense of the city's—and their own—exceptionalism. "Outsiders"—transplants more than tourists—have always played a role in noticing and valuing local cultural features deemed as unique.

Bourbon Street continues to be the city's most iconic street—a competition with Frenchmen as instructive as it is pointless. We're talking about a competition between symbols, not business zones. While the über-hip among us like to demean Frenchmen as the "New Bourbon," it's more accurate to say that Bourbon Street was the old Frenchmen.

Not so long ago, Bourbon was *the* place for live music, what with Louis Prima, Al Hirt, Pete Fountain, and other legends holding forth. Many of today's older musicians, from Ellis Marsalis to Herlin Riley, honed their chops at Bourbon Street gigs. It combined vice (striptease) with live music in a way that invoked a lighter shade of Storyville, continuing to feed America's sense of New Orleans as a place that parties in an exceptionally transgressive manner.

Frenchmen Street has succeeded in severing sexual vice from live music, an achievement that says a lot about New Orleans and America in the late twentieth and early twenty-first centuries. Back in the Storyville Era, the state's repressive Gay-Shattuck laws sought to curb sexual commerce, drinking, and interracial mingling by, among other measures, banning live music in bars.[1]

There's no real competition between Bourbon and Frenchmen because they cater to different audiences, people of differing social and cultural backgrounds (as well as those enlightened cosmopolitans able to enjoy both).

People with a greater degree of cultural capital—both locals and visiting aficionados—prefer Frenchmen. The ultra-hip have concluded, of course, that Frenchmen Street is already too well-known to confer "underground" cred, so they're branching down St. Claude and pooh-poohing the poseurs left behind. Thus, we see again how the anxiety of authenticity has become more acute than ever in the post-Katrina boom years, even if the hipster compulsion for cultural distinction has degenerated into just another consumer niche.

The comic irony is that Frenchmen Street today is nothing like it ever was before, so it can't be a passed off as a continuation of a traditional use of the area. We need to accept that the explosive downtown cultural renaissance that Frenchmen Street presides over is the result of a romantic vision of what New Orleans should be, more than a continuation of how it has been. Frenchmen Street represents a re-creation of New Orleans in a particular version of its own image. Change, yes, shaped by myth. As naturally New Orleans as vegan gumbo and milk punch daiquiris.

I Miss My Schwegmann's—and I Got a Right To 2014

The City Planning Commission has OK'd the new Robért supermarket on the corner of Elysian Fields and St. Claude. If it goes up—and there's no reason to think it won't—it will signify the changed status of the neighborhood as much as the original Schwegmann's Giant Supermarket did when it opened on that corner in 1946.

The proposed structure has a Whole Foods look to it: sleek comfort, dressed-down luxury. It will be shiny and clean and will probably not have the funky features defining the effort of the Healing Center, a few blocks down St. Claude, to represent neighborhood culture—the voodoo vévé out front, Devin Myers's NOLA primitivist mural out back.

I have personally come to appreciate the riverside downtown corner of Elysian Fields and St. Claude the way it is right now, but I know I'm on the fringe. My favorite thing about the corner now is its function as the Megabus depot. I love watching the crowds line up and board the buses to Houston, Birmingham, etc. And maybe a large abandoned building is best for anchoring a neighborhood struggling to remain affordable. I remember messing around in the old Jax Brewery when it was condemned. The Quarter was never the same after it was redeveloped.

My personal preference for getting the old Schwegmann's property back into commerce? Put it back exactly how it was in 1979, which is very close to how it still was in August 2005. But I also realize that my personal sentimentalism isn't shared by the majority of neighborhood residents, however pleased I am that sentimentalism is a viable argument in New Orleans.

I still wake up today and realize I had been in the narrow aisles of the old Schwegmann's seconds ago, in dreams. I could walk you straight to the coffee or toilet paper or headache medicine. I could do it blindfolded.

I bought beer and cigarettes there for my parents as soon as I was old enough to walk over on my own—about eight or nine. The staff all knew me. Schwegmann's had a house liquor brand labeled "Piety and Burgundy" that intrigued me, since in my mind Piety and Burgundy was quite far from Elysian Fields and St. Claude. I later learned that the label was an homage to the original Schwegmann's, which stood at Piety and Burgundy and was known as the Bell Foods grocery store when I was a kid.

One time I was mugged on the way to Schwegmann's. It happened alongside the Paris Theater, a porn cinema on the corner of Elysian Fields and Burgundy. It was a couple of well-known neighborhood toughs. I knew their names. They passed a pocket knife between them and advised me firmly to hand over my grocery money. The police came quickly and knew Schwegmann's was the first place to look. I remember walking across the parking lot with the uniformed cops and seeing the two older boys coming out with foot-long hot dogs doused in chili and mustard.

The cops were optimistic about the pocket knife. They said it might make an armed robbery charge stick. They confirmed that these guys—brothers or cousins, everyone in the neighborhood knew their names—were bad seeds. They might benefit from a stint at "Juvenile," the cops said, which I knew meant jail for kids.

I also saw my first gunshot victim at Schwegmann's. He was an older Black man, balding, wearing a polyester dress shirt and slacks. He sat on the ground by the parking lot side door. His left leg was in a pool of blood and he had a bunch of bloody paper towels all over and around the wound, in the thigh. They said the police were coming.

I remember a guy died in the Schwegmann's once, too. I don't think it was nefarious, probably just a heart attack or something. He was in the back corner by the paper goods, cleaning supplies, and pet food, three aisles that jutted back at a perpendicular angle to the other aisles in the store. They had employees around him and some uniformed professionals of some type. I just saw his feet. But I was happy to help spread the word around the neighborhood: "They had a dead guy in Schwegmann's!"

It was the first store I shoplifted from. Never got caught, either. I was almost as comfortable there as in my own house. I went there almost every day.

I bought my first condoms that weren't out of a machine there. My brother was audibly breaking into a giggle-fit a few yards behind me. We were that kind of giddy teen-stoned that never works after age twenty-five or so. The lady behind the pharmacy counter had known me since I was riding in a cart. She must have thought something about kids growing up and getting stupid.

I'm happy that my son got to experience the place. It was called Robért by then, but in the early years of the twenty-first century had barely changed. They had closed the pharmacy and put the liquor there. They no longer served beer and snacks at the lunch counter, but the layout of the aisles was mostly the same, and they still had a window where you could pay utility bills, something that I doubt Robért will have when they reopen. As my son grew from infant to toddler, the staff all got to know his love of bananas. I'd roll him in past the old pharmacy, turn right into the produce aisle, and he would point and beam and squeal: "Banana!"

Katrina didn't fundamentally alter everyone's life, especially close to the river, but the loss of the Schwegmann's (which we still called it years after Robért had taken over) was felt deeply. Joshua Clark depicted the scene inside the store during the Katrina aftermath in his 2006 memoir, *Heart Like Water*. It's well written, but differs from the account of my mother, who also made forays into her old neighborhood grocery after the storm. Clark's account is frightening, alarming, with a rumor of a senseless murder in the aisles. My mom reports that she was scared to go in, so she stood on Rampart and watched people go in and out until a friendly elderly man offered to go in with her. He took her through the rear delivery entrance, on Rampart, which worked for her because she was after cat food, which was way in the back. She said it was dark and quiet, with footfalls and murmuring, but no screams or gunshots.

I was mightily offended to read the notice the Robért people put in front after the building was boarded up for its long coma. It said it would take a while to reopen because of how severely damaged it had been by looters. I was more of the mind that they should have thanked the looters for taking out their meat and other perishables before they rotted in there. I swore I would never shop there again, whenever they opened.

But the post-Katrina adrenaline has worn off, taking with it the deeply personal grudges of that angry and paranoid time. For years, though, I felt abandoned by my old Schwegmann's, and I blamed Robért—despite knowing that Schwegmann's and Robért were locked in a legal battle about whose insurance should pay to fix the place. During those years, other businesses came through, and I'm reluctant to abandon them.

The first was Mardi Gras Zone, a corner store whose eccentricity fits right into the cultural fabric of the neighborhood. Then the New Orleans Food Co-Op, planned since well before Katrina, finally opened in the new Healing Center. The co-op's slogan—100 percent owned by the 99 percent (I'm an "owner" myself)—is far more in keeping with my kind of Marigny identity than whatever attempt Robért will make to appeal to neighborhood authenticity.

Between Mardi Gras Zone and the co-op, unless Robért can match Rouse's prices, I really still don't see why I'd go there. It won't be anything like the mystic Schwegmann's of collective memory, but then, how many neighborhood residents today share that memory? And of those, who remembers it more fondly than not?

In my more rational moments, I remember that, before Katrina, I was a lot less nostalgic about the city in general. One of the psychological effects of Katrina on me, which has only increased with the recent demographic changes in the old neighborhood, is a knee-jerk defensiveness about the pre-K status quo ante. The more I hear about how terrible the city was before the storm, the more I remember its un-terrible charms.

Before the storm, however, I was one of the people loudly wishing for a Marigny that's a lot more like it is now than it was then. During all the years I lived away from New Orleans, I told every hipster I met (though the word had different connotations then) that they needed to get to New Orleans to help realize the bohemian utopia that had been nascent in Marigny/Bywater for decades already. I wanted more innovative restaurants, bars, coffeehouses. I wanted gourmet grocery options, not the same old Schwegmann's (whatever the name on the sign) with its unimaginative product list and bad hot dogs at the snack bar.

So, I can critique my own nostalgia, but I still don't like it when newer transplants dismiss older residents' refuge in memory. The "Ain't Dere No More" mode is something we treasure. Newer residents sometimes feel that such nostalgia is an effort to challenge them on the local authenticity scale, so they overcompensate by bad-mouthing the dear, shabby city we all loved (though often critically) before they got here.

Allow us to cherish our memories and don't take it the wrong way. Youthful memories are, in fact, a chief distinction between how native-born locals and transplants view the city. Even if the whole city is bought up by folks from somewhere else—folks with more money, ambition, whatever—our weepy nostalgia will be one thing that the new New Orleans won't be able to colonize.

So, in my more rational moments (which I treasure less than my sentimental moments), I think it's a great thing that Robért has opted for a total redesign of the riverside downtown corner of Elysian Fields and St. Claude, and I'm glad the design doesn't resemble an oversized Creole cottage. One commercial corner of totally new buildings—to replace a 1946 structure—will not damage the neighborhood's tout ensemble; it would be far more embarrassing to see Floridian pseudo-colonial architecture at that spot. I'm just glad I've already signed a fixed-rate mortgage, because the effect on property values could be more detrimental than the aesthetics of the building. The rising cost of housing is what will certainly transform the Marigny we grew up in, replacing a neighborhood social character defined by affordability for the first two centuries of its existence.

A Chic Makeover for a Shabby Economy 2015

New Orleans was shabby chic before shabby was chic. But today we witness how the more chic the city gets, the more un-shabby it becomes. Unable to alleviate poverty, we can at least sweep it into the corners, where it won't clash with our spiffed-up historic renovations. It may be decadent of me, but I remember fondly the visual aesthetic of the city when it looked more roughly lived in, and when a more densely packed working class filled the streets with a festival air of public congregation, with all the messiness of a daily parade.

Every new era promotes its own greatness by turning on aspects of the era before it, patting itself on the back for solving long-standing problems, becoming the city "we always knew we could be." Part of the sales pitch for the new New Orleans is overplaying the alleged complacency of previous generations, to seem always like finally, something is being done. But much of the trumpeted social healing of our ancient problems amounts to little more than a visual argument. The pervasive ills of poverty, inequality, unreliable employment, and attendant symptoms (crime, addiction) haven't really gone away, as we see every night on the evening news or hear in the chatter carried from stoop to stoop. But pains have been taken to push visual evidence of capitalism's collateral damage further back than "back of town" used to be, and the seams of poverty that used to stretch through the riverfront neighborhoods, adding social variety and keeping property values down, are on their way to total extinction.

Meanwhile, we see a new wave of warnings about New Orleans's loss of its historic identity,[1] even as its blend of the modern with the traditional is declared by others to be a tricentennial triumph. Creole déjà vu, since we see these messages go mano a mano at least every twenty years. New Orleans exceptionalists will keep complaining, but the Americanization continues, because guess who's got the money?

The latest round of hand-wringing over our inevitable but apparently glacial Americanization emphasizes the recent smoking ban, the end of skinny dipping at the Country Club on Louisa Street, and various items in the proposed new Comprehensive Zoning Ordinance. Most concerning are the draft CZO's recommendations for acceptable noise levels and higher height limits on the river below Esplanade. But these are all symptoms, not causes. This is a time to remember the basic Marxist wisdom that economic change also changes every other aspect of society. The 1996 H. U. D. grant to tear down the St. Thomas projects in the Irish Channel was the first step on the long road to luxury condo high-rises on the river.

Alice Walker's great short story, "Nineteen Fifty-five," has an Elvis Presley character deliver a priceless line to his Black blueswoman mentor: "They want what you got but they don't want you."[2] This is the anxiety that haunts many a New Orleanian today. Unless the much ballyhooed economic boom can hire the people who are already here, like the 26,000 unemployed New Orleanians between ages eighteen and twenty-four, it just spells doom for people trying to stay in a city where people from somewhere else get the good jobs and make life increasingly unaffordable.

The economic changes bring on changes to the city's appearance, too. A more sanitized look. The opening of Jim Jarmusch's 1986 film *Down by Law* features a montage of New Orleans street scenes that captures well the look of the city in my youth: peeling paint, litter, aimless-looking loiterers, and, of course, the ubiquitous housing projects. Today you can see remnants of the last one right next to Marie Laveau's tomb, which, for the first time in history, you now have to pay to visit. Bringing those projects down was an emotional act that spoke volumes about the city's uncomfortable relationship with the working people it needs to feed the fortunes of the entire metropolitan region and state.

I attended a lecture last fall at Loyola given by American studies scholar Julia Faisst. She spoke about the demolition of St. Louis's Pruitt-Igoe public housing development in the 1970s. She argued convincingly about how the modernist architecture of the Pruitt-Igoe complex (and similar developments, like Chicago's Henry Horner and Robert Taylor homes), represented a utopian vision in which economic problems were treated with an aesthetic solution. Lipstick on a pig, as it were, and of course doomed to fail. But the same conflation of optics and economics is with us to this day. It's reflected in the way anger at the continuing social disaster of American capitalism has been directed at aesthetic rather than economic targets. Thus, the response to long-standing, racially inflected poverty and violence was to "Hope VI"—i.e., tear down—the housing clusters that once seemed to represent a similarly facile solution to an entrenched problem.

The New Orleans projects were rooted in the same inequitable economics as the massive high-rises of the industrial Midwest but were markedly different in design. Porches and balconies on low-rise structures faced each other across grassy quads.[3] I was charmed by them as a child, regaled with stories from a first-grade classmate at McDonogh 15 about how fun life in Iberville was. I wanted to do a sleepover at his house, but my mom forbade it out of safety concerns. That was my first inkling that something shameful lurked in these leafy housing developments. Indeed, they looked so much like university campuses that mayoral candidate Virginia Boulet actually suggested moving the University of New Orleans to the Iberville Project in the heady, visionary election of 2006.

If the aesthetic of Pruitt-Igoe and similar developments was futuristic, our housing projects conveyed a more paternalist message. Not a radical break with the past into a bold future, but a more consummately New Orleanian effort to enshrine aspects of the past into solutions for the future (at least visually). Both architectural styles, however, would eventually be tarred with the shame of government assistance, the ultimate degradation for gung ho American individualists. For their own self-respect and to assuage the guilt of others, the working poor now needed to be housed in a way that camouflaged the role of government in mitigating the abuses of capitalism.

The reworked developments take pains to send a very different visual message than the projects they replaced. The new structures don't face each other across quads; they face the street, dispensing with the interior park-like atmosphere of yore. Some redevelopments—like River Garden, which replaced St. Thomas—invoke traditional New Orleans residential models, the signature approach of Pres Kabacoff's HRI (Historic Restorations, Inc.) Others, like the Magnolia and St. Bernard redevelopments, go with a more generic suburban look. Maybe if it looks like an affluent suburb of Washington, DC, subsidized residents will shake bad habits like destitution and the violence it breeds.

The names of these new developments are the most telling detail of all: River Garden, Harmony Oaks, and—the kicker—Columbia Parc at the Bayou District (that's what used to be the St. Bernard Projects, and yes, "parc" is spelled with a "c"). Who needs satire when farce becomes social policy? Significantly, the old project names had become iconic in the cultural history of the city—St. Thomas, Magnolia, Calliope, St. Bernard. But enough New Orleanians were so deeply ashamed of that aspect of their social history that they started changing the names before the money for the bulldozers was available.

High priests of the city's triumphant neoliberal gospel have required that other names and buildings associated with the less fortunate also be unstitched from the city's semiotic weave. Charity Hospital, for example—gone and not coming back, after a 250-year run. "Charity," it seems, is now shameful, a symptom of dependency in a society that hangs its hat on a particularly antisocial version of "freedom." Now more than ever, Kris Kristofferson was right that "freedom's just another word for nothing left to lose." Our local, affordable public university isn't looking too healthy, either. Be thankful that you're free to be unable to afford college. After all, we can get college graduates from other places.

To their credit, some preservationists joined advocates of the working poor in (vain) resistance to the city council's unanimous 2007 decision to redevelop the "Big Four" projects. The scattered-site units peppering riverfront neighborhoods were less architecturally significant and have found fewer friends. Yet they served the purpose of preserving the working-class character of the area and keeping property values affordable for a broader swath of residents. The Faubourg Marigny Improvement Association groused about the scattered sites and greased the skids for their elimination; now they're worried about the inevitable proposals for luxury condo high-rises on the river.

I'm a proud sentimentalist when it comes to preserving what I feel to be distinct cultural attributes of New Orleans, but fighting the cultural fight after the economic one has been decided is like tearing down buildings that came to represent poverty, racism, and crime rather than addressing the actual problems.

When it comes to culture and economics, post-Katrina New Orleans has witnessed an odd reconciliation of formerly hostile ideological camps. New Orleans Americanists—champions of business and economic development—have made common cause with culture-loving New Orleans exceptionalists by converting culture to money (the "cultural economy"). The exceptionalists fret about the city losing its identity while the Americanist masters of the cultural economy stay busy packaging that identity.

Maybe the only tonic for worried exceptionalists is good old New Orleans fatalism. Hey man, cultural change happens. I'm an English professor facing the death of print culture. How does that feel? You get over it. And then you die.

In his 1924 tome, *Literature and Revolution*, Leon Trotsky surmised that after the revolution, art and literature would disappear altogether. What's more likely is that a truly just society would have less need of the kinds of art—social realism in literature or the blues in music—that are responses to and coping strategies for the victimization the haves repeatedly inflict on the have-nots. Judging from the ongoing assault on economic equality in Baton Rouge and Washington, we have no cause to fear the end of gritty, edgy, angry art. We may in fact witness a glorious rebirth of the blues.

We'll need to look in different neighborhoods to find it, and there will be arguments about whether the new art forms are legitimate or authentic. But when those aesthetic quarrels subside, we can grab the real estate and put up plaques in honor of the cultural pioneers, while their descendants pack up and try to find housing they can afford. After all, compulsory mobility is the American way. Enjoy the boom!

Got the Airbnb Blues?
Get Hip to Creative Disruption!
2016

I was despondent about the city council decision to allow whole-home short-term rentals for up to ninety days and about how it might make it impossible for permanent residents to continue living in New Orleans.[1]

So, I met with my Libertarian friend, Gary Rand, to try to look on the bright side. We met at Mimi's in the Marigny, which is where he hangs out since Bootie's in the Bywater closed. He likes bars that announce the name of the trendy neighborhood on their signs. I had suggested my usual haunt, St. Roch Tavern, since that also has the neighborhood name in it, but he said the beer selection was weak, that less than twenty hoppy microbrews on tap is below market standard. He also warned me about going anywhere behind the new St. Roch Market. "Good luck trying to get an Uber back there!" he chortled.

We bellied up to the bar and I got an Ugly Bastard Organic Molasses IPA. It was ten bucks, but he was buying. "Aren't you worried about Airbnb making it impossible for regular people to live and work in New Orleans?" I asked him.

"Dude, you're looking at it the wrong way," he assured me. "New Orleans is just *resistant to change*. Platforms like Airbnb give us just as much opportunity as challenges. We need to embrace the new, and we're doing that. New Orleans is on *Creative Capitalist* magazine's top ten list of innovative extractors of wealth today. Instead of whining about getting left behind, we need to get in front and lead."

"But how can somebody do that if they can't find a place to live where they can afford the rent?"

"Great example. Instead of whining about not being able to afford the rent, people need to buy up properties and start building their portfolio."

Gary Rand knows what he's talking about. With a small loan from his parents in Connecticut he was able to buy some wrecked houses after Hurricane Katrina that he converted into artist lofts. He's very proud of the work he put in to rebuild the city and make it able to compete for creative talent from around the country.

"But Councilman Jared Brossett says it could erode the character of our neighborhoods," I pressed.

"Great point," he conceded. "We do need to be wary of that. Local people are part of our brand, even though they're sometimes a drain on our resources. But the good news is that you can become local really fast here in New Orleans, because the locals are so friendly and easy to imitate! *Alternative Travel* magazine listed New Orleans in the top ten for people who are eccentric but also friendly and cooperative. We want to keep New Orleans weird, but we need to do it like Austin does, like weird in a way that's fun for visitors and not scary or put-offish. Like how Whole Foods is alternative but also high-quality and with a price point that discourages troublemakers and people who are just depressing to be around because they can never afford anything."

"But if eccentric locals can't afford to live here anymore, will the tourists still want to come? How will they do their—what is it called?—'people watching'?"

Gary Rand also writes a travel blog—it's called "How to Not Look Like a Tourist." He knows how to walk the walk. He was wearing a cap from a coffee shop in Asheville and a T-shirt from a snowboard shop in Park City. His shoes were limited edition New Orleans-themed Nikes. He's given lots of tips to New Orleans visitors, like don't wear beads when it's not Mardi Gras and be sure to bad-mouth Bourbon Street. His latest post added Frenchmen Street to the list of places to loudly complain about.

"The city council needs to get creative about how we can preserve the city's character," he continued. "But that doesn't mean caving to the people who aren't directly contributing to brand development and brand sustainability. Nobody comes here to see some boring, normal-looking schoolteacher or nurse or bus driver or whatever. It's about focusing on the culture bearers, giving them a way to capitalize on their authenticity."

"But where are the culture bearers supposed to live? If a nonresident can rent a whole house for up to ninety days, how can they also rent it out to a local for a one-year lease?"

"Dude, you're the one being conservative," he retorted. "It's called the 'sharing economy' for a reason. It's called 'house sharing.' People need to learn to share. It's especially selfish for people living in New Orleans's old neighborhoods to refuse to share their housing with others. New Orleans is a national treasure. It belongs to everyone."

"But how can somebody live in a house if they have to give it up for a tourist three months out of the year?"

"You need to be more creative. Old solutions are not going to work for the twenty-first century. Consider the wisdom of the market: When do most tourists come to visit?"

"Mardi Gras? Jazz Fest?"

He guffawed. "You're thinking too small! That's the problem with you old-fashioned socialist types. Always wanting to shut down the energy of the marketplace. New Orleans is a draw all year round now, even in summer, with festivals every weekend!"

"So, we can't live here at all?"

"Not what I said. I agree with the council's ninety-day limit. But people wouldn't rent out for three months in a row—they would probably Airbnb their properties on the weekends mostly. See?"

"See what?"

"That means traditional renters could still occupy the properties during the week."

"What would they do on the weekend?"

"Lots of possibilities there. Let's brainstorm. The city could use tax revenues generously shared by the platforms to build temporary housing units in New Orleans East for culture bearers to go over the weekend and fund a special shuttle to get them to their jobs in the city, just for those couple of days. During the week they could maintain the properties. Maybe the wealth creators—the property owners—could be induced to help the locals even more by renting their units, just on weekdays, below market value, like, say $1,500 a month instead of $2,500. It would be worth it because the people without enough money could help keep things authentic. New Orleans needs its locals! They know what little knick-knacks and hot sauces and stuff to stock so that the apartment seems like a real New Orleans place, not some hotel for tourists. And—who knows?—forward-thinking home sharers could also maybe keep like a little backroom or outbuilding to house the culture bearers on site. That way the guests could have like a real local on the stoop to greet them and help them get situated. But remember, a large homeless population isn't quite so bad here as it would look in other places. The homeless just need to stay upbeat about it."

He started crooning a Gershwin song, "*I got plenty o'nothing, and nothing's plenty for me-ee.* Like that, see? It's all about having the right attitude. That way our visitors won't be made to feel uncomfortable. Basically, we need to license the locals and monitor them to make sure that, you know, when they're hipping visitors to out-of-the-way bars that only locals know about, or just acting weird on the streetcar, that they don't take it too far."

I asked him about muggers, about whether our reputation for crime was also part of our brand that we wanted to continue to promote. He said it could be done as long as tourists didn't actually get hurt—but it might be a perfect nightcap to a New Orleans adventure to witness some locals having a catfight or shooting at each other. "All part of gettin' wild on the weekend, yeah you right!" He slapped me on the back and winked.

I had never thought of all these ramifications. That's why I always go to Gary Rand when the creative disruption of capitalism, Mother Nature's economic system, gets me down. He's a real creative guy. He's designed lots of local microbrew names and labels, like "Big Easy Misery," just voted the sourest triple-hopped gutbucket ale in the Deep South by Hop Hip, an influential beer blog. I think he also helped design the New Orleans-themed décor at the Starbucks on Canal and St. Charles.

I wanted to talk more but he got an urgent text. New guests were arriving at a property of his in Desire Garden, a former housing project where he'd managed to wrangle a market-rate unit. He wanted to get over there to spin an old Meters L. P. on the vintage turntable and put on a costume, to show them what New Orleans is all about. "I love sharing my city with people from all over the world!" he beamed.

He hopped on his custom titanium bicycle and sped off, turning his head for one last piece of shouted advice: "Relax, man! Enjoy the revolution!"

Restless Super-Natives:
New Orleans and the Anxiety of Authenticity
2018

The anxiety of authenticity is a disease affecting many of us today with untold damaging symptoms, especially in New Orleans. It can be seen in the constant hand-wringing over our ever-evolving music, parading, culinary and festival scene, and even in the proliferation of short-term rentals. While many of us feel that the loss of permanent residents damages the authenticity of any residential neighborhood, the whole reason people seek out Airbnb accommodations, rather than traditional hotel rooms, is the desire to experience a place in what is felt to be a more "authentic" manner.

The specter of cultural appropriation is one symptom of authenticity anxiety. It affects how we view the nature and evolution of local culture. In strikingly ahistorical logic, critics of cultural appropriation argue that only "authentic" members of a group are licensed to express that group's culture. The term "poseur" used to be hurled at people who engaged in some kind of "inauthentic" cultural performance, but now the stakes are higher. The "poseur" has become a thief, even an imperialist, whose unbounded sense of entitlement and privilege enables him to invade, "colonize," and deprive "authentic" subjects of their sole right to produce and trade in their exclusive cultural forms and tropes.

New Orleans has become a laboratory for the anxiety of authenticity in the years since Hurricane Katrina, largely because of the ideology of New Orleans exceptionalism—the idea that certain sectors of New Orleans society offer an alternative to Anglo-Saxon America's puritanical capitalist value system, with its emphasis on work, delayed gratification, and social mobility.

There was a great resurgence of New Orleans exceptionalist attitudes immediately after Hurricane Katrina. The post-Katrina recovery years witnessed a veritable renaissance of parading, arguably the most distinctive aspect of New Orleans culture in the American context. Free public festivals also exploded.

At first, this renewed embrace of distinctly New Orleanian cultural practices promoted solidarity among the reduced population of people who couldn't imagine living anywhere else, despite the difficult conditions (limited amenities, frequent power outages, etc.).

But then came the post-Katrina boom years and attitudes quickly changed. Many of the older parts of the city that had remained affordable for generations suddenly saw huge increases in property values and, accordingly, in rents and tax assessments. Growing economic anxieties led, predictably, to recriminations of a cultural sort.

After the storm, many young people came down to participate in the recovery effort, for economic or altruistic reasons, and became enamored of the city's current sense of itself in the high exceptionalist mode. Many fell in love with and embraced a distinctive New Orleans cultural identity, founding new parading societies and street festivals.

In 2013, New Orleans studies guru Richard Campanella penned an influential essay entitled "Gentrification and Its Discontents."[1] In it, he pointed to demographic changes in Bywater, a gentrifying area in the city's Ninth Ward. He took special interest in a new kind of post-Katrina transplant dedicated to embracing traditional aspects of the city's culture (public celebration, cuisine, music, voodoo). He labeled these culturally precocious newcomers "super-natives," implying that their efforts to embrace the local cultural identity were some kind of unearned appropriation.

I had always considered it a point of local pride that many people who moved here wanted to become New Orleanians, rather than just Americans living in a different city. And there's nothing new about transplants settling here with the express aim of embracing and preserving a culture they view as unique. But now, the embrace of New Orleans culture by new arrivals had become suspect, even sinister. It was around this moment that the anxiety of authenticity in New Orleans became acute.

There have been many flashpoints since then, among them a "second line" parade to honor David Bowie after the international pop star's death in 2016. "Second line" parades are traditionally held on Sundays and sponsored by various social aid and pleasure clubs, which are, of course, African American fraternal organizations. There are also plentiful faux parades put on for tourists, conventions, even wedding parties. Chicago stand-up comic Hannibal Buress has a hilarious routine about organizing a bachelor party parade in the French Quarter for four guys.[2]

The David Bowie event wasn't a traditional African American "second line" parade, but it wasn't a tourist knock-off sponsored by a convention, either. It was local residents putting on a parade on short notice to commemorate an important global event (in their eyes), in a distinctively New

Orleanian way: with traditional New Orleans brass bands winding through the streets playing Bowie standards.

Of course, the blowout got hammered anyway, for "appropriating" a traditional practice in some kind of "inauthentic" manner. Similar charges flew later that same year when a Carnival club, the Intergalactic Krewe of Chewbacchus, staged a Princess Leia memorial parade after the death of *Star Wars* star Carrie Fisher.

The latest chapter in the drama was the social media sniping in 2018 about a new Carnival club, Krewe du Kanaval. It added a Haitian element to the dynamic mix of Carnival traditions that continue to evolve in New Orleans. The boilerplate Facebook mini-outrage about cultural appropriation was much less creative than the new parade itself and not well thought out.

The crux of the resentment appears to have been the view of some New Orleanians that the Canadian band Arcade Fire—involved in the new krewe as well as the 2016 Bowie parade—was too "super-native" in the way it adopted and adapted New Orleans cultural practices. But band member Regine Chassagne is of Haitian descent and is active in supporting Haiti and diasporic Haitians, so that solves one part of the bogus authenticity challenge. And co-founder Ben Jaffe, who attended McDonogh 15, the same New Orleans elementary school I went to, solves the other part—unless you deny even people who grew up in New Orleans the right to their local culture. (His father was instrumental in establishing Preservation Hall, which Jaffe now runs.)

The thin foundations of claims about lack of authenticity, in all these cases, shows not only that people are too quick to judge, but that those whose local authenticity is the most tenuous are the quickest to judge. Simply put, it's basically people who moved here five minutes ago taking heat from people who moved here ten minutes ago.

The sad thing about anxiety of authenticity in New Orleans today is how it makes lovers of New Orleans culture enemies of each other. Instead of the solidarity of the immediate post-Katrina years, now it's a competition to out the poseurs, the appropriators, the ones accused of not deserving the culture they embrace.

The cultural spats obscure the economic foundations of our fear and anger, but they can also have economic repercussions.

The anxiety of authenticity has fueled the rise of short-term rental apps, for example, because the promise of authenticity to people who are deathly afraid of being recognized as tourists is the go-to pitch for Airbnb and similar listing services. My neighborhood, Faubourg Marigny, has had the misfortune of recently being labeled "hip" and "trendy," though it has been a haven for low-income bohemians (the truly "hip") for a hundred years. Today, short-term rentals are eating us alive, as the city council struggles to find enforceable ways to license and regulate them. There are blocks where over half of the residences are short-term rentals,[3] and the number is growing, forcing out permanent residents because the landlord's income can be so much greater when renting to stealth tourists.[4]

Price is not the reason people choose Airbnb. The prices are comparable to suburban motel rooms. The wording of the ads makes clear that an "authentic" local experience is the selling point. "Underground" tourist guides offer the same escape from the dreaded "tourist" label, as if it's a badge of shame, something that needs to be concealed. Today's tourist wants to experience New Orleans (and other tourist destinations) "like the locals do." And so, technology and the anxiety of authenticity converge to empty beautiful old neighborhoods of authentic full-time residents—who maybe aren't really "authentic," anyway, because they're probably "super-natives" rather than "real" natives.

The problem for residents of the old Creole districts is that too many of our fellow New Orleanians seem ready to write our neighborhoods off as cash cows for tourists, their assumption being that no "real" New Orleanians still live there anyway.

A recent review in the *New Orleans Advocate* of the new Bravo series, "Southern Charm: New Orleans," is a good example: "In a media landscape saturated with post-Katrina documentaries and shows like 'Tremé,' which are tributes to New Orleanian exceptionalism and fodder for the class of transplants that Tulane geographer Richard Campanella calls 'super-natives,' Southern Charm feels surprisingly . . . authentic."

Why? Because "they don't all live in shotgun houses and busk in the French Quarter. They live in Gentilly, Old Metairie and the north shore."[5] Two of those three neighborhoods aren't even in Orleans Parish, and Gentilly is the throwback American-style suburb that Americanists gushed over when "authentic" New Orleans writer Walker Percy put his protagonist there in his 1961 novel, *The Moviegoer*. Yet we're told that the rich suburbanites of Bravo's new "reality" show are more authentic New Orleanians than residents of the city, and certainly more authentic than the working people who struggled to pay the bills on HBO's *Tremé* (which, by the way, had several native New Orleanians in the cast and on the writing staff).

The disdain of residents outside the Creole districts toward people in them is not new. I experienced it as a Marigny resident attending school in Gentilly in the 1970s. The issue then was the "fruits" in the area—as I was told by both white and Black classmates. Mid-twentieth-century writers like Tennessee Williams and John Kennedy Toole document well the conviction that the Quarter was a place for freaks, feared and despised by those New Orleanians who just wanted to be good (conservative) Americans. As the bohemian population has been forced further and further downriver by rising prices, the disdain has also shifted to include, apparently, anyone who lives in a shotgun house.

Today, terms like "hipster" and "super-native" are additional tools for demonizing people who choose to live a lifestyle that's an alternative to the suburban American Starbucks dream of commercialized and sanitized homogeneity. It's not PC to call them "freaks" anymore, so now the implication is that they're inauthentic, culturally appropriating yuppies, even though most of my (non-tourist) neighbors are schoolteachers, waiters, social workers, contractors, musicians, and artists—as they have been for generations. I wish Richard Florida had never coined his well-meaning "creative class" label,[6] because it falsely conflates traditional urban bohemians with "gentrifiers," even though the bohemians don't have any money.

City Council District C is a microcosm of the social divide between urban bohemians (now maligned as "hipsters") and the suburban Americans who resent them, since it's perennially represented by a West Bank resident who views the East Bank part of the district as a constituency of real estate developers and tourist industry leaders.

Outgoing council member Nadine Ramsey has consistently voted against the will of East Bank riverfront neighbors to preserve the small-scale residential character of the area, favoring instead developments pushed by real estate and tourism interests.[7]

We might be tempted to hope for better from returning District C member Kristin Palmer, but I still recall that in 2012 she designated my childhood neighborhood in the Marigny Triangle an "adult-oriented section" that children had no business living in.[8] Her recent sponsorship of a bill to halt new STR licenses is, however, cause for hope.[9]

A widely shared story on the Airbnb threat told of a lawyer in Tremé who was shocked to see an inflatable dildo installed by Airbnb tenants nearby.[10] He said that he didn't want to have to explain the dildo to his young child. As it turns out, he wasn't a long-term neighborhood resident anyway, but a suburban transplant (and a lawyer with deep-pocketed clients, so he certainly wasn't helping to keep rents down).

The problem isn't the dildo, and complaining about risqué practices in neighborhoods that are traditionally risqué totally misses the point. What many people who did not grow up in my neighborhood don't realize is that for generations there has been a coexistence of family life and "adult-oriented" behaviors in urban districts of this type.

Krewe du Vieux paraders who complain about seeing kids on the route also miss the point. Those of us who are from the neighborhood grew up in a sexually open environment and we and our kids are not shocked by nudity or sexual innuendo. We want neither an American-style family suburb, nor an "adult-oriented" district that no one actually lives in. But my fear is that other New Orleanians—not to mention Trump-voting suburbanites—may be less amenable to the kind of traditional mixed bohemian neighborhood I grew up in than transplants from other cities are.

After Hurricane Katrina, the Urban Land Institute advised against rebuilding newer, flooded neighborhoods like Broadmoor and New Orleans East. I was at first receptive to their recommendation, until I heard from residents of those neighborhoods who were aghast that the city might consider moving on without them.

Today, we in the older, unflooded neighborhoods need our fellow New Orleanians to stand with us, to help preserve our way of life, even if it seems either too freakish or too "inauthentically" New Orleans exceptionalist for their tastes. A "super-native" makes a better neighbor than an incognito tourist in a whole-home Airbnb.

There's a huge difference between a tourist from Brooklyn and a transplant from Brooklyn who lives and works here. And suburbanites who deride transplants for continuing to "appropriate" and adapt the local culture (as they have for hundreds of years) shouldn't take out their resentment on those of us who still live in the historic neighborhoods.

So, let's limit short-term rentals to homes with homestead exemptions—and insure that inflatable dildos only be made available to permanent residents. And please, stop shaming transplants who choose to live here because they love our culture. Let them be New Orleanians, too.

New Orleans in the Age of Social Distancing 2020

A couple of months in, it's dawning on us that this COVID-19 thing is the biggest threat to our lives and bank accounts since Hurricane Katrina. Unlike Katrina, however, this is a global event. That means moving away won't solve anything and also that we can actually measure our handling of the crisis against other jurisdictions and hit back against all those charges of some innate New Orleans dysfunction that comfortably dry critics wielded against us fifteen years ago.

On the whole, we've comported ourselves admirably, joining together under trusted local elected leaders to bring about a more positive outcome than much of the rest of the country. Together, we have "flattened the curve" (in New Orleans) and thus avoided the catastrophic inundation of our hospitals that social distancing was designed to prevent. On the other hand, age-old divisions, enmities, and anxieties, egged on by today's toxic American political culture, have erupted into boils. Among these are the unbounded arrogance of the white southern conservatives who beset our city on all sides and the demoralizing misrecognition of New Orleans by national political and media voices, often on the Left. Hostility from the Right and misrecognition from the Left puts the overwhelmingly liberal, feminist, and anti-racist population of New Orleans in a quandary.

The more provincial New Orleanians lash out at local government and culture with well-worn rhetoric about how the "backward" city lacks unquestioned American virtues like individual initiative, work ethic, and allegedly more efficient and less corrupt government. These are the reasons, in the Americanist New Orleans imagination, that New Orleans doesn't get the national attention gracing Atlanta, Austin, etc. Thus, a citizen complained in a letter to the *Times-Picayune* on March 20 that Mayor LaToya Cantrell should have closed bars and restaurants a couple of days earlier than she did, claiming, "Other states had already closed public venues except for grocery stores and pharmacies."[1] The letter writer then worries that people in other places will be infected because of New Orleans's negligence.

The first question is which other "states" had shut down bars and restaurants before March 14. The answer: none. A couple of days later, the state did move to shutter bars and restaurants and was in the first handful of states nationwide to make that move (and the first southern state to do so). It also needs to be noted that the mayor and other city leaders had strongly advised people to avoid crowds and even shut down several major events scheduled for that weekend, including St. Patrick's Day parades and Super Sunday. Oh, but we had Mardi Gras, which is certainly the reason the city became an early COVID hot spot, though no one anywhere in the country canceled anything—not indoor concerts or sports events, megachurch revivals or Trump rallies—before this year's Fat Tuesday back in February.

The misrecognition of Carnival is an ongoing irritation for New Orleanians who care what other people think of us. Terry Gross, interviewing Tulane professor and author John Barry on NPR's *Fresh Air*, offered the typical misrepresentation, which has become so stubbornly pervasive and oblivious to facts that I have come to view it as a microaggression. After Barry described Philadelphia's 1918 war bond drive parade, which was held well after influenza had begun spreading through the city, Gross asked if that incident reminded Barry of how "New Orleans held its Mardi Gras parade" despite the dangers.[2] Mardi Gras parade, singular? Clearly Gross's understanding of Carnival in New Orleans comes from Disney's *The Princess and the Frog*, which also partakes in the common misrepresentation that Carnival consists of a single, official, city-sponsored parade on a certain day. Why is it that New Orleans is the one place in the world about which a modicum of cultural literacy isn't required before people open their mouths to criticize?

This pandemic has shown once again that the national perception of New Orleans is akin to how some people see a person with a distinctive mole on their nose. The mole is Mardi Gras. To some, it is unsightly; to others, it's a charming beauty mark. But the point is that every other feature of that person's physiognomy (shape of eyes, size of mouth, hair, etc.) is totally ignored because the viewer can't take their eyes off the mole. On the other hand, the person with the mole knows it's there, has learned that, though it's different, it's not necessarily repulsive (well, some of us have not reached that stage), and does not walk around all day obsessed with its existence.

What's upsetting is how every other feature besides the mole is ignored. If New Orleans comes up in the national conversation of COVID-19, it will be some offhand reference to Mardi Gras, usually derogatory. Without some reference to the mole on our nose, we fade into invisibility.

How often have we heard the report that "states in the Deep South, for the most part, are not engaging in serious mitigation measures"? Why won't they just add the three words, "except in Louisiana"? The *Huffington Post* reported on April 20 that Michigan "appear(ed) to be the first state to create a panel to address racial disparities seen during the pandemic."[3] Actually, Louisiana Governor John Bel Edwards did that more than a week earlier, on April 10. Louisiana was also among the very first states to release racial data on infection rates and deaths, on April 6.

It's a truism that pandemics exacerbate existing social co-morbidities, and clearly race is one of those. At least America is recognizing that the racial disparity data is consistent all over the country and not confined to that basement of the American imagination called "the South." Indeed, racism is more national in the Trump era than perhaps ever before. Confederate flags are as ubiquitous at the Michigan state capitol as anywhere else. Of course, the Trump poison is very potent in Louisiana, though perhaps less so in this particular moment because of the careful, triangulating leadership of John Bel Edwards. Trump has been predictable in this crisis in the way he has divided, damaged, and disrupted, while eschewing any semblance of an effort to unite the country and provide stable, coherent leadership. All he has ever offered is rhetoric, but his rhetoric has its effects, and they are always deleterious.

The racial disparities in COVID-19 outcomes are bad news not only because they expose (again) racial disparities endemic throughout the country's history, but because reminders of those very disparities make racist white people even more racist. The absolute lack of concern for the lives of African American citizens is probably the most offensive thing about the Republican rush to "re-open" America, but other disturbing features of American über-capitalism are also being exposed. Some of the most illuminating local texts have come in comments from Jefferson Parish Chamber of Commerce head Todd Murphy,[4] New Orleans & Co. CEO Stephen Perry,[5] and a full-page ad in the *Times-Picayune* on April 19 by four local, entitled, rich white guys attacking our elected leaders' mitigation efforts. Each of these shows the unbounded sense of entitlement felt by self-anointed "business leaders," as well as their conviction that the primary role of the people of New Orleans is to make money for them, even if they must sacrifice their lives in the process.

It's hard to decide which paragraph of the April 19 full-page rant, signed by Franco Valobra, Robert Lupo, David Monteleone, and Jay Batt, is the most offensive. It may be that the most innocuous statements are the worst. For example, when they say that "protecting the health of our citizens from this deadly virus and protecting our citizens from economic depression and despair is not a choice between the two but rather a decision should be made to address both at once."[6]

No, it's not the mangled syntax that bothers me. It's the insinuation that our local elected officials do not feel exactly the same way. Why do they suggest that only they, the authors, want to balance medical safety and economic survival? "Staying closed is not a plan," they gravely intone. But since when was it anyone's plan to stay closed forever?

The weirdest statement in the April 19 diatribe concerns the future of the French Quarter: "The deeply unsustainable cancellation of all public events in our city for 2020 will irreparably damage, if not destroy, our city's culturally important French Quarter."

I'm in the Quarter every day, just as I was in my childhood and youth. It doesn't look "destroyed" to me. Do we really need to point out that no physical damage to structures has taken place as a result of the pandemic? Why do they equate a cessation of mass tourist attractions in the neighborhood with "destruction"? The reason is a core principle of capitalist ideology: The only value is exchange value. If something can't be exchanged for money, it has no value. Thus, a beautiful work of art is useless—until somebody pays a lot of money for it. Food, too, has no value unless somebody pays something for it. Need we point out, finally, that human lives also lack value if other people can't make money off them? We don't need to say it, because the Republican zeal to sacrifice lives for profits during a pandemic (and in every other circumstance) is clear on its face.

People who treasure the Quarter as a beautiful neighborhood—you know, with people living in it—might come to quite a contrary conclusion: that the destruction of the Quarter happens when it is converted entirely into a cash cow for tourist industry profits and no longer has any value besides that.

Tourist industry magnates are livid that Mayor Cantrell thought it wise to cancel—for one year—major attractions that draw people from all over the world to the city. Do the whiners really think that it's prudent, as COVID-19 peaks in places that were too Trumpy to take necessary measures, to invite hundreds of thousands of people into a city that has just painfully done what it needed to do to nip the virus in the bud?

It's not Mayor Cantrell who has put a multi-year crimp into the tourist business. It's the virus itself, and the failure of the United States to produce sufficient testing to even know where it's spreading at any given time.

The other sad lesson we've learned is that the United States government is just as incapable at economic mitigation as it is at public health. I still haven't seen the check—with Donald Trump's name on it—that was supposed to float me through April. America's state-level patchwork of unemployment insurance has proven itself utterly inadequate to the task, small-business relief got sucked up by large corporations, and people are losing their employer-based health care during a pandemic. In this mess, Americans realize that we're on our own and may have to risk our lives for the paltry scraps our employers are willing to throw at us. Conservatives call it "freedom," and we can celebrate it by refusing to wear a mask around the people who are forced to serve us.

If self-appointed "business leaders" really cared about the well-being of people with low-end tourist industry jobs, they'd join the rest of us in demanding universal health care, a higher minimum wage, a unionized work force in all major hotels, and federal funds to help cover losses of states and municipalities that have met this crisis head-on while the president fiddled in the White House.

Since their bosses only care about wringing profits out of them at the cost of their lives, and since conservatives in Washington and Baton Rouge refuse to sufficiently tax the billionaires who have enriched themselves on the backs of the rest of us, what can we do to help our many neighbors who depend on tourist industry jobs? We have to get creative.

Local New Orleans grassroots cultural institutions are stepping up, including Mardi Gras clubs. The Krewe of Red Beans is doing its part. They've begun delivering food from local restaurants to our frontline health care workers, crowdsourcing the cash to pay for it.[7] We can also go to our favorite musicians' websites and download their music or order CDs. Measures like these are more like emotional support, of course, than the kind of financial support that can float hospitality workers through the total cessation in cash flow that they're experiencing. That's why, in addition to signs of personal support, we need to continue to advocate for the kind of government that recognizes how many Americans rely on gigs. Obviously, that means universal health care, as well as a safety net that does not rely on getting fired from a job in order to get unemployment benefits.

The other question is how to love New Orleans in a way that can help us emotionally at a time when we can't enjoy restaurants, coffeehouses, bars, live music, and public gatherings, all of which fill our sense of identity as much as our weekly schedules.

While it's true that the culture of public dining and public celebration is one of the high points of local pride, another feature of local culture that's been celebrated for centuries is simply love of beauty, the idea that aesthetic appreciation is as central to a well-lived life as social status, career success, capital accumulation, or even community life. It means loving something for itself, just for how it looks, sounds, feels, smells, or tastes, not for its exchange value in the capitalist marketplace. If you've got one, enjoy your porch, balcony, back patio, or garden. The city is still beautiful. That's the upside of living in a museum. We can still stroll its streets—maintaining distance from others, which isn't as difficult with the decline in tourists. We welcome tourists, especially because they pay us, but this city is first and foremost for us—that's why we live here. So, get out and enjoy some live local scenery, and stay healthy for the day when we can meet up together again in our favorite restaurants, clubs, streets, and festival grounds.

I'm proud that New Orleans and Louisiana have been a model for dealing with this crisis, even though I know we won't get recognition for it beyond the 504. The national myths of dysfunctional New Orleans are too great—and too internalized by locals—to overcome with the good governance we've witnessed these past weeks. We were among the first to put strict social distancing guidelines in place, and now we're seeing the fruit of our efforts.[8] We don't know when or how it will end, but we've handled the initial moment of the outbreak with grit and grace. Unfortunately, regardless of public health outcomes, the political side of this is just going to get uglier. It's scary enough to wonder how long the pandemic will extend, how and whether schools will start in the fall, how we will be able to feed and house ourselves. The abdication of government responsibility outside New Orleans, most notably in Washington, means that we will probably suffer a great deal more before this is over.

PART II
AMERICANISM
VS. EXCEPTIONALISM

Bobos Go Native:
Gentrification and New Orleans Exceptionalism 2013

The rapid demographic changes in some of New Orleans's older neighborhoods have sparked consternation among locals as well as professional observers of the city. The firestorm over Richard Campanella's recent article on the subject, cutely titled "Gentrification and Its Discontents" is only the most recent flashpoint.[1] Is what's happening in places like Bywater best thought of as a renaissance or mere gentrification? And is there a difference?

As always, word choice is the lifeblood of any good dustup in the public square, and there are certainly other ways to frame the current debate. One of them, dating at least to 1803, pits New Orleans "exceptionalism" against "Americanism" as a model for progress. In the simplest terms, exceptionalists savor the distinctive features of New Orleans culture as an alternative to American lifestyles and ideology perceived as mainstream. Americanists, on the other hand, bemoan our distinctive cultural and political quirks as detrimental. They're what's "holding the city back;" why we've "fallen behind" Houston, Atlanta, etc. The Americanists smell mystification and self-delusion in exceptionalist paeans to New Orleans's "uniqueness."

Exceptionalism's modern trappings date to the last decades of the nineteenth century, when writers like George Washington Cable, Lafcadio Hearn, Grace King, and Alice Dunbar-Nelson began packaging accounts of New Orleans culture and social customs for consumption by the American general reading public. While Cable often promoted an Americanist view, bemoaning the city's cultural inheritance as rife with racism, nepotism, xenophobia, corruption, and bad business decisions, Hearn constructed an identity for New Orleans that touted the city's polyglot diversity while mourning that so unique a cultural island would inevitably be crushed by the steamroller of American capitalist "progress."

Both of these writers, as well as King and Dunbar-Nelson, draw liberally on *decadent aesthetics* in their portrayals of New Orleans's physical beauty. That is, they acknowledge that crumbling, dilapidated buildings have always been a source of the city's moody beauty and allure. A question that concerned those writers continues to rankle both residents and non-resident aficionados of the city: To what degree is New Orleans defined by its physical identity—its built environment—and to what degree by the culture we share?

Indeed, this is the question at the heart of the gentrification debate. If we keep the same buildings but replace the residents, has the city been successfully "preserved"? The popular catchphrase after Katrina was, "New Orleans isn't the buildings, it's the people." I admit that, at first, I found the formula too reductive. The buildings matter. Yes, people built them, but architecture also shapes future people. To a degree, this put me in stride with the exceptionalists, who had long viewed our shotguns-and-stately-homes cityscape as part of its charm—an attitude the Americanists once dismissed as sentimentality and an obstacle to "progress," whether embodied in the riverfront expressway struggle of the 1960s (an eventual triumph for preservationists) or the post-Katrina fights over tearing down the mid-century housing projects and building the giant hospital complex now going up where a Third Ward neighborhood used to be.

But casting architectural preservation as an alternative to American-style economic development pivots on a woefully outdated duality. In our own era, the far more common phenomenon is architectural preservation in the service of economic development. Neither tourists nor newcomers (shopping nationwide for a place to reside) are interested in a New Orleans that can't be recognized as such in an easy iPhone photo posted on a Facebook page. So, the more germane question for our times is whether distinctive cultural traditions can have the same durability as structures. Can certain cultural practices be learned by newcomers not raised with them and then perpetuated and adapted in the manner of all living cultures? The answer is yes, though nagging questions of authenticity and sustainability remain.

In his Bywater-focused essay, Campanella outlines a cycle of gentrification common to many American cities over the past fifty years. Using my own terms rather than his, it basically begins when starving artists and assorted dropouts and desperadoes are drawn by cheap rent and a sense of adventure to an economically depressed urban neighborhood. In New Orleans, that's going to mean areas like the Eighth and Ninth Wards, home to low-income groups, increasingly African American in the decades after desegregation, when so many blue-collar white ethnics took to their heels. Ideally, such a neighborhood is a stroll or bike ride from a more thriving area, where the newcomers can panhandle, busk, or work for tips—i.e., the Marigny Triangle or the French Quarter. These "pioneers" are followed by better-educated hipsters and yuppies (or "creative class" or "bourgeois bohemians" or "bobos"). These second-wave winners are folks responsive to cheap but rising real estate values and hungry for the cachet that comes with being at least in proximity to a cultural cutting edge.

The losers are obvious: the low-income households, usually rife with kids, that are forced out of the neighborhood by rising real estate values, if not cultural estrangement. Campanella goes on to identify further stages of gentrification, including, as in today's French Quarter, the eventual elimination of the pre-gentrification population and its replacement by tourists and the soulless rich.

Again, this cycle is not unique to New Orleans. So, is it still shaped by the older New Orleans duality of Americanists versus exceptionalists? Yes, indeed. But not without an interesting synthesis having occurred, one that champions social and cultural relics of the displaced population, as well as the architecture in which the working poor were housed.

It's the preservation of this cultural overlay that prompts urban boosters to declare Bywater-style gentrification a "renaissance," a still meaningful alternative to what they perceive as mainstream Americanism. That they are irked to be lumped in with garden-variety gentrifiers is apparent from the overwrought kicking and screaming in the comment section below Campanella's wry and erudite essay.

As always, however, bourgeois appropriations of bohemian ideologies contain some contradictions. Exceptionalists have celebrated New Orleans as a place where leisure is more meaningful than labor, aesthetics trumps functionalism, and the very notion of social mobility (the American Dream?) is held in suspicion. Yet the "creative class" movers and shakers who are now buying up the real estate are all about their careers. They demand a level of convenience comparable to other American cities (with their constant worry about parking), and have the ambition of putting New Orleans "on the map" when it comes to competing nationally for the continuing infusion of people like themselves ("brain gain"). In that respect, they are indistinguishable from the most unrelenting Americanists.

But here's the difference.

As Campanella perceptively notes, many of these newcomers are deeply engaged with what they perceive to be the most unique features of New Orleans social and cultural practice: Carnival, parading, cuisine, music, and, of course, the architecture. Campanella calls them "super-natives," and the shoe fits. It also pinches when, along with enthusiasm for the working-class culture, the moneyed hipsters flock to the overpriced restaurants and precious boutiques that have effectively driven out the indigenous economy of corner stores and lunch counters.

Indeed, the new "super-native" celebration of New Orleans's distinctiveness smacks of tourist industry branding practices utilized for decades by the city's Convention and Visitors Bureau and other civic boosters. A shining example is the Idea Village's development of a "festival season" for vetting and financing new companies. Thus, New Orleans's public frivolity and American competitiveness are at least superficially joined.

There's nothing new about the most ardent exceptionalists being transplants. It was true of Hearn and in every generation since. In the era of my birth, the 1960s, culturally sensitive transplants were responsible for key efforts to preserve unique New Orleans cultural practices, of which Preservation Hall is a perfect example.

In a sense, we could view the smitten newcomers as a socially constant class that replicates itself by means other than birth. The French sociologist Pierre Bourdieu notes that the petit-bourgeois class "endlessly remakes the history of the origins of capitalism."[2] Similarly, waves of newcomers reinvent and nourish New Orleans exceptionalism. Every couple of years, it seems, especially since Katrina, a new arrival pens a column on how special New Orleans is compared to other places. A typical example of the genre, entitled "Love NOLA: A fool's journey," was penned by Brett Will Taylor for ViaNolaVie's first anniversary last year.[3] New outfits like ViaNolaVie and WGNO's *News with a Twist* trade in exceptionalist superlatives faster than Café du Monde shovels beignets.

But newer transplants also overlap with previous generations of like mind, as Christine Horn has noted in a well-researched critique of Campanella's analysis.[4] Horn also points out the way institutional interests, from local government agencies to national urban design firms, collude in redefining exceptional (or "historic") as salable, thus bringing an area once perceived as an alternative to the national economic rat race, right up to the starting gate of a classic American real estate boom.

Which brings us back to the central question of whether New Orleans can continue to feel exceptional if the buildings are preserved but the people are largely replaced. If transplants buy into certain tenets of exceptionalist ideology—our regard for public performance and embrace or at least toleration of sensuality, for example—will they and their descendants be culturally recognizable New Orleanians? (How about they start calling each other "darling"? Will that do it?)

The paradox is that the final triumph of exceptionalist rhetoric, convincing the nation how special New Orleans is, also represents the greatest threat to preserving the city's exceptional social character. This is where Americanist goals and the utopian daydreams of the exceptionalists must finally part ways. Because the Americanist vision of a thriving economy and high property values clogs the paradoxical wellspring of much of the city's exceptional culture: the proposition that grace and elegance can arise from cheap materials and a legacy of trouble.

Implicit in decadent aesthetics was the reality that beautiful and crumbling mansions bespoke economic decline. The only reason the French Quarter didn't get torn down in the early twentieth century was because developers weren't interested. Economic desuetude was like amber. Could it be that a good chunk of the rest of the culture was also tied to a shortage of cash? A meal at Bywater's Maurepas Foods is much more of an investment than a pound of crawfish and a forty taken right on the sidewalk—or on somebody else's stoop.

The racial situation is even more alarming: My Marigny neighborhood is suddenly way whiter than it's ever been in my lifetime. True, my new neighbors are not openly racist, as many of the old white residents certainly were. But Black neighbors are becoming exceedingly rare—a major shift *away* from the city's traditional (and unusual) residential mix.

Finally, and perhaps most significantly, too many of my newer neighbors are keen to have their fabulous New Orleans experience without children. The Marigny of my youth was poorer, more rundown, and less self-consciously exceptionalist, but it was also far more diverse in terms of race, ethnicity, age, and sexual orientation—and kids were everywhere.

With such a thin claim to social diversity, no amount of exceptionalist posturing can hide the fact that the old downtown riverfront neighborhoods are actually becoming more like old school American suburbs (culturally and socially segregated), rather than more distinctive. The older, non-assimilated exceptionalists, who dreamed that a move to the Creole districts would be an escape from the rat race, are waking up to discover that the rat race has come to them.

Music and Murder: A New Orleans Story 2013

So, a couple of knuckleheads starting shooting at each other in the middle of a crowd on Mother's Day. But hey, nobody got killed. And if they had been?

It's easy to get fatalistic about murder in New Orleans, to see it as almost a side effect of the climate down here, like humidity and hurricanes. Such fatalism is only affirmed when you peel back the layers of history and find that the unjustly dead have been profuse in every era of the city's past. This last shooting isn't particularly remarkable except for the number of injuries. Happily, it resulted in no deaths, but that's really a matter of luck, fatalism's divine arbiter.

New Orleans writer Tom Dent (1932–1998) wrote a play in the 1960s about the senseless killings we hear about or personally encounter every day. He called it *Ritual Murder*. In it, the mother of the perpetrator describes homicide as a kind of communicable disease: "You hope you and nobody you know catches it."[1]

A local paper took a more distant perspective in 1870: "Judging by the amount of poor shooting lately, it cannot be denied that our people are very inefficient marksmen. One man fires six shots at his assailant, and made only one ball tell . . . while another fires three shots and harmed, by accident, a disinterested citizen."[2]

Sounds about like last Sunday. This particular instance of gunplay is attracting a perhaps unusual degree of attention for a couple of reasons: because it took place at a second line and because at least one of the victims, blogger and videographer Deb Cotton, has been a champion of second line culture and a voice against violence. Cotton, aka "Big Red," wrote from her hospital bed a moving appeal to the city about preventing violence through more effective means than after-the-fact arrest and prosecution.[3]

Cynics will be tempted to emphasize that the public hand-wringing over this latest of routine outrages is due to recent marketing of neighborhood second line parades through "Follow Your NOLA" and similar tourism campaigns.[4] If the tourists see it, it's real.

On a deeper level, the relationship between distinctive New Orleans cultural practices and the city's high level of violent crime touches a perpetually sore nerve. The American popular imagination has long insinuated that our culture is a fundamental cause of our murderousness and associated social pathologies. Linking New Orleans culture with crime and political corruption is nothing new. It made Herbert Asbury's lurid, voyeuristic *French Quarter: An Informal History of the New Orleans Underworld* a 1936 bestseller. Asbury and others portray the city's laissez-faire approach to living as a stew of spiritual corruption spiked with murder and flavored with racial difference.

The crime isn't new, and neither is the culture. What *is* new is mainstream (read: white American) embrace of customs once confined to the city's backstreets. Fear of crime, and the conflation of crime and Blackness, kept white tourists out of majority Black areas for much of the city's modern history. But the trickle of white tourists shouldn't be seen as evidence that American racial anxiety is on the wane.

Indeed, in the national shouting match over New Orleans since Katrina, a jolt of American racial anxiety has served to flip the switch from the common American view of New Orleans as the "Big Easy" and the "City that Care Forgot," to what Fox News celebrities Bill O'Reilly and Geraldo Rivera recently called the "Big Sleazy," the city that forgot to care, the very emblem of the nightmare that ensues when Black people are allowed to slip their traces and run out of control. O'Reilly maintained that everywhere outside the French Quarter was a "vast urban wasteland."[5]

African American voices aren't immune to this brand of racial hysteria, either. Sonja Steptoe dished out the loathing in a *Time* magazine piece a few months after Katrina, when we were still dazed, heartbroken, and grimly plotting our survival. She called New Orleans, among other things, "dirty . . . dangerous," "a mess of a city," and "only slightly better" than "Port-au-Prince, Bangladesh, or Baghdad"—though she admitted that she "never lived in the city."[6] Foreign, poor, lawless, and a few shades darker than white—why would any decent American want to live in a place like that?

The insidious conflation of race, moral laxity, and New Orleans street culture dates back to the Louisiana Purchase, when large numbers of free Blacks and a perception of unchecked interracial sex alarmed the Americans newly arrived from points north. In this regard, the overrepresentation of Storyville brothels in the history of jazz is telling, the insinuation being that the city's distinctive culture is rooted in moral turpitude. Movies like 1947's *New Orleans* and 1958's *King Creole* emphasize indelible bonds between music and criminal activity. The taboo is what makes the mix so titillating.

Let's not mince words: The city's voluminous history of violence forms a great part of its national appeal. The gothic imagination comes alive in New Orleans, as the several ghost tours, horror movies, and, yes, my own 2002 ghost apocalypse novel, *Soul Resin,* attest. These cultural expressions repackage the worst, most frightening aspects of the city's cultural gestalt as pleasurable aesthetic experiences. But here we have to remind ourselves of the obvious: Sublimation of collective trauma into art is not the same as actual trauma experienced by individuals.

As we lament the Sunday bloodshed, bear in mind this incontrovertible fact: While pervasive public parading is unique to New Orleans, shooting people is a venerable American tradition. I don't need to remind readers that the cultural producers behind second line parades—the clubs, the dancers, musicians, and members of the high-stepping, tagalong public—are not the ones pulling triggers. Deb Cotton and a host of others, including Tamara Jackson, spokesman for the anti-crime group Silence Is Violence, have forcefully made this case already.

What I'd rather do is point out a silver lining, if it's not too early to do so. The silver lining lies not in the crime itself, but in the way it's being interpreted. The post-Katrina era has led to a newly uncontroversial approbation of exceptional features of New Orleans culture, especially Black culture. This means that locals, at least, are more and more able to deplore a common American crime at a cultural event without deploring the distinctively New Orleanian culture surrounding it.

The mayor and others have vowed that explosions of violence will not put a damper on second-lining. And indeed no one really expects that street-level parading will vanish from the city's "urban wasteland"—Bill O'Reilly's term for everywhere outside the French Quarter. Second lines in New Orleans have become as uncontroversial as going to the movies in Colorado or running in the Boston marathon.

According to Police Superintendent Ronal Serpas, his officers are now partners with social aid and pleasure clubs and Mardi Gras Indian organizations. That's right, *partners*—not antagonists, as they have been perceived for generations, for as long as New Orleans street culture has existed. I've never heard a New Orleans mayor, much less the police chief, so piously bow toward the Black street culture of the city's working-class wards. We can call that progress.

We need to recognize that city hall's friendlier attitude has everything to do with the expanded interest in such practices, not only by white people and tourism interests but by African American transplants like Cotton. In combination, they have been celebrating and preserving cultural practices that native-born New Orleanians (Black and white) often ignore or dismiss.

The mayor's emphasis on the cultural economy, whatever its shortcomings, does provide an incentive for the city to protect and foster these traditions. Fears that the smothering embrace of commerce will make them less authentic should probably be set aside, especially if the brass bands and social clubs stand to gain more money and more safety in the bargain.

But the key will continue to be untangling the peripheral murderousness from a culture that undeniably was birthed amid violence—check out the lyrics of "Didn't He Ramble" and many another trad standard. Bloodletting is ample in the lyrics of Black street music in New Orleans (and other vernacular lyrics), because art depicts what it sees. Art responds to social ills and provides spaces for people to process them collectively. We need most to remember that traditional New Orleans music, dancing, and street community are palliative medicines for the killing, not causes. But not a cure, either.

An American Vegetable in Magical New Orleans 2014

The fault line under New Orleans is rumbling again. It acts up every few years, but it's different than most fault lines since the people who monitor it nationally are always new and always seem to think they're the first ones to discover it. Local people have known of its existence for centuries, of course, but national self-appointed culture experts must verify for themselves, because of their profound distrust or disregard of locals' analytical abilities. The fault line is an intellectual one; the two plates that periodically scrape and jar are the will to mystify New Orleans and the will to debunk the mystification. I've referred to these two tendencies as New Orleans exceptionalism (the will to see in New Orleans an alternative to mainstream American values) and New Orleans Americanism (the notion that New Orleans is not more special or valuable than the rest of the United States, just weaker, poorer, lazier, dumber). Both points of view depend on viewing New Orleans as "other" than the rest of the country, but one is positive and celebratory, while the other is simply insulting.

The funniest thing about every flare-up of this debate is how the participants, especially new transplants, seem so unaware that they're reenacting an age-old script. The latest flashpoint came in a *New York Times* piece that unleashed "kalegate" in the local blogosphere. Many locals were amused that one of the recent transplants interviewed for the article claimed there was "no kale" in New Orleans.[1] There were lots of responses on Facebook and in the local press, one of the best coming from Jarvis DeBerry at the *Times-Picayune*.[2]

Some wondered why she couldn't find kale in the city, since it's been around for years in a variety of grocery stores and restaurant tables. Others wondered why we needed kale in our diets to attain some kind of national legitimacy, especially since, as DeBerry pointed out, cooked leafy greens like collards, turnip greens, and mustard greens are so common in Deep South cookery. But the most remarkable thing about the *Times* travel piece was that the reporter dispensed altogether with what might have been thought a basic requirement: to talk to someone actually from New Orleans.

Lizzy Goodman's "research" involved talking to a handful of folks who had just moved here within the last couple of years. These newcomers could see the city, in Goodman's words, with "fresh eyes." Yet their impressions were patently not fresh. They were as ancient as the earliest exceptionalist-minded transplants, smelling magic wafting from every sagging, vine-covered gallery. Yet, it's true, night jasmine does have an intoxicating fragrance. So does sweet olive.

The *de rigueur* Americanist debunking of this viewpoint came from Dave Thier in *Esquire*. Magic? Mystery? All bunk. Take away the climate and New Orleans isn't much different than Cleveland, Thier contended.[3] He declares that he's become just as bored here as he's been everywhere else (whose fault is that?) and has taken to watching Netflix—which, no worries, is available here. I guess that means that kale is here, too, and I guess kale must be some kind of ammonium salt or cold shower.

Thier presents his credentials for finally seeing through the mystification: He's been here three years already. He must have had quite an Ash Wednesday hangover this year. But, of course, his sober refusal to grant a few crumbs of fantasy to the romantic exceptionalists isn't new either, even if he seems to think that Hollywood invented New Orleanian magicalism. When? I guess right around when Thier showed up in town.

What's arrogant about both the newly transplanted exceptionalists in the *New York Times* and the newly transplanted Americanists in *Esquire*, is their total disregard of the history of the debate they engage in. Charles Gayarré set the tone in his first history of Louisiana, back in 1846, by insisting on the "poetry" of his subject, rather than the "scrutinizing, unimpassioned, and austere judgment of the historian."[4] The predilection to favor romance over factual objectivity then continues through many another writer and literary character. Tennessee Williams was one of the great mystifiers, too, and a smart one. He has his Blanche DuBois famously say, "I don't want realism. I want magic!"[5]

Yes, Blanche is viciously punished for her love of fantasy, but I'm no fan of the Blanche haters, especially since Blanche is so often held up as a symbol of New Orleans itself (even though she's not from here). Ignatius Riley, too, of John Kennedy Toole's *A Confederacy of Dunces*, has the guts, like Don Quixote, to insist on his own cognitive individuality, cost him what it may.

What the debunkers of magic don't get is that the will to imbue New Orleans with magic is in fact the source of that magic. It's like a *gris-gris* bag. We can laugh at the silly superstition of wearing a pouch stuffed with customized and secret ingredients, as if it could protect you from getting hit by a bus. But the wearer of the *gris-gris* bag doesn't believe that. In voodoo terms, it's about intentionality, about focusing a strong and emotional intention, like prayer, and how that makes people feel safer and more empowered, regardless of the scientific facts. In a similar fashion, the people who "want magic" *will* their lives to be more magical because it enriches their experience. It's called cognitive freedom, the will to embroider a pissy world with beautiful myths (after a rational assessment that the American social world is, in fact, pissy).

Not that all of us are susceptible to the magic. Freud confessed in *Civilization and its Discontents* that he was unable to sense in himself that "oceanic feeling" to which people of faith lay claim. But he at least acknowledged that their feelings were real for them.[6] To translate into NOLA vernacular: You gotta believe.

Americanists like Thier (and the scores who have written pretty much the same thing before him) suggest that the will to fantasy, to magic, is somehow a cause of material social ills, or a factor in neglecting them, but this charge relies on a disregard of history more egregious than the exceptionalists' addiction to night jasmine's intoxicating vapors.

New Orleans has had plenty of muscular political and social movements, from a centuries-long Civil Rights struggle to a once vigorous radical labor movement. Lafcadio Hearn's love of the moonlight didn't prevent waterfront unions from organizing across racial lines in the late nineteenth century (until a state commission stepped in). Just in the past twenty years, New Orleanians voted to raise the city's minimum wage (until the state shut it down) and a mayor sought to sue gun manufacturers (until the state shut it down). Today, of course, the levee authority for the East Bank of New Orleans is filing suit against oil companies to help pay for coastal damages (though the state is fighting it). Wearing crazy outfits and pretending to be other people during Carnival doesn't seem to prevent these kinds of committed efforts in the real world from taking place.

But, of course, we can't expect the new transplants arguing about New Orleans on their big national stages to know about any of this, and they're clearly not interested. Yet they claim to know the city better than an average tourist would. Worse, whether they celebrate the magic or debunk it, they don't accord the city the dignity of an intellectual history. Lavender Ink, a local publisher, just released a new anthology, *NOLA Lit: 200 Years of New Orleans Literature*. Maybe transplants that are truly into the place should pick it up and give it a read. Until they acknowledge the New Orleans that existed before they got here, they'll just be typical colonists, imposing whatever their uninformed and youthful imagination wants on what they falsely perceive to be a blank slate.

The natives have opinions, too, y'all, and have been engaged in defining their own city for generations. The national press shows, as often in the past, that it's not really interested in New Orleanian self-analysis. Apparently, we're not qualified. Once again, American intellectual life sees New Orleanians as inarticulate native subjects who need their experience interpreted for them, subalterns unable to speak for themselves, and thus in need of qualified experts from a less magical place.

So, if we're doomed to be subjects rather than agents of our own definition, which master do we choose: the exceptionalist magic lovers or the Americanist anti-magic crowd? If the choice is between beautiful savage and dumb yokel, I guess I'll go with the former. I've got the perfect outfit for it, and the right mood music, too. The fantasy is working its magic—I feel better already.

Waving the Trashy Shirt:
Class War in the French Quarter
2014

The French Quarter is the scene of many of New Orleans's most contested battles over New Orleanian style, identity, and wish fulfillment. The target of one of America's first architectural preservation ordinances, it has a venerable tradition of civic oversight of its commerce.

The battle last year over reducing legally permissible noise levels was hard fought, until the forces for a quieter, classier Quarter withdrew from the field, withdrawing the proposed stricter noise ordinance. Shops selling T-shirts and souvenirs are another bête noire, especially despised by the Vieux Carré Property Owners and Residents Association (VCPORA), the neighborhood association that claims to represent the interests of Quarter residents. Despite the association's earnest efforts, T-shirt/souvenir shops have only mushroomed over the past thirty years, particularly on Decatur Street.

Last fall, the city (with ample prodding from VCPORA) raided and cited seventeen shops for noncompliance with city rules against trashy souvenir merchandise.[1] The usual legal delays ensued, and the Board of Zoning Adjustments will consider the fate of several of these malefactors.

All parties to the fracas acknowledge that many of the shops have been operating in the same way going on thirty years, but VCPORA and its allies on the city council offer the same argument used to defend pulling the plug on unlicensed live music venues: Lax enforcement in the past is no excuse for not enforcing the law in the future.

VCPORA's executive director, Meg Lousteau, is stern on the subject of scofflaw T-shirt pushers: "It is one of most common complaints we hear in the French Quarter from people who live there, visit there and work there. They can't understand why this beautiful historic gem allows the proliferation of T-shirt shops. We have yet to find anyone who thinks they add anything of value to the French Quarter."[2]

Lousteau's survey of public opinion cannot be quite as comprehensive as she would have us believe. What about people who own or work in T-shirt/souvenir shops or the many visitors who patronize them? We can more easily accept her claim that Quarter residents abhor the shops. But the reasons for this deeply held animus bear closer examination.

Decibel levels, sexual commerce, alcohol sales, parking hassles, garbage—it's easy to see how each and all of these issues could impinge directly on a resident's quality of life. But the beef against the T-shirt shops is essentially that they're aesthetically offensive, and that's an argument that can't be understood without factoring in preferences that break along lines of social class. The inescapable conclusion is that Lousteau's "beautiful historic gem" is being violated by trashy people and the way they express themselves.

That the debate reeks of class bias is not lost on the targeted "violators." The very first item in the statement to the Board of Zoning Adjustments offered by shopkeeper Sadiq Khan goes like this: "Personal views and feelings about the taste, value, or beauty of our legal, non-conforming use have no relevance to the factual question before the board . . . The board should discourage and dismiss comments based on sensationalism, stereotypes, preferences, or artistic disapproval."[3]

The visceral rejection of T-shirt shops and the wares they peddle is intimately related to the routine bad-mouthing of upper Bourbon Street by many locals—that is, those locals anxious to be thought of as legitimate, "authentic" locals.

The role of Bourbon Street—or the avoidance of it—in establishing an exclusive, separate local identity was on display in a Thrillist.com "listicle" of the "22 Things" locals supposedly have to explain to outsiders. It's a series of photographs with cute captions. The photo of upper Bourbon Street is emblazoned with the words "Don't Ever Go Here."[4]

In one sense, the hating on Bourbon Street and T-shirt and souvenir shops is simply an effort by natives to flaunt our local capital and differentiate ourselves from tourists. But then why not demonize Jazz Fest, too? Or streetcars? Or elite restaurants? The issue isn't that tourists patronize Bourbon Street and buy T-shirts, it's that *trashy* tourists do it. And it's untrue that locals don't go to Bourbon Street. Doubly untrue that locals don't purchase "souvenirs"—the abhorrent merchandise that supposedly cheapens the "gem" of the Quarter. The new zoning ordinance curls its lip not just at T-shirts, by the way. The condemned wares are defined broadly as "items . . . which serve as a token of remembrance of New Orleans and which bear the name of the City or geographic areas or streets thereof or of events associated with New Orleans including but not limited to events such as Mardi Gras, the Sugar Bowl, or the World's Fair."[5] But how many locals went and got that fleur-de-lis tattoo after Hurricane Katrina? Should flesh thus inked also be banned?

The fact that many locals celebrate their enthusiasm for the city by consuming the same stuff tourists haul back to Peoria and Hoboken is troubling to some. In his book *Authentic New Orleans*, Tulane University sociologist Kevin Fox Gotham sees the development of a "touristic culture" in New Orleans, which he defines as "a process by which tourism discourses and practices increasingly frame meanings and assertions of local culture and authenticity."[6]

Does your dentist have a picture of a streetcar or French Quarter balcony in his lobby? That's "touristic culture," and every New Orleanian with a fleur-de-lis keyholder, Dr. Bob sign, or framed stencil of the Sewerage and Water Board logo in their kitchen is participating in it.

On the other hand, so what? I've grappled personally with the issue of how to express local belonging and ended up caring less whether I could be mistaken for a tourist or not.

I was reared in the Quarter and, when I was a teen, many flea market stalls and cheap tourist shops carried wide-brimmed straw hats that brought to mind an old-time riverboat gambler. I grew a moustache, wore white broadcloth shirts, boots, and donned the hat. I even got a cape. I had everything but the Bowie knife. I was my own rich fantasy of a Creole gentleman in magical New Orleans, a hodgepodge of powerful but ahistorical images. I was cured of the hat when a buddy saw it on me and remarked, "*Que tourista!*" I felt deep shame, but only for a while.

OK, so local celebrations of place interact with touristic branding—big deal. It's not like people from all walks of life are as hung up on authenticity issues as the bourgeois bohemians now flooding Mid-City and the downriver neighborhoods. The anxiety over New Orleanian authenticity is a symptom of a particular social class and has roots as old as the Romantic movement's search for a perceived lost authenticity among the fading peasantry of Europe (since the new urban industrial poor weren't sufficiently picturesque). My own relationship with Bourbon Street and NOLA souvenirs in general is illustrative.

As a downtown teenager in the 1980s, my yat[7] and Black neighbors showed no revulsion against Bourbon Street or French Quarter souvenir vendors. They partied on Bourbon Street, as many locals continue to do, and, as expressions of local pride, had items in their homes that could be defined as souvenirs. By early adulthood, I had begun to hate on the T-shirt shops, decrying them as an ugly incursion of crass consumerism on my own very personal fantasy of what the Quarter should be. But then I read books and grew up and realized that the Quarter was never remotely close to the misty incarnation of post-Renaissance Venice that I wanted to superimpose on the architecture.

I also realized that I was unconsciously trying to employ my own growing cultural capital (as a young self-identified artist and intellectual), to set myself apart from the masses of people—tourists and locals—who express their appreciation of the city in a different way.

Today, of course, not all T-shirts are the same. Especially since Katrina, they've reached a new level of sophistication in expressing sense of place. Magazine Street's Fleurty Girl, which offers "shirts with yatitude," is careful to signify to locals that their T-shirts offer local cred in the way the average Bourbon Street variety cannot.

But why is it that working-class people, local or visitor, don't have the same negative feelings about Bourbon Street—or your average, un-ironic New Orleans souvenir T—as do many people of higher educational attainment? Pierre Bourdieu writes that working-class people are more interested in expressing solidarity than personal distinction in their aesthetic taste; sports-fan gear is a classic case in point. Working-class culture also celebrates hedonism and the body in less refined, distanced ways than bourgeois taste finds acceptable. Thus, while some people find the shirt reading "I Got Bourbon-Faced on Shit Street" to be a funny and apt expression of an unarguably unique aspect of New Orleans culture (the country's most liberal alcohol laws), others see it as tasteless, unrefined, embarrassing, inappropriate, and all those other adjectives that speak to bourgeois notions of proper comportment— the whole purpose of which is to distinguish the better people from the trash that come for Wrestlemania, etc. (but who love the city with equal ardor).

What really drives the loathing of T-shirt shops in the Quarter is the fear that New Orleans will be seen as a minor capital of the Redneck Riviera rather than as a paragon of elite culture.

This insecurity got a big stoking back in 2006, when *GQ* restaurant critic Alan Richman outed the French Quarter as "an illogical mix of characterless housing, elegant antiques stores, and scuzzy bars, a destination for tourists seeking the worst possible experience. The entertainment values are only marginally superior to those of Tijuana, Mexico." He opined that New Orleans, at its best, was a "three-day stubble of a city."[8]

The problem is that I find the three-day stubble rather endearing, also very much in keeping with the aesthetic of the French Quarter of my childhood—indeed, of the past hundred years, at least. A touch of Tijuana doesn't bother me, though too much Soho or Rodeo Drive certainly would, and that's the vision for the Quarter's future that the VCPORA set seems to cherish.

Sure, the Quarter's changed over the past few decades. But it's become a lot less sleazy, not more so. The junk shops, used bookstores, and quirky storefronts have largely disappeared, like the old Vieux Carré Hair Store in the 800 block of Royal Street or the Chinese Shop at Royal and Orleans. They haven't been replaced by T-shirt shops, but by pricey art galleries. Many of these galleries offer products that the cultural elitist in me wouldn't deign to call "art," either. Indeed, many of their products fit the city's own definition of a "souvenir," and are distinguishable from T-shirt shop fare only by their price tags.

There are lots of uses for the T-shirt shop locations that I'd rather see, but they don't include galleries with thousand-dollar souvenirs instead of five-dollar ones. The tasteless hordes have a right to enjoy New Orleans, too, and to do it in a way that they find comfortable and affordable, even if more refined sensibilities get ruffled in that messy jostle called urban living.

New South Quackery:
The Cultural Politics of *Duck Dynasty*
2014

An offensive logo loomed behind the many New Orleans-hating conservatives who addressed the Republican Leadership Conference here earlier this month: a dancing elephant holding a camo umbrella in its trunk.

I was relieved when the commentator I was watching on TV failed to make the connection between the umbrella and New Orleans second line traditions. New Orleans is a city that twice voted overwhelmingly for Barack Obama and that has no Republican in city government. A Republican at a second line is like a Taliban mullah (or Southern Baptist preacher) leading a prayer service in nothing but a jockstrap and a feather boa.

The reason the umbrella was camo was to honor keynote speaker and aptly titled "patriarch" of the *Duck Dynasty* reality TV series, Phil Robertson. *Duck Dynasty* is a new chapter in an old story, the conservative movement's effort to politicize cultural identity in the South. It uses the classic strategy of casting elites as victims, of portraying establishment insiders as rebels. Such political tactics date back to the Confederacy, but it's always interesting to see the new bottles that the old Kool-Aid is poured into.

The first step is to fabricate easy and narrow markers of cultural authenticity. The Robertsons are from Louisiana, so it wouldn't appear necessary to accessorize their legal residency with the numerous cultural icons they have worked into their public image. The problem is that other people are from Louisiana, too—people who don't wear camo, who don't hunt, and who even, God forbid, may be gay vegetarians.

The political Right has long assailed what it sees as identity politics on the multicultural Left, insisting that race, gender, ethnic background, sexual preference, and religious difference are overemphasized at the expense of a common national identity. Yet *Duck Dynasty* proves that today's most avid practitioners of identity politics are in fact conservatives.

As reality show stars, the Robertsons are supposedly "just being themselves," though the beards they grew before the cameras were turned on suggest that their natural, authentic selves needed a bit of a tweak to be ready for prime time.

Before Phil Robertson made the ugly politics of the Robertson clan more explicit, first with a provocative *GQ* interview, and, most recently, by delivering the keynote address at the Republican Leadership Conference, the family's main claim to fame was in the world of design and fashion. This, too, shows how today's conservative movement appropriates values of that vague cultural enemy they're always so fired up about. *Duck Dynasty* fashion is now to white southern rural conservatives (young ones, anyway) what hipster fashion is to many blue state urbanites. "We've got style, too!" their outfits shout from the marshes. But the more important message sent by their camo, beard, and bandanna ensembles is, "We, too, are marginalized by the mainstream!"

Public disgust with Robertson's "deeply held beliefs" lets him posture as a victim of cultural bias—no matter that conservatives usually decry just this kind of sympathy bid by traditional "minorities" (African Americans, gays). But *Duck Dynasty*'s carefully designed casual wear also makes a self-contradictory statement.

Tom Wolfe coined the term "radical chic" in 1970 to denote how the world of fashion sought to absorb some of the verve of radical political movements without sacrificing comfort. The Robertsons sell a similar product, a southern variant we might call "rebel chic." It, too, has its roots in the 1970s, among southern rockers like the Allman Brothers, Lynyrd Skynyrd, and Molly Hatchet.

These guys helped distance the white South from the longhair-bashing cultural politics of George Wallace's 1968 presidential campaign, and it seemed that the white South, still voting Democrat in those days, might finally transcend the burning cross it so long had to bear. On the other hand, Confederate iconography features plenty of glorious longhairs, too, so identification of hirsute hairstyles with hippies was always historically short-sighted.

The "rebel" rockers of the 1970s, especially Lynyrd Skynyrd, helped to transform the sense of a southern "rebel"—Confederate battle flag included—into a celebration of hedonism and rock 'n' roll spirit, "freedom" in the rolling stone, "Ramblin' Man," "Free Bird" sense. Today the band is attempting to distance themselves from the neo-Confederate politics indelibly associated with the flag they tried, without much success, to rebrand as a rock 'n' roll symbol.

Whatever the politics of the southern rockers, their lifestyles fit the "rebel" mystique implied by their tonsorial style much better than the straitlaced squares of *Duck Dynasty*. Far from being rebels, in terms of money, ideology, and lifestyle, these millionaires are scions of the status quo. As such, they reflect the need of the Republican Party's Libertarian wing to steal some of the glory of American anarchism, a far more colorful and less contradictory political sensibility. Before Phil Robertson identified the usual suspects as the enemy, Jase Robertson's ejection from a New York hotel (for looking like a rebel) was their greatest claim to outsider cred.[1]

The *Duck Dynasty* role as conservative tastemakers fits well with GOP wooing of young Libertarians. It's an effort to fashion a kind of southern conservative hip, a visibly countercultural style as a reflection of supposedly embattled mainstream conservative values.

The key to the Robertsons' role in the broader cultural irruption on the right is not to be found in the antics of the carefully crafted "rednecks" in front of the camera, but in the political commentary surrounding them, which is essentially a form of marketing. Phil Robertson tells *GQ* of his principled aversion to gay sex and his memories of happy African Americans in the pre-Civil Rights era.[2] Clearly, he intends his comments to be incendiary, but he plays innocent. The ensuing uproar is first branded as "controversy," then as "persecution." With that foundation laid down, Willie and Korie Robertson can show up on the cover of *Us Weekly* with the headline, "Defending Our Beliefs," as if anyone was threatening those beliefs.

Of course, there has to be a threat. That's the crux of right-wing cultural movements, driven as they are by fear. Richard Hofstadter's 1964 essay, "The Paranoid Style in American Politics," is still the go-to text for deciphering conservative cultural politics in the United States. Hofstadter nailed it with his description of the ever-present enemy of America's cultural conservatives: "a kind of amoral superman—sinister, ubiquitous, powerful, cruel, sensual, luxury-loving." This "cosmopolitan intellectual," in the mind of the cultural conservative, also "controls the press." Finally, Hofstadter identifies that secret longing of the cultural conservatives to become like their enemies.[3] This is the tendency that the Robertsons—media and fashion moguls, themselves—best exemplify.

Identification of the enemy is easy on one level: Barack Obama. But whose interests does this evil mastermind from Hawaii, Chicago, Harvard, and Kenya represent? The rhetoric on the Right works better if that's left quite vague. Phil Robertson put it this way in his Republican Leadership Conference speech: "We're up against evil like I've never seen in my life." But he didn't specify what it was.[4]

Bobby Jindal's comments placing *Duck Dynasty* in the broad context of American pop culture are more revealing. Defending Phil Robertson's views,

Jindal slammed the "politically correct crowd" (a favorite pointedly vague designation roughly analogous to Hofstadter's "cosmopolitan intellectuals"). "Miley Cyrus gets a laugh and Phil Robertson gets suspended," Jindal quipped.[5]

The suspension, of course, was not much more than a ratings stunt, since the "liberal media" had soon found another place at the table for the Robertsons. (Jindal should be so lucky when his governorship ends year after next.) What's interesting is how he singled out Miley Cyrus, presumably for sexually suggestive dancing. Toleration of overt sexuality would seem to have been renewed as an omen of the coming cultural apocalypse—as it has been since Sodom and Gomorrah.

I found another clue to the political subtext in a meme shared on Facebook last year. It showed a charming picture of Phil and Kay Robertson with the caption: "The world needs more Phil and Kay and less Kim and Kanye."[6] But what do Kim and Kanye have to do with Phil and Kay? Obviously, they're the "them" to help define the "us" of the southern family-values crowd. But what "evil" American future do Kim and Kanye portend? And why does a choice between second-rate pop culture celebs have any larger significance at all?

Ask Chris McDaniel. Mississippi's upstart GOP candidate for US Senate has singled out hip-hop as a mortal threat to America's moral fiber.[7] Like Phil Robertson, but with slightly greater specificity, he declares it "the evil we're up against." Here's why: "There are millions of us who feel like strangers in this land, an older America passing away, a new America rising to take its place," McDaniel laments. "We recoil from that culture. It's foreign to us. It's alien to us. . . . It's time to stand and fight. It's time to defend our way of life again."[8]

OK. This "foreign" menace is the world of Kim, Kanye, and Miley, but what does Washington have to do with it? Phil Robertson's nephew knows. Not content simply to endorse candidates, the Duck Commander machine is now fielding its own. Zach Dasher, running for the Duck Congressional District (Louisiana's 5th), has vowed to take the fight to the "intellectual elitists in Washington."[9]

These are the snobs who sneer at *Duck Dynasty* but enable Kim, Kanye, and Miley. It's a twisted version of the old southern populist notion of the Bourbon coalition, which posited an economic symbiosis between the planter class and poor Blacks, at the expense of white working people. Refitted for cultural politics, our righteous Duck Commanders now imply that "intellectual elitists" celebrate African American urban culture and lewd young women, while snubbing the caricature of white southern culture the Robertsons try to pass off as genuine.

Cultural humiliation is the fuel that drives the paranoid-style Tea Party resentments lurking behind every blind on *Duck Dynasty*, the shame at the perceived snub of their culture by "intellectual elitists" in some faraway decadent city, be it Washington, Hollywood, or New Orleans. Yet the show also fuels the misapprehension of southern culture at the root of that humiliation, by trading in the most banal icons of white southern identity.

Fifty summers ago, Lyndon Johnson, a white southern Democrat, signed the Civil Rights Act into law. Today no Democrat dares even sign up to run for Congress from Louisiana's 5th District. I wish I could just laugh at the frightened dumb yokels making another spectacle of themselves down South. Being a white southerner myself, I can't do that. For me, the phony innocents of Ouachita Parish are more depressing than cute.

New Orleans as Subject and Object
2014

I was a very interested guest at a recent Tulane University conference entitled, "New Orleans as Subject: Beyond Exceptionalism and Authenticity." I attended the keynote lecture in the Lavin-Bernick Center (formerly known as the "UC") and panel discussions in the equally opulent Goldring-Woldenberg Hall.

I couldn't help but reflect on the days when I was often on Tulane campus, as a local high school student drinking in the Rat (the old UC's dark basement bar) and partying on the Newcomb Quad at the now legendary "TGIF" parties that were thrown every Friday in the 1980s. Thirty years later, I still felt somewhat like a townie crashing the quad, even though the purpose of the conference was ostensibly to study my hometown.

The very concept of "New Orleans as Subject" presents an interesting problem for us natives. New Orleans has been the subject of intense, often critical scrutiny for hundreds of years. This poses challenges and opportunities for the locals. W. E. B. DuBois famously wrote of African Americans that they have a "double consciousness." They see themselves through the eyes of their own communities as well as through the eyes of an often critical national (i.e., white) consciousness.[1] New Orleanians, especially after Katrina, have faced a similar dilemma.

But the conference didn't much concern itself with distinguishing the ways in which natives, transplants, visitors, and non-native scholars interpret the city. The main gripe of the conference organizers was how myths of New Orleans exceptionalism and authenticity can serve to mask real social and economic problems.

An overemphasis on distinctive cultural forms, and, especially, how these cultural features are marketed in a tourist economy (music, cuisine, etc.) can blind local as well as national observers to deep inequalities and human suffering. Adding insult to injury, the musicians, artists, and restaurant workers who create that authenticity (or the illusion of it) get short shrift themselves when it comes to compensation.

So goes the theory, but I'm not sure that either the exceptionalism myth or the authenticity myth contributes to creating, or even masking, the social problems the Tulane scholars tried to connect them to. I guess I just don't see how "moving beyond" deeply rooted New Orleanian myths like exceptionalism and authenticity would result in the desired social improvements, i.e., a more economically just society. It's the same old assimilationist bargain that's been offered time and again to marginalized peoples: Give up everything unique about your identity and maybe we'll accept you then.

Let me take my analysis a step further: I came away from the conference convinced that its assault on New Orleans's sense of being exceptionally authentic is just the latest style in which this yearning for authenticity dresses itself.

I've always heartily agreed that New Orleans exceptionalism and authenticity are "myths," or, if you prefer, "ideologies." But I just don't see how excising such myths and ideologies would leave the patient better off. I also think my reluctance to jettison this ideological heritage has a lot to do with my being a native son.

In other words, when I observe New Orleans, I do so as both observer and subject. I have a sentimental stake in how people think about New Orleans. Such sentimentalism may indeed undermine what the nineteenth-century historian Charles Gayarré called "the scrutinizing, unimpassioned, and austere judgment of the historian,"[2] but I don't have enough faith in the "science" of culture to feel that disposing of my native sentimentality would yield fruitful results.

Authenticity as a category of value has been on the outs for decades among scholars of culture. As a colleague of mine recently put it, "I'm an English PhD, I don't believe in authenticity." Neither do I, if authenticity requires some kind of unselfconscious innocence or naiveté that somehow exists outside the pressures of consumer culture and capitalist hype.

New Orleanian identity, in particular, brings with it lots of symbolic baggage—vulgar signifiers that are passed off as badges of local cred: knowing that Frenchmen is hipper than Bourbon Street, for example, or that Krewe du Vieux is cooler than Rex. The ideological game of locating the "real" New Orleans is largely precipitated by the tsunami of tourist hype that's been building for over a century.

New Orleanian "double consciousness" in the face of these profit-motivated representations confuses the issue further. African American cultural authenticity is equally contentious, as is queer authenticity, and both have been made more so as the cultures of Black and gay people have become more incorporated into the dominant culture. Marginalized groups who resist total assimilation into a larger hegemonic body often emphasize features of their own culture to hold up as emblems of empowering difference, and there's always a struggle when the hegemonic culture then incorporates that difference and reifies aspects of it. Are we then to reject those distinctive signifiers, once empowering, which have been appropriated? Or try to preserve them somehow?

In the words of Tulane conference organizer Matt Sakakeeny: "Our aim is to go beyond the caricature of New Orleans, as one friend put it, as if everyone in this city was a Mardi Gras Indian second-lining down the street, po-boy in hand, on the way to Jazz Fest."[3]

So, the point is that not all New Orleanians engage in the culturally distinctive practices that are thought of as uniquely New Orleanian. But didn't everybody already know that? And how is Sakakeeny's call to move beyond such blatant stereotypes any different than the usual quest for the "real" New Orleans, the New Orleans "the tourists never see," the hankering for authenticity that gained special urgency (and hype) after Hurricane Katrina?

Like many such critiques of local folkways, the implication of the "New Orleans as Subject" conference was that distinctive features of New Orleans culture are the problem, and that if we could just de-emphasize our much-ballyhooed cultural difference then we could be . . . Miami? Houston? Newark? But, of course, these cities have all the problems of social injustice that our narcissistic infatuation with our own culture is allegedly causing or "masking."

Like all the other entries in the old "City that Forgot to Care" cliché, the "masking" idea suggests that New Orleanians do not already vigorously debate the very real inequities that plague the city. But with two local newspapers and sites like *The Lens* (media that include, but do not limit themselves to, cultural analysis), that's also a dubious premise. In fact, New Orleanians have often sought to ameliorate our city's savage inequalities with progressive policies time and time again, only to be blocked at the state level.

As Sakakeeny's caricature suggests, images associated with tourism are particularly toxic for any notion of a truly "authentic" New Orleans. Tulane scholar Kevin Fox Gotham's persuasive notion of "touristic culture," as a barnacle attached to local identity by the ever-expanding tourist industry,[4] clearly seems to have caught on in the thinking of many contemporary scholars. The problem is that the way local people adopt touristic strategies to frame their own identities is basically just an idiomatic expression of what's happened to the vast majority of identities in the postmodern era.

In his seminal essay, "Notes on Deconstructing the Popular," Stuart Hall noted that people imbibe images and ideas from popular culture, but then refashion them for their own needs.[5] So, yes, tourists as well as many locals celebrate Mardi Gras Indians, parading of some kind, po-boys, etc.

But don't locals see something different in these icons or interpret them differently? I would say that we have hybrid identities rather than simply inauthentic ones. For example, when I was a kid at McDonogh 15 Elementary School, we had a resident musician named Miriam Anak who wrote songs—anthems, really—for us to perform. One was called, "Hey, Mister Buggy Man":

Hey, Mister Buggy Man
Let's take a ride today,
Go down Decatur Street
To Jackson Square
French Quarter old and gay.
We meet you on our way,
And there is music, music everywhere.

On a first read, it seems like the most banal touristic tripe imaginable. But for us it was a kind of anthem of local belonging, since we saw the Quarter and its imagery as our neighborhood. Without the blessing of Ms. Anak, of course, we rode the buggies, but did it by jumping up onto the rear axle spans that jut out from the back, until we got shooed off by the driver. We also bellowed the word "gay" in the song to emphasize its sexual orientation meaning, thus reflecting a different marker of local authenticity obvious even to children in the 1970s French Quarter.

The role this song played in my childish sense of self-definition clearly shows that an authenticity construed as totally independent of an external gaze is problematic, if not impossible. Yes, I did incorporate touristic ways of conceiving my hometown in the formation of my own identity. But everyone else in America constructs their identity in a similar way, just with different signifiers.

So, I'm still left wondering why the myth of New Orleanian authenticity is more damaging than any other place's defining myths. Especially because so much joy and fulfillment are experienced by embodying archetypes of local authenticity—the kind of thing we see *en masse* every Carnival season.

In the end, it seems like the rejection of the more stereotypical symbols of local authenticity is simply a ploy to locate authenticity elsewhere. Thus the "real" New Orleans can finally be attained by locating the least distinctive aspects of the city in the national context. A good candidate might be exactly those aspects that are supposedly "masked" by fetishized New Orleanian difference—crime, poverty, racial inequality—since there's nothing unique (in America) about those social ills.

I think the answer lies in the perspective of the non-native scholar, not in the subject. Natives have an uncomplicated way of assessing local authenticity and it has nothing to do with po-boys or second lines. It's usually about where you went to high school. The transplant, on the other hand, has to make an effort to attain authenticity or, of course, give up the game and disparage the very notion of local "authenticity."

Some transplants embrace Sakakeeny's reductive formula (throw together a bunch of clichés and become what Rich Campanella calls a "super-native"[6]); others just don't worry about it. Scholars, however, are also driven by the academic marketplace. Like contemporary hipsters, they're driven to distinguish themselves by discovering trends before anyone else does.

It's true that New Orleans scholarship has been driven for a long time by cataloging the city's distinctive features, so what is a New Orleans scholar supposed to do to stay "hip" in the academic arena? Talk instead about how New Orleans is like everywhere else and disingenuously suggest that we could realize America's first socially just community if we would just stop talking about second lines and po-boys.

I guess I'm just too sentimental to be convinced.

I Want Magic—A Defense of New Orleans Exceptionalism 2015

A recent academic vogue among scholars of New Orleans is to warn against the dangers of an ideology deeply rooted in the local culture: New Orleans exceptionalism. There are two strains of anti-exceptionalist fervor today. One fear is that the will to see a New Orleans that is distinct from broader national cultural norms will result in biased conclusions, in a failure of what is naively referred to as "objectivity." The other is the complaint that New Orleans exceptionalism "masks" serious social injustices that would appear in bolder relief, and presumably be redressed, if not for that old narrative about New Orleans's "unique" culture. The academic itch to debunk popularly held exceptionalist verities has increased in recent years precisely because New Orleans exceptionalism became a great rallying cry after Hurricane Katrina. The more that average New Orleanians wanted to see their city as a special place—perhaps to summon motivation to rebuild lives at the site of catastrophe—the more vigorous became the finger-wagging of a handful of experts who managed to make a career out of specializing in the academic study of New Orleans. It's easy to see how sneering at exceptionalism is partly an effort to promote exclusivity in a narrow discourse community. But it's even easier to see the willful blind spots of the critics of exceptionalism.

To charge that New Orleans exceptionalism will constitute an epistemological "confirmation bias," as Richard Campanella does in the Summer 2014 issue of *Louisiana Cultural Vistas*,[1] is to assume that no other confirmation biases are possible. This dream of absolute objectivity seems dated in today's postmodern intellectual milieu. One chooses one's biases, hopefully in a somewhat conscious manner, and should announce them, rather than pretending that any one of us can be free of bias. More specifically, New Orleans exceptionalism is defined by what it claims New Orleans is an exception to. Whether seen as an enemy of truth or as an enemy of social progress, New Orleans exceptionalism needs to be understood as a response to far more pervasive and dominant ideologies on a larger scale. No form of exceptionalism exists in a vacuum. The claim of New Orleans exceptionalism is not that New

Orleans is an exception to all of human history. New Orleans exceptional-ism expresses a sense of difference on three successive levels, depending on which exceptionalist text is up for analysis. New Orleans exceptionalists have claimed that New Orleans is different from the rest of the United States, different from the rest of the South, and different from the rest of Louisiana. All of these assertions have been made in published texts and in private con-versations. While people do say things like, "New Orleans is the greatest city in the world," this is more of a common expression of civic pride, heard in many a great city, than an expression of specifically exceptionalist sentiment.

So New Orleans exceptionalism has defining oppositions and can only be understood in relation to this broader ideological context, which, at the most general level, is Americanism. The believer in that old myth of pure objectivity, then, may be motivated by an Americanist bias, which suspects in New Orleans exceptionalism some kind of affront to America, some kind of anti-American strain that is deeply blasphemous. Indeed, many an excep-tionalist text, from Lafcadio Hearn, to Robert Tallant, to stuff I see posted on Facebook by fairly typical New Orleans bohemians, is explicitly anti-Ameri-can in a cultural if not directly political sense. In other words, to warn against New Orleans exceptionalism is simply to fall into the trap of some other, un-named bias—better to acknowledge biases and take a position openly, rather than resorting to the disingenuous claim that only the other guy is diseased by ideology.

Another weakness in this latest round of New Orleans Americanist rheto-ric (billed as "moving beyond" New Orleans exceptionalism) is the sharply re-ductive definition and genealogy of New Orleans exceptionalism it trots out. Besides ignoring the tri-level stage that exceptionalist ideologies take shape in (America, South, and Louisiana), detractors like Thomas Adams and Matt Sakakeeny, organizers of a conference titled "New Orleans as Subject: Moving Beyond Exceptionalism and Authenticity," have claimed that New Orleans exceptionalism is "static," "reified," and "ahistorical."[2] But this is itself an ahis-torical observation. Much of what today's Americanist detractors attribute to New Orleans exceptionalism derives from penetrating critiques of the rising tourist industry, and its effects on local culture, by Mark Souther, Anthony J. Stanonis, and Kevin Fox Gotham. But the broad scope of New Orleans exceptionalism is far older and more various than tourism caricatures suggest. I think the way out of the vague, reductive view of New Orleans exception-alism as tourist hype is to think not of New Orleans "exceptionalism," but of New Orleans "exceptionalists," specific names who have authored specific texts. That would have the added benefit of addressing another rhetorical sleight of hand dear to the practice of interpreting New Orleans's place in the national culture. While I have always understood New Orleans exceptionalists as persons who celebrate the idea of New Orleanian difference, and Americanists as those ideologues who berate New Orleanian difference as detrimental, the new anti-exceptionalist movement lumps these very different interests together—since both assume and overemphasize New Orleans's distinctiveness in the first place. But this is finally too violent a conflation of diametrically opposed attitudes: haters and rhapsodists.

Whether in the interest of truth or of social progress, we're told that the danger of New Orleans exceptionalism is that it will somehow hinder our ability to apprehend facts. But what constitutes a "fact?" New Orleans exceptionalism is in itself a fact, accumulated in hundreds of years of written texts in English, French, and German. These texts form a preponderance of facts. Anti-exceptionalist scholars tend to value numbers over texts, quantitative over qualitative research, but the sheer numbers of exceptionalist utterances must mean that New Orleans exceptionalism is an ideology with a long history and a complex series of stages in its development. It began as a species of anti-colonial nationalism, pitting francophone Creoles against the new American administrative power. One of the most distinctive features of New Orleans exceptionalism was evident in those early stages: that it crossed racial lines. White Creoles such as Charles Gayarré had their version, as did Afro-Creoles like Armand Lanusse and the *Les Cenelles* poets. This shows also that there are varieties of New Orleans exceptionalism, different strains that agree on New Orleanian difference as a reservoir of possibility but disagree about specific values enabled by the exceptionalist imagination.

Just as conscious exceptionalists should study the roots of their ideology (though it tends to begin in the gut first), Americanists, if they can admit their own ideology, can see early on the roots of New Orleans Americanism as a counterargument to exceptionalism, most notably in George Washington Cable. New Orleans Americanism doesn't hold that New Orleans does not have certain exceptional historical and social features; rather, it sees exceptionalism as a dangerous ideology that needs to be disabused in order for New Orleans to take its rightful place in America—whose own exceptionalist triumphalism is far more dangerous than our little city's. Indeed, from antebellum Afro-Creole Republicanism to Baron Ludwig von Reizenstein to Lafcadio Hearn, the point of New Orleans exceptionalist arguments was to link New Orleans to non-US influences and thus to escape the straitjacket of American exceptionalism by invoking a more global understanding of the city's culture and historic destiny.

Cable artificially disconnects his Creoles from the broader francophone world in his 1880 masterpiece *The Grandissimes*. Moreover, to make his point that New Orleanian difference is more detrimental than valuable, he engages in some fantastic distortions. Like other Americans of his day, Cable views miscegenation as one of the great evils enabled by an exceptional New Orleans. This conviction leads him to paint the free Afro-Creoles of New Orleans as psychically damaged by the sinful circumstances of their ancestry, and, most significantly, as intellectually and politically impotent. Yet he had personally witnessed how these same people forcefully asserted themselves and their political interests during Reconstruction and before. This is an example of how Americanist bias distorts facts equally as much as exceptionalist apologetics can.

Simply refusing to note the exceptional in New Orleans, rather than misrepresenting it, is also an Americanist intellectual weakness. Thus Afro-Creole exceptionalist Rodolphe Desdunes felt compelled to write a pamphlet in 1907 taking to task none other than W. E. B. DuBois for his inability to recognize the contributions of Afro-Creole New Orleanians or distinguish them from the broader mass of "Negroes of the South."[3] H. L. Mencken's characterization of the South as a "Sahara of the Bozart" led to a similar flare-up of exceptionalist rhetoric in the 1920s. Finally, after nasty national commentators characterized New Orleans as a second-rate Detroit following Katrina, many locals responded by embracing exceptionalism as a badge of honor. Indeed, knee-jerk New Orleans exceptionalism became more widespread after the storm than ever before. The message in all these instances is clear: When Americanists refuse to recognize what their terms don't have words to describe, exceptionalists remind them that their terms aren't the only ones. This is a tendency to be embraced, not shunned as some kind of provincial ignorance. Kenneth Frampton has written of the possibilities of "critical regionalism" as an antidote to master narratives of "modernity" and "progress,"[4] which, in New Orleans, are deeply associated with the meaning of "America." New Orleans exceptionalism has all the features of such a "critical regionalism."

New Orleans exceptionalism represents the possibility of an alternative value system existing alongside, and sometimes in opposition to, American values. The specific content of both of these vague conglomerations of values is variable, historically contingent, and hard to pin down. But the will to offer an alternative to a nationally hegemonic value system is valuable in itself, not something to be ashamed of.

And this leads to the saddest failure of understanding in today's faddish academic critique of exceptionalism, which is the disregard for its utopian character. I've already said that New Orleans exceptionalism doesn't represent a distortion of facts but rather a body of facts—a textual record. But, of course, every body of facts is selected by a governing ideology. At its most imaginative, New Orleans exceptionalism represents a utopian vision of an ideal society, of a way of living that manages to celebrate different values than the prevailing ones in the broader national hegemonic culture. As such, exceptionalism has often been a bohemian ideology. I thought its bohemian character began with Lafcadio Hearn in the 1880s, until I read Baron Ludwig von Reizenstein, who wrote in the 1850s. His *The Mysteries of New Orleans* (*Die Geheimnisse von New Orleans*) was published serially in German in the radical German newspaper *Louisiana Staats-Zeitung*. In many ways it is a typical exceptionalist text. For example, he writes, "New Orleans has always been the leader in the United States in everything that heightens enjoyment of life and makes the dullest people into Epicureans."[5]

We see here some common features of New Orleans exceptionalist ideology as it has developed over the centuries. Most notable is the sense that New Orleans offers a value system seen as alternative to mainstream American values, specifically in terms of sensual and aesthetic fulfillment. For Reizenstein and many other successive exceptionalists, New Orleans throws up an obstacle to the march of Anglo-Saxon capitalist and puritanical definitions of value. It's right and fair to point out that Reizenstein's audience was not representative of all New Orleanians, and that his assumptions about New Orleans might simply be the ravings of one fevered brain—indeed, his work wasn't translated into English until 2002. But the numbers argument misses the point. Like all ideologies, New Orleans exceptionalism is a history of ideas, not of a broad social movement. Indeed, Reizenstein, like many other exceptionalists, might be expressing a wish or a dream of New Orleans more than he is recording an accurate social portrait.

Let's consider just one more exceptionalist text, penned a century after Reizenstein. Robert Tallant said in 1950 that New Orleanians "derive more enjoyment from their lives than do most Americans . . . for even those who cannot afford to belong to a privileged leisure class often act as though they do."[6] There are multiple ways to interpret this statement. We could point out that it's too sweeping to be factually accurate. We could say it masks the reality of economic inequality by suggesting that all New Orleans social classes know how to *laisser les bon temps rouler*, thus negating the need for economic justice. Or we could see in this a call to democratize leisure as well as labor and to prioritize leisure as a more meaningful pursuit than slaving away for the boss in the hope of illusory social mobility (i.e., the "American Dream").

Instead of seeing distinctive New Orleanian cultural practices and attitudes as masking or distracting from economic struggle, we could put the horse before the cart and realize that New Orleanian joie de vivre has often been a response to and a coping strategy for economic distress. We need to be able to deplore economic conditions without also deploring the people who created unique cultural forms and attitudes under such conditions.

This brings us finally to the "problem" of New Orleans "magic." Anti-exceptionalist positivists always sneer when the "m-word" comes up. But invocation of "magical New Orleans,"—or, as Lyle Saxon titled his 1928 book, *Fabulous New Orleans*—represents a will to live a life of awe, mystery, and intensity. Why do some people care so much if others like to color their factual mess of pottage with some fanciful brush strokes? Because, so goes the vulgar materialist critique, fantasy and aesthetics are "mystifications" that "mask" real social inequities. But this is the usual Americanist puritanical charge: that New Orleans's valorization of sensual and aesthetic fulfillment prevents its economic functionalism (that is, these lazy and dissolute dreamers don't want to work).

Regarding the knightly defenders of fact over fiction, Nietzsche reminds us that "truth" is always a matter of distortion anyway, "What we do in dreams we also do when we are awake: We invent and fabricate the person with whom we associate—and immediately forget we have done so."[7] The trick is to be as conscious as possible of how one is fabricating one's own experience. One of the loudest exceptionalist themes in New Orleans literature is that folks like a little fantasy in their lives. So? The will to fantasy is perhaps the most dangerous but also most liberating aspect of New Orleans exceptionalism: The dream that sensual fulfillment is more valuable than social ambition, that a rich aesthetic life need not be sacrificed to the dictates of economic survival. The claim that the imperative of sensual and aesthetic fulfillment simply masks economic injustice is the same old Americanist puritanical suspicion that culture, art, and partying are the enemy of economic progress.

Anti-exceptionalist scholars really just suggest a change in emphasis, from cataloging the ways in which New Orleans is different to checking off ways the city is not. In other words, we should focus on what makes New Orleans most like everywhere else rather than on what makes our experience special. One of the biggest problems with this approach is how tone deaf it is to the aspirations and possibilities of local identity. New Orleanians have broken into the two camps of Americanist and exceptionalist for centuries, yet now we supposedly have an opportunity to end this ideological history by amputating one side of the dialectic. But why would we want to do that?

Why is our rich local mythology seen as the problem? Can it really be that our little city's dream of an exceptional identity is a greater contributor to inequality than capitalist valorization of unrestricted free enterprise, individual initiative, and social mobility? If we could manage to excise our deeply ingrained sense of special identity and see ourselves more like a smaller version of Houston, Atlanta, Jacksonville, etc., who could possibly believe that this cultural mutilation would lead us to overcome the ingrained injustices that are part and parcel of American-style capitalism everywhere? Such puritanical sacrifices of emotional fulfillment are easier said than done, anyway—just as being aware of what drives one's libido doesn't make it go away, being told that we shouldn't think we're so special doesn't erase that urge either.

I can admit that I, too, often roll my eyes at exceptionalist platitudes, especially since they've been harnessed by tourism and embraced by many new transplants in superficial ways. I think it's fair and necessary to distinguish between vulgar exceptionalism—like bashing neighbors who want some peace and quiet as "enemies of the culture"—and a more thoughtful, conscious embrace of exceptionalism as an ideology. Far from being some recent tourism-induced local fad, New Orleans exceptionalism is older than po-boys, jazz, and every local university. To dismiss it as an enemy of knowledge or, worse, an enemy of an equitable society is not only a failure of imagination, but the willful blindness of an ideology unwilling to name itself.

Adieu, Vieux Carré
2015

Is this another piece whining about how New Orleans is changing for the worse? Is this another burst of weepy "Ain't Dere No More" nostalgia? Yes.

It's also about the French Quarter, ground zero of New Orleans history, and once ground zero of debates over gentrification and the changing character of the city. Today the gentrification debates focus more on neighborhoods downriver and back of the Quarter, areas which now still contain many people who fled the Quarter as the rents got too high. Where will they (we) go now?

The transformation of the city's oldest neighborhood into a retirement community for the rich and boring is now too far along to stop, but that's no reason not to cry at the visitation. "Ain't Dere No More" nostalgia is a deeply rooted genre in New Orleans letters, and it's never been staunched by a lack of practical applicability before. Sobbing at the funeral won't bring back the dead, but people do it anyway.

The choice has never been between change or remaining the same. The truism is true: Change is the only constant. But changes are agreed upon—or not—by people, or, to be more honest, people with money. The rest of us get to whine.

Lots of little changes add up to total change, and there have been a few more little changes this year affecting the Quarter. It's now light years removed from the Quarter I knew growing up.

The smoking ban is one of these changes, I suppose, because it definitely changes the daily experience of the Quarter's many bars. But some changes are more sensible than others, and some are more democratically arrived at. The smoking ban had the support of many New Orleanians, including employees of the affected establishments. Getting rid of the Confederate monuments is also a change that most New Orleanians, including myself, see the sense in. But the main criterion for my decision on whether a change is good or not is economic, and neither the smoking ban nor the removal of Confederate monuments makes the city more expensive, thus driving away its historically low-paid inhabitants.

The genius of New Orleans culture was its accommodation of joie de vivre not for the rich—for whom the entire country is an unlimited playground—but for natives of limited means as well. It might sound hard to believe today, but the French Quarter was cheap to live in until very recently. We can see a glimpse of the old Vieux Carré in old movies. Elia Kazan's *Panic in the Streets* gives us a look at the place in 1950. Walter Hill's *Hard Times* shows us a fairly run-down Royal Street in 1975—remarkably, the film was set in the 1930s, and the structures didn't look much different forty years later. Even Clint Eastwood's *Tightrope*, released in 1984, shows us a functioning farmer's market and the condemned husk of the old Jax Brewery, before its renovation anchored the new era of a cleaned up, more expensive Decatur Street.

One of the great ironies is that the Quarter had a lot more families and children at the same time it was also far more sleazy. This past week, the Louisiana Office of Alcohol and Tobacco Control revoked the liquor licenses of five bars in the upper Quarter because of suspected drug and prostitution transactions. But whom are they protecting?

Back when families lived in the Quarter, prostitution was wide open in the street, particularly along Iberville and upper Decatur. To be honest, as a kid I was a little freaked out by the aggressive streetwalkers of the old days.

And the ruins of Jax Brewery were decidedly a hazard, which of course did not stop us from playing in the darkened interior on the way home from school. One day I narrowly missed falling three stories into one of the giant holes left when they removed the brewing tanks. That same day, by coincidence, we were accosted at Jax by heavily armed police. They told us the place was a haven for interstate felons who hopped trains all over the Mississippi valley and came there to hide out.

This is the big dilemma in arguments about gentrification. I'd like to live in a neighborhood where prostitution is more discreet (in bars or brothels rather than on the street) and where condemned structures don't threaten to collapse on passersby or cause the deaths of naturally adventurous children. But can I afford it?

We have a nice new amenity in my neighborhood today, the Crescent Park on the riverfront. It's wonderful to have a formerly closed space open to the public. It's free, of course, being a public park. But some, like Daniel Wolff, have offered very convincing arguments about why public parks are actually something you don't want—why? Because it will attract the wrong element—people with money—who will then see to it that only people with higher incomes will ever be able to live anywhere near the fabulous new park.[1]

Crime is another thing we'd all like to see less of. Or is it? Many older native New Orleanians mutter the cynical hope that good old New Orleans bad guys will eventually scare off the well-heeled newcomers. I believe the dream of a low-crime city—glimpsed for a handful of months after Hurricane Katrina—might actually be possible. But, again, I'm afraid I won't be able to afford it.

The French Quarter is leading the way. On October 24, Quarter residents approved a quarter-cent hike in sales taxes—just in the Quarter—to pay for a more permanent presence of Louisiana State Police in their neighborhood. I don't like the idea of more state cops rather than NOPD—especially since they excel mainly at busting prostitutes and roughing up local musicians like Shamarr Allen.[2] But as in other neighborhoods that have agreed to higher property taxes to pay for beefed-up neighborhood patrols, there's a built-in inequity.

Accepting a higher cost of living in exchange for more police protection is very different from a broad federal or state tax hike that finances improved public services for everyone. The special assessments move well-heeled neighborhoods closer to the suburban dream of a gated community, a barrier that may enhance the safety—and prestige—of those inside, but that relegates the rest of us to the no-man's-land that used to be called middle class America.

So, the Quarter will be a bit safer and a bit more expensive. It will also continue to be less diverse, in terms of race, income, and stage of life. The kids are mostly gone by now, hanging by a thread at the only remaining elementary school in the Quarter, my alma mater, McDonogh 15. Rumors have swirled for years that the school board will sell the site to real estate developers, and today those rumors seem truer than ever, with the lease of the latest tenant—KIPP New Orleans—drawing to its close.[3]

You used to see old folks in their wheelchairs in the 1200 block of Dauphine Street, across from the kids romping in the wading pool of Cabrini Park, adorned as it was with Bruce Brice's mural of multicolored French Quarter children at play. The mural is gone, the wading pool is gone, though a fancy new playground set has replaced the basketball courts. (I guess younger kids are less scary than older ones). And now the old folks are gone, too.

They'd been on the block since Reconstruction. The Maison Hospitaliere was initially built to house indigent Civil War widows, but it continued as a nursing home until 2006. Now it's been partially razed, partially gut-rehabbed, to make room for million-dollar condos—ten of them. "We're confident the market is there," said the developer, "whether it's people who are going to make this their permanent home or a second residence."[4]

More condos are coming on Conti Street, at a site that will go down as one of the most painful "Ain't Dere No More" locations for a couple of generations of native New Orleanians. The Musée Conti Wax Museum will close its doors forever at the end of January 2016. They've already sold the building; architects are already drafting the condo plans.

The Wax Museum, open since the 1960s, was a unique New Orleans attraction in a number of ways. Many tourist destinations have wax museums, but the star of the Musée Conti was New Orleans history, not the latest Hollywood sensation. The museum embodied an older version of the New Orleans exceptionalist imagination, significantly different than what we see in the post-Katrina era, in shows like HBO's *Tremé*, for example. It showcased spectacular, creepy, and odd scenes from the history of the city, each of which conveyed a sense of New Orleans as a place with a history ripe for conversion into myth, and therefore as a place with a special sense of its own identity: Ursuline nuns, Jean Lafitte, Marie Laveau, Madame LaLaurie, Storyville, the 1891 lynching of Italians at Parish Prison.

In the cool, darkened halls, the series of three-dimensional scenes, with their lifelike wax protagonists, unfolded at whatever pace you wanted to walk. The place was too quiet, and required too much interpretation on the part of the viewer, to compete with 4D Imax explosions at the World War II Museum or the aquarium. And many of the historical episodes foregrounded in the museum were dark, even terrifying. So maybe that lack of sugarcoating was too much for today's parents and school administrators to get comfortable with.

You could argue that the framing of the city's history was as dated as the technology—as a "waxworks"—but the charm lay in its loving presentation. The museum was a visual version of a common New Orleans literary genre which we might call "mythography." It's a tradition at least as old as Charles Gayarré's multi-tome antebellum *History of Louisiana*, in which the author acknowledged a bias toward "poetry and romance" rather than "the scrutinizing, unimpassioned, and austere judgment of the historian."[5] Other hoppers of ore from the same lode include Henry Castellanos's *New Orleans as it Was* (1895), Grace King's *New Orleans: the Place and the People* (1921), Lyle Saxon's *Fabulous New Orleans* (1928), and Robert Tallant's *The Romantic New Orleanians* (1950). These are very subjective, unscientific histories in which fact is tinged with the magic of myth.

New Orleanians still like to think of the city as a rare and rebellious place that swims against the swift currents of the American mainstream. But the exceptionalist strain in contemporary culture has lost touch with the moody

Romanticism of its roots. Today's version is often a one-note obsession with music and the lifestyles associated with it—cuisine, of course, and parading included. Everything before the 1980s brass band revival is viewed with the vague fear that it's probably a bunch of racist southern stuff, and we'd best not go there. And, of course, positivist academics remain highly suspicious of the role of myth in culture, since it's irrational and has often served dubious political purposes.

The Wax Museum was a great reminder that, while every city has a history, a city with its own mythology really is something special. If it were being replaced with anything besides high-priced condos, I would be less despondent, but it's hard to avoid the symbolism in this particular change: A commemoration, however flawed, of the myths that form our collective identity is being bulldozed so that more retirees from Dallas can enjoy the sanitized ambience of a neighborhood that New Orleanians used to live in.

A Slap-Down for Old Hickory
2016

The rusty old republic is getting some new detailing, if not the engine work it really needs. Instead of changing the way the money gets divvied up, they're just changing the way the money looks.

Though we know that symbolism is no substitute for economic reality, it's still fun to psychoanalyze what the symbols say about what America wishes it was. Trading Andrew Jackson for Harriet Tubman reflects an admirable effort to revalue some old values, or at least make the older values less visible.

What Andrew Jackson represents to America in general is not the same as what he means to New Orleans. Yes, he's been feted here as "the hero of the Battle of New Orleans" for two hundred years. On the other hand, the context of early American New Orleans gives us a very different way to understand the meaning of the 1815 decision to rename the old Place d'Armes in his honor. Despite that one shining moment of glamorous and unnecessary killing (the war was over before the battle was fought), New Orleans has even less reason to honor Jackson than does the United States in general.

Let's look at Jackson first from a broadly national perspective. The strikes against him are obvious and oft-repeated: Indian Removal and slavery. The two are closely related, of course. Simply pointing out that Jackson was a slaveholder barely glimpses the tip of the iceberg. Jefferson was a slaveholder, too, but also an outspoken critic of the peculiar institution. No such paradoxes muddy Jackson's legacy.

Matthew Rosza, writing for Salon, redundantly points out that Jackson was also an "imperialist."[1] It's a redundant observation because Jackson's expansionist ambitions are tied inextricably to his support for slavery. The "Five Civilized Tribes" of the Southeast needed to be removed to make the region safe for white slaveholders, and the dream of the slaveholding class was to keep expanding into Mexican territories to the west, and even into the Caribbean and Latin America.

But excoriating Jackson today for these policies is a perfect example of the impotence and hypocrisy of symbolic politics—as if Jackson alone is responsible for Native American genocide and slavery, as if the beneficiaries and victims of these historic crimes are no longer with us, and it's just a matter of cleaning up the bloodstains. We know what American conservatives think, so it's really a failure of the mainstream liberal Left, a crowd good at endlessly proposing cosmetic makeovers that don't touch the substance of the unequal world the bad guys of the past bequeathed to us.

In the conservative corner, Donald Trump says the decision to replace Jackson with Harriet Tubman is "pure political correctness."[2] I used to be confused about what "politically correct" was supposed to mean, but Trump and GOP rival Ted Cruz have clarified it for me. It just means any policy or argument that's not fanatically conservative. But the rhetorical effectiveness of the "politically correct" charge lies in nuances and contradictions under the surface of its plain meaning. Like Nixon's "silent majority" ploy back in '68, "politically correct" plays to the persecution complex of America's white rural Christian masses.

On the other hand, we can't dismiss their sense of disenfranchisement as pure persecution fantasy, either. With declining incomes as well as life expectancy, white working people are clearly in crisis.[3] They're also correct to note that America's ruling elites don't really give a rat's ass what happens to them. Like the rest of us, they're fed symbols and rhetoric instead of bread and butter, but Trump gives them the symbols and rhetoric that smell the most like real food to them.

Trump is a master of vagueness. He says Andrew Jackson "had a history of tremendous success,"[4] which we could translate as "Jackson made America great." There's no reason to think that Trump is a scholar of Jacksonian America, but he gets the basic theme right: Jackson represents the idea of America as the land of equality and opportunity for white people, at the expense of people of color. To consider the interests or memory of non-white people is "pure political correctness."

But what does the country gain by a public slap-down of Old Hickory? It's yet another signal to white, southern, country people that their heroes, the greats on whom they model their own identities, are out of vogue, even shameful. If America is ashamed of Jackson, all those kids who grew up revering "the hero of the Battle of New Orleans" must realize that America is also ashamed of them.

Harriet Tubman as Jackson's replacement on the $20 bill is unassailable and not just because, being Black and a woman, she checks off two "politically correct" categories at one stroke. Like Jackson, she's a military hero. Like Jackson, she comes from humble social roots. She's also a revolutionary. It's perfectly fitting that Jackson will be replaced by someone he would have quickly executed if their times and paths had crossed.

The regrettable aspect of Jackson's removal isn't about Tubman or him. The sad and typical lesson of the failure of the liberal symbolic imagination comes from the sudden resuscitation of Alexander Hamilton. Through a downright surreal succession of events, the architect of American capitalism is now an icon of anti-racism.

I hate to break it to folks, but Hamilton was not a Latino hip-hop artist. It would make more sense to put Lin-Manuel Miranda, the creator of the hit Broadway show that saved Hamilton's historical reputation, on a bank note—if indeed the idea is to offer an alternative to rich white men as America's heroes.

Hamilton believed in the necessity of property restrictions on the franchise, that people of modest means should not have the right to vote at all. Jackson, on the other hand, favored much broader political participation and presided over and benefited from removal of property tests for white male voters. The decision to dump Jackson while keeping the suddenly and nonsensically hip Hamilton represents perfectly the contradictory politics of the Democratic Party in the age of the Clintons.

It's a symbolic fantasy of a color-blind meritocracy that does nothing at all to lessen the plight of working people of any color. Thus, Jackson's legacy as a champion of the working poor, once so dear to Democratic Party identity, is utterly eclipsed by those aspects of his politics that we rightly find reprehensible today. Nothing is actually done to improve the lives of the descendants of the people Jackson wronged or to address the obvious fact that America's prosperity, its "tremendous success," in Trump's words, was an outcome of the atrocities that we now self-righteously blame on dead people.

We really showed that racist bigot, we took him off the $20 bill! But nobody's lining up to give Georgia back to the Cherokee or Mississippi back to the Choctaw, and the families that made fortunes off the opening of the South and West to economic development are still pretty much running the country.

What's even worse is how Hillary Clinton has invented a strange new brand of race-baiting in her response to Bernie Sanders's challenge from the Left. Southern conservative demagogues used to distract white working-class voters from their own economic interests by promising to keep Black people down. Hillary, on the other hand, distracts white middle-class voters from their economic interests with symbolic anti-racist and pseudo-feminist appeals rather than racist and sexist ones. "If we broke up the big banks tomorrow," she said in February, "would that end racism? Would that end sexism? No!"[5]

She thus demonstrated in a nutshell the abandonment of the Democratic Party's historic mission to ameliorate economic inequality by implying that racism and sexism are condoned by those who fight for economic justice—as if economic inequality and racial inequality are somehow separate issues.

Bernie Sanders is Andrew Jackson in this twisted scenario, a guy who wants to stick it to powerful capitalist interests and sell out people of color. Sanders's policies might greatly improve the lives of many working women of color, but Hillary wins at "feeling their pain," that great Clintonian ability to acknowledge identities rather than help people with their problems.

While Jacksonian democracy envisioned a world where all white men would strive on an equal playing field, Clintonian democracy projects a future where all millionaires can be treated with respect regardless of race, sex, or gender identity, where Ben Carson and Sheryl Sandberg and Caitlyn Jenner and Bill Gates can all walk into Donald Trump's Palm Beach country club without fear of being snubbed. The underpaid Black and Latino workers in the kitchen will get lots of respect, if nothing else, while the angry white poor will get lectures about white privilege.

The future of Jackson Square, whether or not the Place d'Armes is re-named once again, raises a whole other set of questions, in some ways distinct from the meaning of Jackson for America at large. In New Orleans, Jackson is a symbol of the American triumph over Creole society and with it the Americanization of race relations in the Creole city. To put it bluntly, America in Jackson's time was a disaster for the Black people of New Orleans, both enslaved and free.

While most African Americans had no freedom to lose, many Black New Orleanians did have freedom to lose (half of them, in the 1810 census), and lose it they did. Jackson apologists will point out that he, out of desperation, authorized a regiment of free people of color to fight at the Chalmette battle-field. Yes, the future president appealed to the free Blacks of New Orleans as "sons of freedom"[6] and praised their conduct after the battle. But that wisp of anti-racist sentiment quickly vaporizes when we note that the Spanish had already rewarded enslaved Blacks with freedom in exchange for military service (much different than praising already free men for being free), and that the first business of the new American territorial legislature had been to disband the Spanish free-Black militias.

Indeed, many of the Black men who served under Jackson had been trained by the Spanish or by the French, like the Black hero of the Battle of New Orleans, Colonel Joseph Savary. And Jackson's kind words to the Black veterans of 1815 didn't slow the steady erosion of their freedoms under the

Americans. Ask 1815 veteran Hippolyte Castra, who wrote, "I fought with valor / Wishing to serve my country / I had no thought my reward / Was to become a thing of contempt."[7]

So, I think Jackson has less of a claim to the heart of the Creole city than he does to the $20 bill. I could think of at least twenty people from New Orleans and from the same era that I'd rather see in the square: Joseph Savary, Marie Laveau, Pere Antoine, Henriette Delille, Rodolphe Desdunes. But I'm not writing any letters about it. Jackson's support of slavery did not lead him to start a Civil War that killed 600,000 people, so it isn't appropriate to lump him with the Confederates, either.

I'd love to see New Orleans continue to distance itself from the conservative South through monument shuffling, but of course symbolic politics is ultimately just smoke and mirrors. Jackson should also remind us that economic struggle—this time including all colors—should be the No. 1 priority of the political party he shaped so profoundly. New Orleans is now the sixth most economically unequal city in the United States, based on cost of living compared to average income.[8] Every other city on the list is a blue city where dead racist bigots are not tolerated. Harriet Tubman is welcome here, but she'd have a hard time paying her bills.

Why Hipster Haters Are Worse than Hipsters
2016

The painfully acute anxiety about personal authenticity that has gripped New Orleans throughout the post-Katrina boom years offers lessons on the right-wing backlash that just took revenge on the United Kingdom and threatens to give the United States a punch in the gut this November.

Similarities between the Brexit campaign and Trumpism were noted in the weeks leading up to the lemming vote in Britain on June 23.[1] The connection was made more explicit by the Donald himself on June 24, when he praised the Brexit outcome, saying, "People want to take their country back."[2]

Those of us who self-define as overeducated know-it-alls will want to parse Trump's utterance in the usual ways, by asking which "people" want to take "their" country back—and from whom.

Nigel Farage, leader of the hard Right United Kingdom Independence Party, answered that question when he declared the Brexit outcome a "victory for ordinary people, for good people, for decent people."[3] I know what "good" means (I think), but "ordinary" and "decent" are more illuminating about the international right-wing movement led by Trump and Farage, and also France's Marine Le Pen.

Are these code words for white? Many people will argue that they are, and they won't be wrong. But I continue to believe that the American Left's laser focus on race and gender identity obscures an equally important aspect of the prevailing *Kulturkampf*: social class identity. Though collateral damage falls heavily on Black and Brown communities, what we're witnessing is really a political drama among white people. Some of us want to live in a multicultural society, and other white people resent us for it—in the visceral, almost libidinal way usually reserved for unrequited or ex-lovers.

An even more instructive term used by Farage for Brexit supporters came a couple of days before the vote, when he predicted it would be a victory for "real people."[4] Apparently Brexit's English opponents, urban cosmopolitans, are no longer "real." They are inauthentic as a result of their education and willingness to embrace cultures they were not born into. By insinuation, then, the only authentic people are the ignorant and the incurious.

What do the New Orleans identity wars of the past few years tell us about the broader social crisis afflicting the United States and Europe? The answer lies in the way that economic grievances are misread as cultural ones. Ever since 2013, when Tulane's Richard Campanella coined the term "super-natives" to describe the new transplants who so zealously embrace New Orleans culture,[5] there's been a knee-jerk backlash against "inauthentic" expressions of New Orleans identity. Leading the charge are local people who feel the threat of displacement—no matter that many of them have been local only a few years longer than the newer and much-maligned wave of transplants.

The top derogatory term for inauthentic persons displacing "real" people today is "hipster." American hipitude used to have its own authenticity, associated with the hard-partying cultural Left (from 1920s hep cats to 1950s beatniks to 1960s hippies). But now the deadly fear of being called a poseur (i.e., inauthentic) stifles the creative and performative energies of those who would be hip. Thus, the fear of inauthenticity leads otherwise creative people to dress as drably as Mark Zuckerberg, whose T-shirt is deemed to make the youthful billionaire appear "unpretentious."

What gets lost in the pointless hand-wringing about local cultural authenticity is the cause of the underlying anxiety and resentment: the economy, stupid. "Bywater hipsters from Brooklyn" is pejorative only because the spike in the cost of housing is real. The cultural arguments can be fun, but they obscure the real issue. The rising cost of living amid stagnant wages is making everyone's lives more desperate, no matter their cultural identity.

Arguments about cultural authenticity in New Orleans—who's "real" and who isn't—reflect our distinctive local cultural contexts, but the way cultural struggle stands in for economic struggle is the same across the country, as well as in western Europe. A milestone in today's culture war quagmire took place when "yuppie" got replaced by "hipster" as the demon of urban gentrification. "Yuppie" (young upwardly mobile professional) was a more purely economic category, while "hipster" saddles the cultural Left with blame for displacement caused by unregulated capitalist real estate markets.

But how, exactly, does cultural resentment obscure social class relations?

The answer can be found in French sociologist Pierre Bourdieu's monumental study of social class identity in western capitalist societies, *Distinction: A Social Critique of the Judgment of Taste*. Americans may be world leaders when it comes to analyzing racial and gender identities, but most of us are near illiterate in our understanding of social class identity.

Take me, for example. I was more of a hipster (and less hip) than I realized before I encountered Bourdieu. It was Bourdieu who clued me in to the fact that my hipster longing for rare microbrews and refined but edgy fashion statements was simply a bourgeois "will to distinction," a yearning to set myself apart from the masses in cultural ways, if not political ones. People like me—a published author with a non-tenure-track college teaching job—have what Bourdieu calls high "cultural capital," but low economic capital ($$$).

My relationship with the truly bourgeois—i.e., rich people—is not unlike the one between artists and aristocratic patrons in the pre-capitalist era. Rich people often seek an imprimatur of "high-class" legitimacy by acquiring cultural capital, which they have to pay people like me to get. Elite liberal arts institutions stand at the intersection of cultural capital and economic capital. Sending rich kids to such a place may assure not just that these kids stay rich but that they also become "high-class"—my American translation of "bourgeois" in the cultural sense. Absent talent of their own, the rich can augment their cultural capital by supporting major arts institutions like opera and ballet associations, art museums, etc.—or, in the local context, maybe just traipsing along as second-liners behind a brass band.

The young rich tend to seek out neighborhoods where starving artists (high cultural capital + low economic capital) reside, thus causing the gentrification that eventually replaces practicing artists with their customers.

People like me—"hip" people—tend to be knee-jerk liberals and sometimes in unproductive ways, such as hating on people with low cultural capital (correction: *white* people with low cultural capital), rather than targeting the rich people who are the source not only of our discontent, but of the discontent of many of our political opponents as well.

Supporters of Brexit and Trump are not hip, and they know it. The outdated term "blue collar" is also not useful when it comes to understanding today's social class identities. For one thing, social class identity needs to take into account not only income and type of job, but aspiration as well. The better term for the social class identity of Trump supporters is a textbook example of what Bourdieu calls *petit-bourgeois*. "The petit-bourgeois is a proletarian who makes himself small to become bourgeois," Bourdieu writes.[6] "Proletarian" means working-class, the social class whose cultural attributes the petit-bourgeois is trying frantically to shed, lest they hinder his ascent into the full-tilt bourgeoisie.

The very first aspect of working-class culture a petit-bourgeois can be expected to axe is solidarity with people who remain working-class. American socialist leader Eugene Debs (1855–1926) famously said that he didn't want to rise out of the working class, but with the working class. Unfortunately for American socialism, the United States has a powerful petit-bourgeois myth called "the American Dream."

The problem with the American Dream myth is how it works in cahoots with racism and xenophobia to blind the resentful to the common economic roots of their suffering. The narrative associated with the dream holds that the United States is the country where anyone can achieve anything as long as, to quote a Bill Clinton campaign slogan, we "work hard and play by the rules." So instead of the economic security promised by democratic socialism, we get the dream of social mobility; we get "economic opportunity" instead of the right to a job—even though social mobility is lower here than in social democracies like France that conservatives accuse of stifling individuality and entrepreneurial initiative.[7]

In Jackson County, Kentucky, 34 percent of the predominantly white population lives below the poverty line, yet they voted last fall for a Republican governor who had promised to take away their Medicaid. Matt Bevins won Jackson County even though fully half the population was on Medicaid. NPR interviewed subjects who were themselves Medicaid recipients, and yet they trash-talked their neighbors who also rely on Medicaid: "They want everything they can get for free," said one. Another added, "They think somebody owes it to them—just because. Nobody owes you anything. You earn what you get."[8]

The problem is that, since the "American Dream" has the mythic power of indubitable fact in their lives, there must be some reason it's not working, some scapegoat. But because of petit-bourgeois reluctance to indict their masters (the economically powerful), they kick at the people slightly below them on the social scale, like races once deemed inferior (before the "politically correct" crowd messed that up). Their resentment includes immigrants, of course, but also—and perhaps most of all—those people with high cultural capital who they see as liking international brown-skinned and gay people more than them. It's these forces who tie the hands of the generous capitalist class who would love to give a well-paying job to all the white people of Jackson County, Kentucky—but America-hating liberals just won't let them.

So, the real object of ire for today's petit-bourgeois Republican stalwarts isn't really Mexican "illegals" or Syrian refugee terrorists. It's people like me. Urban intellectuals with eminently hip, condescending smirks on their faces. People who may have more cultural capital, but who also struggle to pay the bills, have zero job security, and limited-to-no assets.

"Liberal" ceased to be an economic term long ago. It's all imagery now, vague impressions of urban people with cosmopolitan tastes who should be on their side but have betrayed them instead. The treachery stems from that hip but shameful "blame America first" attitude, a conspiracy to deprive white, working-class, country people of their birthright: to become masters themselves.

Surely, they deserve that iteration of the American Dream. Aren't they, after all, the truest and most authentic Americans, the "real people?" It's no surprise that the bulk of Trump's support comes from people of low educational attainment.[9] Not only can they not realize the extent to which Trump's rhetoric is flim-flam—or a flat-out lie—they also thrill to the rise Trump gets from educated people, whom they've decided to hate since they don't have the guts to hate what has really messed up their lives.

So, if you're hip, stop worrying about whether you're authentic and take a tip from Jimi Hendrix: Wave your "freak flag high."

In New Orleans that may mean wearing a straw hat, white linen, colorful shirts (the look I favor). You might get called a poseur by small hearts who don't have the guts to be flamboyant. Let them struggle with their own insecurities. If you're a hipster hater, remember: There's nothing metrosexual about your government's refusal to guarantee your economic security.

Donald Trump, Andrew Jackson, and *The Walking Dead* 2016

Season six of *The Walking Dead* began streaming on Netflix this month. As of today, I'm about halfway through the season. In other news, Donald Trump is still running for president, and calls to remove Andrew Jackson from the old Place d'Armes are growing louder and being met with more aggressive opposition. Taken together, these three phenomena tell us a lot about the zeitgeist of 2016.

Based loosely on the comic books of the same name, *The Walking Dead* is one of my favorite TV shows. I've always been a fan of horror, and of apocalyptic disaster stories. I'm a big fan of fantasy in general, dystopian or not, and see a healthful role for the fantastic imagination in a free-ranging consciousness. But fantasy is a lot like drugs. Some people can handle it, some people can't.

There are obvious reasons why many critics see a conservative ideological agenda in *The Walking Dead*, with its depiction of a shattered and Hobbesian world taken over by zombies. Guns are absolutely necessary, no one can be trusted, the government is a pathetic failure. Pacifists will not only get themselves killed, but all their friends, too.

On the other hand, the new community rising from the ashes of the old is decidedly multicultural, including different races as well as a panoply of sexual orientations. The debate over how conservative the show's messaging is meant to be has gone on at least since season three.[1] More recently, some critics have claimed that the show preps the ground for the particular species of right-wing American kookiness known as Trumpism.[2]

The importance of high walls comes to mind, but also the general tenor of paranoia, which is one of those rich veins of the human imagination that, like drugs, needs to be handled with care. I believe it can be spiritually healthy, and fun, to give in and visit with the paranoiac inside all of us—but just make sure the visit's a quick one and that you have a round-trip ticket back home.

Paranoia is, of course, the driving force behind Trump's entire campaign. Not just the fear that "the system is rigged" (which is plausible enough), but that an apocalyptic war for survival is at our doorstep. As his latest ad running in Louisiana puts it, "We are under assault." Who or what is assaulting us? Good horror writers know it's scarier if the threat is unspecified.

One reason *The Walking Dead* carries the smell of Trumpism has to do with the show's Deep South geography. The cities are a lost cause. Atlanta was abandoned long ago. The battle to survive is being waged in the boondocks and exurbs. Thus, the comparatively low cost of filming outside urban areas ends up contributing to a perhaps unintended ideological message. Rural people are the good guys, and most are from working-class backgrounds.

Suburbanites who once engaged in more intellectual labor are hopelessly unfit to survive in the new, leveled world order. They lack "common sense," that ineffable quality that conservatives of low educational attainment are convinced is their special expertise.

On September 26, National Public Radio's *Morning Edition* interviewed a Trump supporter who would be easy to imagine as a minor character on *The Walking Dead*. Jimmy Arno lives outside Atlanta, the ruined city of the series, where the battle to preserve civilization by destroying it first took off. An auto mechanic, Arno is a great fit for the show's ideal of the working stiff with a basic skill of great value after social collapse. He agrees with *The Walking Dead*'s Rick Grimes, the former sheriff's deputy who leads the show's roving band of survivors, that the cities are already too dangerous to go anywhere near: "If you go to Atlanta or to a major city, you're liable to be shot or attacked," Arno opined.[3]

He's counting on Trump to end the lawlessness of the cities—whether that means running off zombies or some other dangerous sub-humans (perhaps the fictitious border hoppers who appeared in Trump's first television ad).

But, unlike the candidate, Arno acknowledges the possibility that Trump will flop on Election Day and is already making plans. He's vesting his hopes in a roving militia group. "And should martial law, civil war, whatever, break out in this country, they will uphold the Constitution and rebuild our laws." The calamity that might necessitate such an action isn't the epidemic that has set the dead walking. Arno is dreaming of "the war that's going to take place when Hillary Clinton's elected—if that happens."[4]

What's most interesting about dystopian fantasies like *The Walking Dead* is the element of utopian wish fulfillment they also make room for. All those social benefits that have accrued to "the elites" (whether economic or cultural) could be washed away in a cleansing tide that bobs with their corpses. The society that once favored Joe College with all the good jobs will finally be gone.

"Away with you," reads a graffiti warning on an abandoned building during the show's opening credits.

In the zombie apocalypse, grit, physical strength, and skilled labor (construction trades, mechanical engineering, agriculture, butchering, shooting) are all that matter anymore. In other words, the sector of society poised to survive catastrophe looks a lot like the rural working class. Of course, the show's multiracial heroes would be odd men out at a Trump rally, if not thrown to the ground and stomped. But perhaps they are not entirely antithetical to the show's message. They fulfill the white populist fantasy that, one day, even Americans of color will recognize the supremacy of white leadership and finally get with the program. After all, Trump's own campaign commercials make a point of zooming in on the handful of non-white folks in his audiences.

Countless articles have been devoted to figuring out why the white working class is in such sad shape (as the candidate depicts it) and yet seems to be so taken with Trump, a rich guy who's added to the millions his father gave him by routinely ripping off tradesmen like Arno.[5]

The problem for the Democrats has been figuring out how to dissuade Trump supporters without insulting them. As Clinton hastened to make clear after her explosively ill-advised remark about "deplorables" in the Trump camp, you can't fit a group as vast and vaguely defined as "white working class" into one garbage can. Social class labels are a poor substitute for ideological choices, anyway. The insinuation that Trump supporters back him because of their social class just plays into the smoke and mirrors of his pseudo-populist campaign.

The lingering question is why some people who should know better do bad things, like back an unstable narcissist with no political experience and a failed business record for president of the United States. Step one is to get over the idea that they're all Jimmy Arnos. Recent analysis shows that a big chunk of Trump supporters are not economically disadvantaged victims of globalism—though low educational attainment does seem to be a common denominator.[6]

Why would people who work for wages with their hands identify with a guy who lives in a Manhattan penthouse and who, I'd bet the whole casino, can't change a tire, drive a nail, or hit the side of a barn with a shotgun? Because he enables *some* people who identify as working class (white, male, older, without a college degree) to express their anger at the rest of us for supposedly not giving them enough credit for their contributions to our country.

This is why Trump's No. 1 selling point is his embrace of "politically incorrect" speech. Giving the finger to fellow Americans is the right most cherished by Trump supporters. Economic anxiety is overplayed by the pundits. If voters were truly concerned with income inequality, including how it's been exacerbated by international trade deals, their candidate was Bernie Sanders.

Sanders offered a rejection of neoliberal globalization, but without the racist and nativist appeals so thrilling to Trump's base. Trump's repeated attacks on "political correctness"—the right to call women "fat pigs" and Mexicans "rapists"—should clarify that the real terrain of struggle for Trump supporters is cultural.

Jimmy Arno, in his interview with NPR's Steve Inskeep, expressed outrage that a school even in his neighborhood was the site of a Black Lives Matter protest. Why are Trump supporters so enraged by a movement that decries police killings of unarmed civilians? Could it be that they feel "under assault" whenever a non-white person opens her mouth?

In New Orleans, the assault on white people is detected, most recently, by calls to remove Andrew Jackson from the square in the French Quarter that has borne his name since 1815.

The first thing to note about this latest battle over symbolism is that it's not really about the historical Andrew Jackson and not really about New Orleans. It's the myth that moves folks, pro and con. That's OK, since public monuments are far more about public mythology than factual history. The main gripe of the people who want the statue down is that Jackson was a slaveholder. It's a slippery slope, but also a hard argument to counter in a nation that claims to love freedom.

Though it's unarguably clear why descendants of enslaved people find Jackson's commemoration offensive, it's trickier to explain the fierce emotional reaction of the people who want to continue celebrating his life. For some, at least, it has to do with shoring up a more positive sense of identity among rural southern whites. The myth of Jackson mixes George Washington and Davey Crockett. He's the kind of boilerplate American frontier hero Charlton Heston should have played . . . oh wait, Heston *did* play Jackson, in Cecil B. DeMille's 1958 epic, *The Buccaneer.*

A year later, another great guide for understanding the Jackson myth was provided by Johnny Horton's country hit, "Battle of New Orleans." The song makes clear that Jackson isn't as significant to New Orleanians as he is to people outside New Orleans who nevertheless want to claim some kind of cultural ownership of the city. In other words, our rural white neighbors care a lot more about Jackson than residents of Orleans Parish do. The very first line of the song lays out a geography of cultural identity in these terms: "In 1814 we took a little trip, along with Col. Jackson down the mighty Mississipp'." In other words, the experience of Americans under Jackson was a lot like a foreign deployment. Cecil B. DeMille's movie also distances the great American general from slimy, girly aristocrats with French accents (New Orleanians).

This version of Jackson comes much more from the 1950s than from the 1830s, but that's the point. TV world of the 1950s is the utopia cultural conservatives seek, if they can't have the more exciting *Walking Dead* dystopia that would allow them more of a free rein to maim and kill.

At least one reason Trump supporters want to give the finger to the rest of us is that they feel the rest of us have given the finger to them. Not so much economically as culturally. They perceive a denigration of their culture in "the media," and they're not entirely wrong.

Two 2016 books, Nancy Isenberg's *White Trash: The 400-Year Untold History of Class in America*, and J. D. Vance's *Hillbilly Elegy*, do a great job, in different genres, of documenting the ways in which white, country, working people have been culturally marginalized. In an interview on the PBS Newshour, Vance, who grew up poor and white in Kentucky and rural Ohio, expressed his concern that Trump's defeat will exacerbate the desperate sense among rural, working- and welfare-class whites that they are alone in a country that has become hostile to them.[7]

Removing Jackson from the heart of one of the white, rural South's favorite tourist destinations will surely add to this sense of alienation and stoke a yen to lash out against those of us who would tear down a cherished symbol. Such cultural re-valuation—however natural and necessary—causes many white, country people of low educational attainment to long for a world where a man of Jackson's sanguinary talents could be great again. A zombie apocalypse might do the trick.

A Death in Bohemia—
Starbucks Comes to Faubourg Marigny
2018

The other day NOLA.com reported that a Starbucks will open in 2019 at the corner of North Rampart and Elysian Fields, in the heart of Faubourg Marigny.[1] Denunciations ensued immediately on Nextdoor Marigny, a social network designed to facilitate discussion of neighborhood issues. Though the vast majority of responses were negative, there were a handful of Starbucks defenders.

So, what's the big deal about Starbucks in New Orleans? Why do so many residents of the city's most historic neighborhoods view it as an affront to their identity?

This is a question I addressed five years ago, when the mega-franchise opened its doors on the corner of Canal Street and St. Charles Avenue.[2] Since then, Starbucks and its customers have been winning the war against New Orleanians who support our own rich and historic coffee culture. As I said then, one of the reasons Starbucks is such a flashpoint is that coffee, and coffeehouses, are an integral part of local cultural identity.

New Orleans exceptionalists wish to emphasize aspects of our culture that set us apart from the broader national culture, and our coffee culture is an exemplary exhibit. New Orleans Americanists, on the other hand, define a successful New Orleans as a place where the "best" of America (major national franchises, Fortune 500 Companies, more rich people) is on display.

The Americanists are winning. Shortly after my anti-Starbucks tirade in 2013, Loyola University, home of the Center for the Study of New Orleans, replaced its local CC's franchise with a Starbucks. The university administration at the time alleged that a poll of students had been conducted and that 77 percent of respondents wanted a Starbucks.[3]

But a large number of students also complained that they'd never heard of such a survey and that the administration was not transparent about the decision. Today, Loyola students complain that the Starbucks on campus is full of Tulane students,[4] which makes me wonder whether it was Loyola or Tulane students who were so gung-ho about replacing a local franchise with a national one (since the two campuses have combined food service under Sodexo).

A few blocks away, another local independent coffeehouse, Village Coffee, was replaced by a Starbucks last year. I used to be able to get non-Starbucks coffee on campus by going to the university center convenience store, which still stocked CC's, but Starbucks closed off that option this year, by replacing the carafes of CC's with a Starbucks dispenser. Now I have to walk over to Tulane to get local P.J.'s coffee.

It's ironic that Tulane, which has a larger proportion of out-of-state students, would preserve the local option, while Loyola, with more in-state students, would want the national standard, but it also makes sense. Many Americans are drawn to New Orleans because it provides an alternative to homogenized American mass culture without requiring that you leave America altogether, just as many New Orleanians would like to experience mainstream American brands without having to leave New Orleans.

A Marigny Starbucks is a whole different can of worms. It's inconvenient for me, when I'm at work, to walk over to Tulane to get my coffee, but the Marigny Starbucks will pose no such inconvenience. I would have to walk by four or five independent coffeehouses to get to the new Starbucks, though it's only a few blocks from my house. That's good, but also a cause for affront. The range of comments on Nextdoor Marigny,[5] though not a scientific sampling of opinion, gives a good sense of how the neighbors feel.

After the NOLA.com link announcing the new Starbucks, the very first response on the Nextdoor Marigny thread reads simply, "Well, there goes the neighborhood." That sentiment is echoed by the bulk of other responses, but some are more nuanced. A minority of respondents voice typically Americanist views, welcoming a national franchise as a sign that the neighborhood has finally earned recognition and approval from the great capitalists of America. One such comment: "Starbucks will generate far more money than some little place with a tenth of the business. Starbucks is number one for a reason. People line up to spend their money world wide [*sic*]. No different here."

In other words, doesn't New Orleans also deserve what's considered the best in the rest of America? Why do some New Orleanians insist on projecting a different cultural identity than what the rest of America proudly embraces?

Another common Americanist rhetorical strategy is minimizing and dismissing the myth of New Orleanian uniqueness, as in this typical comment: "If anyone thinks all of the local present day [*sic*] coffeehouses represent New Orleans culture they have not been around long. How many are drinking coffee and chicory these days."

Limiting New Orleans coffee culture to chicory is like saying New Orleans cuisine consists only of fried seafood. It ignores the long history of coffee in New Orleans and freezes a 1958 tourist brochure into a static image of the epitome of New Orleans identity. A lot happened before 1958, even in the century before chicory was introduced in the mid-1800s, and a lot has happened since, including a proliferation of independent coffeehouses since at least the 1970s. One obvious reason for the major role coffee has played in New Orleans culture is that so much of it is unloaded on our docks and roasted here, even for major national coffee brands (Folgers, Dunkin' Donuts—but not Starbucks).

It's a typically Americanist misrepresentation to view New Orleans exceptionalism as an effort simply to freeze New Orleans at some earlier point of its history. New Orleans exceptionalist ideology has never, in any of its phases over the centuries, been synonymous with cultural preservation.

New Orleans exceptionalism is a utopian ideology, imagining New Orleans as an alternative to what is perceived as mainstream normative national culture. Today, that means everything represented by Starbucks: homogenized, standardized, and expensive, with slick packaging and a whiff of exclusivity.

When New Orleans exceptionalists praise the city's alleged "authenticity," what they're really expressing is a wish to escape the increasing sameness, standardization, and mass corporate branding of identity that characterizes monopoly-capitalist retail enterprises. It's an attempt to escape what Marxists call "reification." A transliteration of the original German term—*Verdinglichung*—is instructive: *thing-ification*.

The idea is that mass consumerism converts human beings into inexpressive and undifferentiated robots whose needs are conditioned by advertising and whose identities are entirely defined by the products they buy. Reification substitutes standardized simulations for living, human practices, subject to individual variations. CC's and P.J.'s are not the best examples of an alternative, since they, too, are franchises. Indeed, Faubourg Marigny's host of coffeehouses does not include the local franchises, either.

As Theodor Adorno wrote of the reifying effects of emergent mass culture in the 1940s, "Not Italy is offered, but evidence that it exists."[6] In other words, you can't go to Italy, but you can go to the Olive Garden (which has Italian names on the menu—as does Starbucks—and a logo with grapes on it). You can't go to an independent urban coffeehouse, but you can have the simulation, which is Starbucks.

One of the most eloquent New Orleanian attacks on the mass reification attempted by American consumer culture comes from Ignatius J. Reilly, iconic protagonist of John Kennedy Toole's novel, *A Confederacy of Dunces*. When his mother tries to get him to voluntarily commit himself to the mental ward at Charity Hospital, he rails against her: "Every asylum in this nation is filled with poor souls who simply cannot stand lanolin, cellophane, plastic, television, and subdivisions."[7]

The utopian wish of New Orleans exceptionalists is to have a space that is recognizably distinct from that world of second-rate, synthetic simulations—perhaps best embodied by New Urbanist subdivisions in Florida, where every "Main Street USA" storefront is a national franchise.

Exceptionalists are the people who want New Orleans to be a distinct place called New Orleans, a place that can't be simulated and that shouldn't be diluted by the encroaching sameness they perceive in much of the rest of the United States. Americanists resent this wish because they feel that national franchises—especially the pricey ones—confer on New Orleans a middle-class American status they feel they have been wrongly denied. Americanists don't want to live on a cultural island apart from consumerist America, but NOLA exceptionalists do.

The best expression of the New Orleans exceptionalist rejection of Starbucks's new Marigny location came in this comment on Nextdoor Marigny: "Now all the PROUD 'business' people can have super happy guests in their wonderful 'income producing properties' drinking crappy, over-roasted coffee. So much WINNING."

This comment points out both the Americanist priority of business profits at the expense of all other considerations, as well as the "reifying" role Starbucks has played by training a generation of coffee-challenged Americans to think that their "crappy, over-roasted coffee" somehow qualifies as "good." What Starbucks consumers really respond to, more than that distinctively thin, burnt taste, is the way the careful packaging conveys an elite—but standardized—consumer experience, one that confers value on their own identities.

New Orleans exceptionalist anxieties are often expressed as worries about the allegedly unique "vibe" of New Orleans. One commenter on Nextdoor Marigny reassures us that a new Starbucks will not endanger the Marigny "vibe," adding, "New Orleans is known worldwide as one of the most unique cities in the world. It is not an oasis and should not be treated that way. It is of utmost importance to preserve the past, but also be willing to allow in what helps this city to move in a positive direction and thrive."

Though the commenter clearly values "unique" (exceptional) aspects of the city, she also endorses the Americanist assumption that Starbucks is a "positive direction" that will allow the neighborhood to "thrive" more than does the currently rich abundance of independent coffeehouses. Why? The only possible reason is the sense that Starbucks confers the recognition and legitimacy of a national chain, that we can't "thrive" without a giant multinational corporation telling us we're OK.

Another argument in favor of Starbucks paints New Orleans exceptionalist Starbucks-haters (like me) as elitist. Thoughtful observers have often wondered why an exceptional New Orleans cultural identity is worth prioritizing at all, given more material challenges that the city continues to face. One Nextdoor Marigny commenter writes, "Yea! Yea! Yea! Steady employment, good wages, health insurance & educational benefits. What exactly is the problem?"

This argument is difficult to counter. It's true that Starbucks is a relatively responsible employer, and that they are able, unlike many smaller businesses, to offer generous benefit packages. Starbucks has earned the ire of Trump conservatives for its alleged "War on Christmas" and other skirmishes in the realm of cultural politics.[8] That's certainly a point in their favor, too.

With Trump taking a chain saw to the social and civic fabric of our country, preservation of a distinctive cultural identity in one particular neighborhood seems like a low priority indeed. Perhaps the New Orleans exceptionalist impulse to drop out and hide from American society is especially counterproductive right now, when the country needs all-hands-on-deck to resist the disgusting new America Trump and his supporters are trying to foist on the majority of us.

That may be, but there's still no reason for friends to let friends go to Starbucks in Orleans Parish. Let the tourists go, if they're too afraid to part with their cellophane subdivision coffee even on vacation. Will they also avoid the local cuisine by seeking out Chipotle and Panera restaurants? A Marigny Starbucks isn't the end of the world; it's just the end of an era, at least fifty years old, when this neighborhood attracted people who longed for an alternative to the standardized, reified aesthetic that paints the rest of the country in the same copyrighted shades.

Starbucks is a symptom, not a cause. It signals the passing of a great American bohemian neighborhood, distinguished by the care it took to link myths of place to its vision of a more meaningful alternative lifestyle. Not many will mourn the demise of a bohemian enclave, especially not those who blame true bohemians—people of limited means—for attracting the "creative class" yuppies, who then make the average Starbucks customer comfortable enough to also settle in—thus destroying the bohemian "vibe" that started the process in the first place.

Gentrification's economic impacts are more disruptive than its aesthetic consequences, but our neighborhood will now be less distinctive in appearance as well as less affordable—a lose-lose.

Wine from Sour Grapes in Whodat Nation 2019

So, I guess we don't get to have another black and gold day until next fall. And I was planning the perfect outfit for Friday, February 1 to kick off a Whodat Super Bowl weekend. Now all I have is righteous indignation: Botched refereeing robbed us Whodats of the NFC championship.

That's a familiar feeling. After all, persecution fantasies are "naturally N'Awlins." Randy Newman's popular anthem commemorating the 1927 flood crystallizes the paranoia in its refrain: "They're trying to wash us away, they're trying to wash us away."[1]

Historian Shannon Lee Dawdy, in her study of French colonial New Orleans, *Building the Devil's Empire*, noted that, "By the 1720s, writers were characterizing the colony of Louisiana with a language of failure and abandonment."[2] The reasons for early fears of abandonment are easy to understand. The French largely left the colony to fend for itself after the financial collapse of the company authorized to develop it.

That abandonment became the first of New Orleans's many opportunities to make lemonade out of lemons. It inspired self-reliance and interdependence among the people who were here—French, Africans, Native Americans. It also fostered illegal trade ties with nearby Spanish and British colonies, creating a culture that would one day be celebrated for its polyglot distinctiveness.

Centuries later, Hurricane Katrina resurrected the sense that the broader national community doesn't give a %&*$ about us. New Orleanians worked together as neighbors in the storm's aftermath, rescuing people, checking in on others, distributing "looted" goods to hungry residents, organizing waste disposal. It was a marvelous display of grassroots self-government. But the national media spun an entirely opposite tale, instead emphasizing what *Time* magazine columnist Sonja Steptoe called our "lawless depravity."[3]

OK, pro football is just a game, but the cultural practices and emotional responses around it are a game of a different sort. The game on the field is governed by strict rules and an insistence on factual accuracy—with glaring exceptions like the missed pass-interference call in the 2018 season playoff against the Los Angeles Rams. But sports fandom is a less strictly regulated game, a theater for enacting mythical identities.

The eardrum-shattering decibel levels we achieve in the Dome may be an exception, but most of our well-known cultural practices—from crazy costumes to conspiracy theories—have no bearing on game play. Yet NFL football would not be recognizable as a cultural institution without the off-field creativity of fans. In *A Short History of Myth*, Karen Armstrong reminds us that myths are expressions of unconscious "desires" or "fears."[4] Deeply rooted modes of New Orleanian self-expression make Whodat Nation a poster child for Armstrong's understanding of myth.

It's not surprising that the fans of New Orleans's NFL team are particularly adept at spinning a weekly hour of game time into a rich and complex cultural phenomenon. Whodat Nation magnifies the business of an NFL team into a cosmic struggle of the forces shaping local identity.

One of the most fascinating aspects of the performance of Whodat identity is how it juggles the competing ideologies of NOLA identity in general: New Orleans exceptionalism and New Orleans Americanism. New Orleans exceptionalists want to see the city as an alternative to a default American identity, while New Orleans Americanists simply want to be recognized as legitimately American.

Too many students of New Orleans get bogged down in knee-jerk debunking, trying to prove this or that aspect of our collective mythology is poorly rooted in historical fact. But these true-or-false exercises miss the point. Myth always cherry-picks fact, emphasizing certain truths at the expense of others. We need to understand myths as myth—as quasi-factual projections of subconscious fears or desires—and stop vainly groping for levels of facticity more appropriate to science or history. In other words, no, there is not a broad national conspiracy to deny the Saints a shot at another Super Bowl title. But the conspiracy theories do tell us a lot about how we view ourselves in the national context.

On a general level, there is no enterprise more Americanist than fielding an NFL team. The whole point is to earn national recognition, to hear the rest of the United States acknowledge our city as "the best" at that quintessentially American pursuit, pro football.

The persecution fantasy that many Whodats are now giving vent to reflects a very Americanist fear—that "they" won't let us succeed on the American playing field, that for some reason New Orleans is singled out and denied the fair play that Americans are supposed to have a right to. This fear is supported by a conglomeration of inconclusive but suggestive facts: Officials in the Dome last Sunday missed an egregiously early and high hit against Saints receiver Tommylee Lewis, a call that would (most likely) have sealed a New Orleans victory. AND (big reveal coming) . . . many of the refs that day had vague ties to Los Angeles.[5]

The last time Whodats descended into persecution fantasies was similar. The 2012 season could have ended in the first-ever home stadium Super Bowl, since the game was slated for the Superdome and the Saints were still contenders, two years after their glorious 2010 Bowl. Then came "Bountygate" and penalties—including a yearlong suspension of Coach Sean Payton—that struck Saints fans as excessive.[6] Thus the crippled team fell out of contention for a home-turf Super Bowl.

NOLA exceptionalists counter Americanist fears of exclusion from the American community with bravado, falling back on aspects of our culture that are cherished precisely because they distinguish us from the rest of the country. We see the exceptionalist side of Whodat Nation in the way fans customize their team appreciation and adorn it with local signifiers. The pervasive faux French spellings are the most visible sign (e.g., "Geaux Saints"). The local arts of costuming and parading are also front and center, in ways often misunderstood by outside observers. I still remember washed-up conservative comedian Dennis Miller's bewilderment, when he was briefly a Monday Night Football commentator, upon seeing Tom Benson dance with an umbrella after a game. He just couldn't figure out what the umbrella was about and wrongly assumed that it must be a personal idiosyncrasy of Mr. Benson's. Now the Saints have the umbrella, with the late Benson's initials, sewn onto their game jerseys.

The suggestions that we should have a parade for the Saints anyway, in defiance of the national assumption that parades go only to Super Bowl victors, and that we turn Super Bowl weekend—arguably a more American holiday than even Thanksgiving—into a celebration of local identity, these are notably exceptionalist responses. The city that celebrates frivolity for its own sake is also now adding new meaning to the idea of "frivolous" lawsuits, as a couple of Whodats sue the NFL for "loss of enjoyment of life."[7] The demand that life be enjoyed rather than just endured is certainly one of New Orleans's exceptionalism's defining features.

But we hear the defensive and resentful side of the exceptionalist spirit in the trash-talking against other NFL cities. In an era when area bumper stickers proclaim, "This is LA, not L.A.," Los Angeles is a stand-in for an America perceived as boring, aesthetically homogeneous, and unattractive (though wealthier). And, of course, Atlanta is the eternal sign of southern

Americanism, a city, at least in the New Orleans imagination, that is far more successful on the American economic and social playing field, but less imaginative and less beautiful. Now is the predictable time for the memes proclaiming, "We will wake up tomorrow in New Orleans, while they have to wake up in bland, old, boring ___."

The implication of those memes, seen after many a Saints loss, is that life here is more meaningful, magical, and playful than the drudgery faced daily by those poor Americans who don't live in New Orleans. It's a foundational principle of NOLA exceptionalist ideology. It might be made from sour grapes, but it's a great tonic for Whodats in this moment of such flagrantly unfair treatment by an American institution like the NFL. Thus, even the most ardent Crescent City Americanists imbibe NOLA exceptionalist draughts when they sense a snub from a national institution.

So, it's time to box up the extravagant black and gold feathers, sequins, and whatnot. Fortunately, unlike rival NFL cities, we have other avenues for senseless beauty.

Happy Carnival, everybody!

PART III
NEW ORLEANS AND RACE

American Horror in New Orleans
2014

I came home from work the other day and found a notice taped to my front door. It had the logo for the FX television series *American Horror Story* on it. They would be filming on my block that weekend. It gave information about dates, parking and traffic restrictions, and people to contact in case of a problem. One number was the mayor's Office of Film and Video, which, the letter said, could "verify [the] credentials" of the production. We were also assured that "Law Enforcement Officers" would be on hand to help things run smoothly.

It was a relief to learn that horror is so well managed and courteous in New Orleans, certainly a far cry from my childhood days.

The shoot made for a fun evening in the neighborhood. The weather was cool as they set up the lights on the narrow sidewalks. Neighbors came out with cocktails and stood behind the yellow tape, looking out for stars—Kathy Bates or Jessica Lange—and chatting about horror. Nothing much happened before we went to bed, and it was a quiet night. I slept soundly until my neighbor's rooster woke me up around 5:30 a.m. I went out on my stoop in my robe and saw most everything was gone. There was still one big light on a rolling scaffold on the corner. A couple of security guards leaned on it, looking tired. They were unarmed and wore khakis and polos. They resembled Best Buy employees. Further down the street was a house with heavy black plastic hanging over half of it. Workmen came out of it with rolls of cable to toss into the back of a lone truck. It was odd to see no cars on the block, but the parking restrictions had cleared the street and the neighbors hadn't woken up to move their cars back yet. It was enough to provoke a sense of the uncanny, and my imagination began to drift.

I knew the guy who owned the house with the black plastic over it, and I saw him chatting with the crew worker in the truck. I went over and he told me they'd done an interior scene in the unrented half of the double shotgun house. Many of the houses in the neighborhood are double shotguns, interspersed with single shotguns (some with an open gallery on the side), and Creole cottages on the corners. Shotgun houses are comprised of a narrow series of rooms connecting directly, with no hallway. The pattern is usually three rooms, the kitchen—with doors leading to the sole bathroom and back-yard or side alley—and sometimes a rear bedroom.

I grew up in one of these. I don't know if it's my personal history or the design of the homes, but something about the rooms just going into one another in a row with no hallway makes them seem like dream rooms, like you're suddenly in the next room, which looks a lot like the one you were just in, though just slightly off.

My friend Mike's double shotgun is raised about four feet off the ground. Each side has its own little concrete porch and railing—a glorified stoop. He stood on the little porch and asked me if I wanted to see where they filmed inside. He asked the workmen, who were still dragging gear out, and they said it was fine as long as I didn't take pictures.

The first couple of rooms were clean and empty, ready to show to pro-spective renters, with white-washed walls and mantels, high ceilings and fans, high narrow windows, and wooden floors. The next room was furnished. It was the dining room. There was a common wooden table and chairs in the middle, a dresser against a wall, and framed black-and-white family photos on the mantle. The wallpaper was a brownish red, and, on closer inspection, not applied very carefully, not trimmed neatly along the ceiling line. I gath-ered we had wandered back as far as the mid-twentieth century. The next room was the kitchen. It had a sink (with no plumbing underneath), a rustic white wooden china cabinet, and a stove that struck a chord in my memory: the exact kind of stove we had in the shotgun house of my early childhood. It was up on legs, with burners on one side and broiler and oven right next to them, instead of under. The finish was the same white and green swirl baked right into the metal.

The rear bedroom was the scene of the horror. Blood splattered every-where. Pooled in big splotches on the narrow bed and on the floor next to it. The rear door had a broken panel, so you could see the back steps leading down into the yard. My neighbor explained that the broken panel was where the axe murderer had gotten in. No, the blood didn't look real. But the house looked real, which is different than how an axe murder crime scene appears on TV. Lighting, framing, etc.—not to mention the camera itself—create that distance that can make an axe murder fun. Maybe it was the four walls around me that creeped me out. Especially since the four walls of this shot-gun house rear bedroom were so familiar. Though I was never in this partic-ular apartment, it could have been the same room as numerous other rooms I had spent time in, time enough to seed the fabric of my earliest memories and lifelong dream geography. I felt the horror, faint but firm, from some deep-seated interior room that had been locked for years.

When I was in fourth grade, one of my classmates disappeared and was found later, chopped up in a garbage bag. It happened in a house like this. She was an African American girl named Ingrid. She used to wear her hair combed tightly into pigtail twists with those big plastic marble elastics to secure them. She was a bit bigger than the other girls and had a little paunch. We weren't close, yet I can picture her better than almost all my other class-mates of that year. I even have a clear memory of her dad, a guy I never for-mally met, and I can't remember any of my other classmates' parents. She was missing for a few days and the school was involved in putting out the word, helping with the search. It turned out it was her next-door neighbor that got her. With the grisly news of the outcome, the fleeting images of a few days must have seared themselves deep inside me, to stay forever.

Just a couple of weeks ago, I was at a funeral for a dear friend taken finally by disease in old age, and I noticed a stone with her name on it, my murdered classmate. I hadn't ever known where she was buried, but here was her me-morial. Apparently, she died just days before her birthday. She was probably looking forward to her happy day, to promised gifts and a party. Before the Lord decided to subject her to a special kind of hell that only He is capable of devising.

I was watching the Catholic channel one day and they were asking a priest about the position of the church on ghosts. He reported how Catholic teaching holds that there is a finality to death—no survival of the soul as a ghost wandering earth—and said that people probably invented ghost stories to take the terror out of death. A consideration of ghost tourism in New Orleans would seem to confirm that view. Everybody knows that New Orleans is famous for its ghosts; indeed, in the words of one tourist website, "America's Most Haunted City."

But that's not good. It means there are more unhappily dead people here than anywhere else. On the one hand, we have personal memories and statis-tics to scare the bejesus out of us (if we dwell too much on unpleasant details). On the other hand, we get to reap the fun that our sublimation of that terror results in. Aestheticized horror and the genuine article go hand in hand—the wicked witch of a history of cruelty and the good witch of the erotically charged voyeuristic thrill that aestheticized horror provides. Add race to the mix and you have the peculiarly American horror called "the South."

Ghost tours in New Orleans have boomed in the past twenty years. So much so that French Quarter residents file frequent complaints about the drunken crowds lapping up the tour guides' lurid tales on the darkened street corners of the safest part of town. A routine stop is at a house that I was warned away from by neighbors in my childhood. The house of Madame Delphine LaLaurie stands on the corner of Royal and Governor Nicholls. Nicolas Cage owned it for a while, but then he went mysteriously bankrupt and had to sell. The actual Madame LaLaurie was a white Creole society woman who often entertained at the mansion. She would reportedly excuse herself periodically and the guests would pretend not to hear the muffled cries from above. She had a torture chamber in her attic—just for kicks—where she kept enslaved people chained and undernourished for purposes of recreational cruelty. Until one day a little girl, fleeing Madame's blows, leapt to her death in the courtyard below. The resulting community outrage led her to flee New Orleans, first to New York, then to France, but the FX version leaves out these details. Madame LaLaurie is played by Kathy Bates in *American Horror Story: Coven*.

I don't like Bates in the role, but that's not a professional opinion. The reasons are very personal. Though she lived over a century before my birth, Madame LaLaurie is someone I saw often as a child, and she always filled me with the kind of magnetic terror that forms the basis of aestheticized horror, if only it can be kept at a safe emotional distance. I walked by her house and thought of her, however briefly, almost every day of my childhood. I noticed how other people would sometimes cross themselves when they went by it. And I saw her in person, in raven hair and a rich pink evening gown, with candle in one hand and a whip in the other. It was at the Musée Conti, the wax museum where to this day she raises her hand against helpless chained starving victims, as long as the air conditioning holds up (blessedly, they had a generator for Katrina).[1]

The Musée Conti depicts her as strikingly beautiful as she hisses threats in the dim light. In front of her are two chained adults, a standing man and a woman on the ground. The man's hands are shackled high above his head, and the woman seated on the ground has one wrist chained tightly to her neck. Both are emaciated, both twisting their heads to look at her— which can only mean she'd commanded them to. They're Black, but so is the well-dressed butler next to Madame, who brandishes a rope for the little girl running toward the stairs. The eyes of the chained adults, whom I always imagined to be the girl's parents, bulge out of their sallow faces as they twist to heed the famous cruel beautiful white woman in the elegant dress.

As lagniappe, the Musée Conti's New Orleans history exhibit is followed by the "Haunted Dungeon," a series of middlebrow Hollywood horror scenes, from Frankenstein to Dark Shadows. But none of them compare to Madame

LaLaurie's attic, which captures so succinctly the emotional essence of slavery as the handmaiden of sadism. Sadism is, of course, the thrill tapped into by aestheticized horror—the erotic kick of watching other people terrorized. The fact that Madame LaLaurie is in the history section of the museum, rather than the "Haunted Dungeon" section for the kids, is a stark link between a history of horror and the horror industry. Contrary to Freud's "talking cure," though, reliving the trauma doesn't exorcise it, though it does lead to rituals of aestheticized reenactment that must serve some emotional purpose. Sometimes, as in *American Horror Story*, the result is an erotic form of fun. In other cases, there are other intended purposes, though I wonder if emotional results can be accurately generalized and predicted.

Steve McQueen's Oscar-winning *12 Years a Slave* also puts cruelty on the screen, though the intended effect is supposed to be revulsion rather than aesthetic pleasure. Since the 1970s, graphic depictions of historic American racist violence have also come to be a kind of ritual in movies not intended to be "horror" films. But some aesthetic affinities are hard to ignore. Hollywood South regular James Franco made that clear enough in his own review of *12 Years a Slave*: "We like watching humans get beaten, and if such beatings are framed in the right way, in this case, in an *important film about American history*, then we will lap up all that brutality and want more. I know I did."[2]

I think Franco's basically right, as long as we see the "important film about history" part as a thin fig leaf for indulging our sadistic fantasies. More generic horror movies, without claims to social uplift, are perhaps more honest. The other problem is that the aesthetic appreciation of scenes of brutality can easily be ruined by emotional discomfort, and distance from the experience of actual horror might be a precondition for enjoyment of aestheticized horror. Unless, of course, a cathartic effect is possible, the purging of repressed emotions in a controlled environment, sometimes a social one. This is probably the purpose of films like *12 Years a Slave*. But it also can't be ruled out that more "fun" films like *American Horror Story* don't also function on that level. At any rate, both projects' intended effects rely on the viewer's ability to maintain emotional distance from the subject matter. Those Americans who opine that *12 Years a Slave* made them see or feel for the first time the terror of slavery have obviously spent a lifetime not feeling some form of that terror already. Because of my New Orleanian upbringing, however, because of the palpable presence of Madame LaLaurie's legacy, and because of the more random racial identity of my murdered childhood classmate, I developed at a young age a painfully emotional sense that there was something terrifying (not in a fun way) about being Black in America.

One night this past fall, when *12 Years a Slave* was being screened and *American Horror Story* was being shot, edited, and aired, seven young men broke into a dilapidated antebellum mansion in Arabi, an older, immediate suburb of New Orleans. The newspaper reported that their original purpose was to smoke marijuana and search for ghosts. But before they left, they set the old LeBeau plantation alight and it burned to the ground. Community outrage naturally ensued, since one of the area's oldest cultural landmarks, which had stood since the 1850s, was now destroyed. In the film version of Anne Rice's *Interview with the Vampire*, the young vampire Louis de Pointe du Lac burns down his family's plantation home because, as he tells his rebellious slaves, it's been occupied by the devil. Who's to say the LeBeau plantation wasn't also? Who knows what psycho LaLaurie activities went on there? Being from New Orleans means living with the paradox of beauty rooted in blood. Are we to be sad or triumphant when some lovely torture chamber with wide galleries and stately columns burns to the ground?

It's not that New Orleans or the South is unique in the interconnection between suffering and sublimated aesthetic enjoyment. As Walter Benjamin put it a hundred years ago, "There is no document of civilization that is not also a document of barbarism."[3] It's just that Americans have designated the South, perhaps especially New Orleans, as the anti-Jerusalem of American sin, therefore American horror. The problem with being from New Orleans is that there may not be sufficient emotional distance to enjoy it.

South of the South?
2015

South of the South, below the Bible Belt, the northernmost point of the Caribbean: These are all monikers embraced by well-meaning New Orleanians to remove the city from the cultural geography of the South, which often results in distancing us from the state of Louisiana as well. Is New Orleans in the South? It's a silly question on its face, since a quick glance at a map settles it. There is also no doubt that New Orleans has faced the same historical dramas as the rest of the region. Instead of pretending that New Orleans isn't in the South, it's better to think of New Orleans as an "other" South, one that's always existed alongside the popular image of the South that so many of us—including me—cringe to behold.

Many have reflected, especially since Katrina, on the gap between the myth of New Orleans and the various realities of the place. But, of course, the South is laden with myth, too, concocted by natives and onlookers alike. Sadly, southern identity is often hijacked to support radical right-wing political agendas. American leftists are wrong to call American Far Right conservatives Nazis—they're actually Confederates. The conflation of "southern" with "Confederate" is at the heart of the political myth of the "Solid South," and, as ever, the successful marketing of that myth has resulted time and again in political ugliness.

Thus "our" values, to folks such as Governor Bobby Jindal, require limiting the pool of citizens. The *Dred Scott* decision in 1857 said a Black man had "no rights" that a white man is "bound to respect." Just change "Black" and "white" to "gay" and "straight," and you've got the gist of Jindal's "Marriage and Conscience" order.[1]

Explicitly excluding African Americans is no longer politically viable. State-sanctioned racism is a thing of the past, albeit the recent past. But to Jindal et al., the South's stewardship of "traditional values" entails a last-ditch effort to throw up a bulwark against gay citizens. Jindal's executive order protecting people's right to discriminate—by, for example, refusing to cater or provide flowers for a gay wedding reception—is meeting with widespread outrage here in New Orleans. I'm proud of that, but it's no surprise. Even outside Orleans Parish, Louisianans can be found who are offended by the governor's kamikaze-like decision to hold the tourism and convention economy hostage to his quixotic dream of acceptance by Iowa caucus-goers. It's not the first time a southern conservative has sought to build alliances with fellow travelers far from home.

The myth of the "Old South" followed a similar career. It was first dreamed up by southern segregationists like Thomas Dixon Jr., author of *The Clansman* (1905), a celebratory tale of political terror bringing down Reconstruction in a shower of blood. But then Hollywood picked up Dixon's novel and made it into a blockbuster movie, *The Birth of a Nation* (1915), and the image of the South designed by the worst among us became official representation.

Today, Jindal foists an unpopular law on the state, against the will of his legislature, and then runs an ad in Iowa trumpeting the righteousness of his stand against . . . discrimination? Yes—just as the Confederates were outraged at the infringement of their freedom to hold others in bondage, Jindal's wacky but moneyed minority insists that its right to discriminate against others not be discriminated against. Confusing, yes, but self-evident in the minds of true believers.

They understand freedom in a mercantilist sense, as a limited resource—if everyone has the same rights, what are they worth, after all? Rights should be privileges, earned by hard work and obedience to "traditional" values (theirs).

The immediate backlash in New Orleans has been appropriately virulent. Most interesting is the repeated declaration that this executive order is "not us," not what "we" (New Orleanians) are "about." According to Mayor Mitch Landrieu and many other vocally aggrieved locals, we are about "tolerance" and "diversity." Fear of lost revenue, rather than a broad-minded acceptance of alternative lifestyles, is what drives the statewide resistance to Bobby's latest cry for attention, but New Orleanians can rightfully claim a history of live-and-let-live attitudes in regard to personal lifestyle choices.

Then again, the myth of New Orleanian cultural tolerance can be disabused by history as much as confirmed by it. We can look at Tennessee Williams's personal narrative of self-discovery in one of America's most visible gay communities in the 1930s, or we can look at District Attorney Jim Garrison's targeted persecution of gay New Orleanians in the 1960s. Sex across the color line, from *plaçage* to Storyville, remains the central exhibit in the Big Easy's famous (and notorious) disregard of the private lives of consenting adults, but these examples entail exploitation along with unbridled freedom (for possessors of money and power).

"Oh, New Orleans is such freedom!" gushes the major gay character, a trust-fund transplant, in John Kennedy Toole's novel *A Confederacy of Dunces*.[2] But "such freedom" remains elusive for Burma Jones, the novel's African American working stiff, and for Ignatius Reilly himself, an iconoclastic intellectual loudmouth in a world of repressed and repressive socially conservative yats. We could even say that New Orleans's historic tolerance of sex across the color line radiates an especially southern ethos—absolute white privilege for those who can afford it. New Orleans was able to realize the logical outcome of a principle that the rest of the South was simply too squeamish to pursue so openly.

The accusation of racism is the way to go for the jugular when reminding New Orleanians of their southernness. Like many other (white) locals, I was incensed by the way national media emphasized racism in their coverage of Hurricane Katrina. Recent acts of state-sponsored racism in places like Ferguson, Cleveland, and Baltimore usually come with disclaimers like "as in the rest of the country." I don't recall that courtesy in the post-Katrina coverage. New Orleans was made to appear like an average southern city, with white people up on a hill, and Black residents in the swampy bottomland down by a flood-prone creek. Think Sparta, Mississippi, the fictional town of TV's *In the Heat of the Night*. Mayor Nagin had to remind national observers that the "sliver by the river," the higher ground that escaped catastrophic flooding, was also majority Black.

But, of course, New Orleans can't escape its typically southern racist past. All it can do is emphasize a handful of meaningful aberrations from it. Yes, New Orleans was the largest slave market in the country before the Civil War. On the other hand, New Orleans also had the largest population of free Blacks during that era. Yes, school desegregation was ugly here, with national cameras recording "crackers" shouting the n-word at little girls. But were they "crackers"?

Hollywood often insists on giving white New Orleanians redneck accents (like John Goodman's "Big Daddy" La Bouff in Disney's *The Princess and the Frog*), but we know the Ninth Ward yokels cursing out six-year-old Ruby Bridges at Frantz Elementary School in 1960 were yats, not crackers. What's the difference? Urban, ethnic, working-class descendants of nineteenth-century immigrants are more comparable to the racists who took to the streets during the New York Draft Riot of 1863, or the 1919 Chicago Riot, than to impoverished Scots-Irish hill country agrarians. Racist, yes, but southern? Also yes, if we're willing to realize how the urban South differs in many ways from the Hollywood myth of an agrarian South.

We also can't ignore that Jim Crow descended on Louisiana just as it did upon every other former Confederate state. On the other hand, "separate but equal" was valiantly resisted by groups such as Rodolphe DesDunes's *Comité des Citoyens*, who brought their *Plessy v. Ferguson* challenge all the way to the Supreme Court—where, shamefully, Justice Edward White, a New Orleanian, won the day by backing the "separate but equal" opinion that formed the legal basis for Jim Crow. His statue stands once again in front of the state supreme court on Royal Street—why doesn't anyone protest that?

Often, it's the smaller, less public incidents that remind us of our roots in southern racism and associated "traditions." One such private insult took place May 21 at a second-rate tourist bar and grill on Decatur Street called Huck Finn's. The insult was the typing of the words "N----, 100% Dislike" on the check presented to an African American diner. This is the kind of thing that goes viral, and it did.[3]

However you dice it, it will be easy for many to come to the conclusion that this is a typical act of southern racism in a southern city. The employee was immediately fired, and I don't know where he/she hails from. A strange irony is how the offensive word printed on the receipt is uttered throughout the novel narrated by the restaurant's namesake: Huck Finn (in Mark Twain's *The Adventures of Huckleberry Finn*). This is ironic because flinging that word at a modern African American is indubitably a racist act, while the novel itself is one of the great anti-racist texts of American literature. Few people today are aware of the book's anti-racist message, because they won't read it for fear of seeing the n-word. The appearance of the n-word in quite different context in a restaurant irrelevantly named after an anti-racist hero thus tarnishes America's anti-racist literary record as much as it does our city's.

Twain was a big fan of New Orleans and buddies with another great exemplar of the "other" South, New Orleanian writer George Washington Cable. Cable well reflects the fate of that "other" South, the South that defines itself outside the constrictions of conservative propagandists like Jindal. He spoke out loudly against racism, but finally had to flee his hometown because conservatives nostalgic for the "Old South," drummed up so much ire against him.

One of his under-read gems alleges to be a Civil War memoir by a New Orleans lady who resisted the war and spoke out against it, earning the retribution that conservative southerners visited upon neighbors opposed to their catastrophic decision to wage a war in defense of slavery. The story is found in a volume entitled *Strange True Stories of Louisiana*, published in 1890. The word "strange" in the title reflects the challenge faced by an author attempting to counter the dominant myth of the "Solid South," a place of charming backwardness and homespun bigotry that new southerners such as Bobby Jindal, the rabid *Duck Dynasty* fan, are all too happy to continue promoting.[4]

Which drives many of us to the desperate claim that we're somehow not really in the South. Instead, we should be proud that New Orleans has long been a magnet for southerners who wish to remain in the South and celebrate their southern cultural identity without the millstone of hate that southern conservatives attach to it.

Cable's willingness to resist the southern orthodoxy of his day (and ours) doesn't make him any less southern, despite the claims of his enemies. He envisioned a more congenial, more tolerant, more diverse South. A freer South. The New Orleans establishment named for his friend Twain's protagonist serves Cajun burgers and catfish, but the help has been reminded that they are supposed to do so without invoking the n-word or indulging in the gay bashing encoded in Jindal's latest decree. That way, we get to take in an extra helping of tourist dollars—a venerable New Orleans economic tradition that Jindal, as he seeks to extend his lifelong tenure on the public payroll, is being reminded not to fool with.

From *Passé Blanc* to *Passé Noir*
2015

We appear to be in the "conversation about race" era of America's long racial struggle. The problem is how circular the conversation seems to be. The same conclusions keep getting arrived at, the same rhetorical teams keep trotting out the same old plays. It may just be that every generation needs to hash out this hoary American debate for itself.

New Orleans has been having a conversation about race longer than most places because racial identity here has been more complicated, and more nuanced, than in areas with less racial mixing. The whole nation experienced a cataclysmic revolution in race relations over fifty years ago, during the administration of Lyndon Johnson, the last liberal and only Civil Rights president to ever occupy the White House. But racial consciousness has been evolving more slowly since then, notwithstanding the Obama presidency—more a matter of optics, perhaps, than profound social change. Certainly, a Black "first family" in the White House helps erode the insurmountable deficit in social capital that once attached to Black skin, but that doesn't necessarily lead to greater economic capital for Black citizens.

The latest twist in the national debate is brought to you by Spokane NAACP chapter president Rachel Dolezal. Though Black people "passing" as white were a staple of the "conversation about race" before the Civil Rights era, a white woman "passing" as Black, as Dolezal managed to do until recently, has provided a fresh enough twist to light up the Twittersphere.

Ebullient postmoderns celebrate the freedom of all to invent their own identities, regardless of biological restrictions like skin color or sex. They point out that, in physical terms, Rachel Dolezal's identity migration has involved nowhere near the striking visual turnabout that Caitlyn Jenner's move from male to female did.

In another corner (there are more than two in this boxing ring), many African Americans see Dolezal's choice to self-identify as Black as yet another arrogant expression of white privilege. While she can choose her race, many Black people are too dark to do that. There's a sense, too, that a white person is colonizing the limited sphere of Black privilege, at a time when white privilege still brings many more rewards and remains more fiercely guarded against Black intruders.

Other African Americans are willing to overlook Dolezal's embellished racial identity out of respect for her commitment to racial justice.[1] Then, of course, there are the white anti-racist liberals who seek to enhance their own cred by agreeing loudly with aggrieved Black people that Dolezal's appropriation of their limited "racial capital" is unconscionable. Conservatives try to devalue Blackness as a social asset by calling it "victim capital," forgetting, I guess, that Black cool is a currency held in high regard by many a white liberal, and only tangentially associated with victimhood.

Unfortunately, white supporters of racial equality are often inhibited in the scope of their analysis by fear of treading on the authentic Black subject's license to have the last word in any discussion of race.

Finally, aggrieved white right-wingers, convinced they are being condescended to by other white people, whine that they are somehow being stripped of their right to have any opinions at all about race—those opinions often being racist, but perhaps not always.

The problem people have with Dolezal is not that she's a white anti-racist or even that she assumed a leadership role in the NAACP, but that she has chosen to fight racism as a Black person, rather than as a white person.

Michael T. Jeffries, writing in the *Boston Globe*, has offered one of the most cogent responses to the Dolezal incident.[2] Obviously, a white person passing for Black is not a simple symmetrical inversion of a Black person passing for white. Jeffries points out that Black people "passing" for white (*passé blanc* in old New Orleans parlance) can be a form of resistance to racism. But this is an iconoclastic view in the context of African American literature, where passing has most often been represented in negative terms.

Two famous novels on the theme are Nella Larsen's *Passing* (1929) and James Weldon Johnson's *Autobiography of an Ex-Colored Man* (1912). While Larsen and Johnson were celebrated figures of the Harlem Renaissance, New Orleans writers were way ahead of the curve, exploring the arbitrariness of racial categories at least a generation earlier. Local writer Alice Dunbar-Nelson captured the haziness and variety of racial identities in nineteenth-century New Orleans, as did white writer George Washington Cable before her.

Passé noir—white passing for Black—is a less common literary trope, but John Howard Griffin tried it in his 1961 book, *Black Like Me*, and Nell Zink does it in her hot off-the-press *Mislaid*.

The New Orleans contribution to the national obsession with racial identity is rooted in racial *indeterminacy*—with being neither Black nor white, with being both, or not being able to tell which. It was a big theme in New Orleans literature and culture before race relations here became firmly Americanized in the Jim Crow era. Judging from how people wrote about it, the streets of New Orleans offered a bewildering spectrum of skin tones, hair, and facial features. Race mixing was a factor in the confusion, but so was the presence of many darker-skinned ethnicities—immigrant and native—who nevertheless were considered legally white, since white was defined as non-Black.

Lafcadio Hearn wrote of New Orleans in the 1880s, "Every race that the world boasts is here, and a good many races that are nowhere else."[3] Obviously, the races that "are nowhere else" are simply indeterminate, beyond the ability of arbitrary racial categories to classify.

In one of the most striking scenes in Cable's 1880 masterpiece *The Grandissimes,* a transplant from Philadelphia discovers that his landlord is . . . well, what is he? "Ah ham nod whide, m'sieu,"[4] the landlord advises the bewildered northerner. He is Afro-Creole, of course, but the American is unable to determine his race, and so assumed he was "white."

As New Orleans became more American and more homogenized, linguistically as well as ethnically (immigration tapering off after the 1920s), the color line became ever more stark.

Dunbar-Nelson's "The Stones of the Village," never published in her lifetime,[5] is a tragedy of racial determinism, depicting the unhappy fate that befalls an Afro-Creole man who, feeling neither Black nor white, tries to live on the white side of the growing racial divide. He ascends to the heights of elite New Orleans society, but is emotionally torn apart by fear of discovery and by resentment that he has been required to make such a choice. In this and other works, New Orleans's racial indeterminacy offers an escape from racial determinism, but at a high emotional cost.

Another story of Dunbar-Nelson's, "The Pearl in the Oyster," published in 1900, is more like a comedy of errors. The protagonist first outrages his Afro-Creole family by attending a Black university. "You shall not go," his mother moans, "my son wid what dey call Negre! Non, Non!"[6] Later he decides to go white, blending in with the Irish in the Irish Channel. Then he tries to go home again to his people in the Creole districts, only to discover that they resent his dalliance among whites too much to take him back. He resolves to leave New Orleans forever, saying to his wife, "We will start life again, but whether we decide to be white or Black, we will stick to it."[7]

One of the great meditations on the arbitrariness of racial designation in America is Charles Chesnutt's 1889 essay "What Is a White Man?" Though not from the city, New Orleans's reputation as the site of racial indeterminacy caused him to set a novel here, *Paul Marchand, F.M.C.*, exploring the intersection of racial indeterminacy and racial determinism in the antebellum era. In a revolutionary plot development for when the novel was written, in the 1920s, the protagonist chooses to *passer noir* after learning late in life that, contrary to his own and everyone else's assumptions, he had been legally white all along.

The arbitrariness of racial categories was understood well by illiterate enslaved Afro-Creoles, too, as some of their tales collected by Alcée Fortier attest. In "The Marriage of Compair Lapin," the titular trickster rabbit schools his friend Master Fox, "They will say: 'That's a fellow with long ears; he is a mule; let us take him.' Even if I protest, and say that I am a rabbit, they will say: 'Oh, no! look at his ears; you see that he is a mule.'"[8] In other words, power decides what categories subjugated people are to fall into. One way to escape, if not directly challenge that power, is to cheat, since the categories have zero validity rooted in either reason or morality.

With the Americanization of race relations in the Jim Crow era, New Orleans became much less racially imaginative. My dad reports, however, that in the Ninth Ward shortly before my boyhood there, many racial self-identifications seemed to hinge on trust, perhaps owing to the lingering presence of dark-skinned non-Black ethnicities. I learned, for example, that one of our neighbors who identified as "Spanish" was actually "Creole" (meaning Afro-Creole, as it generally always does today). My dad joked once that the funny thing about a David Duke rally in New Orleans was how many rally-goers would be denied admission to the Klan in Alabama.

There have, of course, always been some white people who have elected to cross over into Black society on a more permanent basis, if they could win admittance, including white women. I don't mean furtive slumming adventurers, but actually living full time with Black families. The women I remember from my childhood in the Ninth Ward were not exactly passing—they were just being white people who chose to live on the Black side of a segregated society. And, of course, there was no turning back and rejoining white society once they made the choice to have Black children.

But did a socially established white person, with a degree of power, ever actually assume a Black identity, long-term, in the era before Rachel Dolezal? According to University of New Orleans anthropologist Martha Ward, that's exactly what the love of Marie Laveau's life, Jean Louis Duminy de Glapion, did in the 1820s, so great was his commitment to love the Voodoo Queen as a peer. They never legally married but lived together full time and had many children.[9]

The Americanization of race brought a hardening of racial categories, though "Creole" continues to exist—at least in the minds of many Afro-Creoles—as a category not entirely synonymous with "Black."

When will America be able to relax about people choosing their race, in the way that, liberal Americans agree, we should be able to determine our own gender? Probably not soon.

In her 1976 novel *Woman on the Edge of Time*, Marge Piercy depicted an anarcho-syndicalist utopia of seductive charm. It's a post-racial utopia, where the cultures that evolved in an era marked by racism have shed racial identifications. A wide range of identities are available in Piercy's imagined American future: African and Native American villages and a host of other cultural models. But the citizen gets to choose which culture to live in, regardless of her own racial or ethnic background. Naïve, perhaps, but sweet.

Monumental Decision: Who Should Be Honored in Place of the Confederates? 2015

I never would have guessed getting rid of the Confederate blemishes on our cityscape would become politically feasible—and suddenly it's almost a done deal! I'm elated.

Yes, my nostalgic sentimentalism gave me pause for about five seconds. I have many fond memories of Lee Circle, including swimming lessons at the old YMCA. And I always thought the Beauregard statue at the entrance to City Park looked cool, mainly because of the excellent horse.

The greatest loss will be an end to the periodic defacement of Jefferson Davis with swastikas and other markings appropriate to the ideology he stood for. More than the others, the Jeff Davis monument, on the parkway that bears his name, seemed to inspire political expression by our intrepid local population of anarchist vandals.

There's a petition going around on social media to save the place names and monuments, Lee Circle in particular. But I question how many of the signatories actually live in Orleans Parish. You might think Beauregard would be getting more defense than Lee, if only because he was from here. Indeed, it's hard to think of an historical figure that has less to do with New Orleans than Robert E. Lee. But they all need to go. The only question is what to replace them with.

One historic marker up for removal doesn't need a replacement. The Liberty Place monument, hidden behind the Canal Place parking garage for the past twenty years, could be tipped over and just tossed in the nearest dumpster. The diminutive obelisk should have been a monument to the victims of the 1874 coup, in which Crescent City White League thugs shot at the backs of an integrated New Orleans police force, but it glorified the coup plotters instead, so just throw it out.

Since Confederate sympathizers no longer have the guts to argue baldly for white supremacy, they now claim that the Confederacy was a part of "history" (like everything else) and should be enshrined in stone and bronze for that reason. I agree with them to this extent: The sites of the three statues commemorating leaders of the Confederacy should be replaced with figures from that time period or earlier.

I think we play into the arguments of Confederate sympathizers if we feel we have to replace these old statues with people from a more recent time. We can't just turn our eyes in horror from the whole saga of New Orleans prior to the day before yesterday, in some vain search for a conflict-free historical moment that will never exist. I also think we need to avoid the easy, touristic solution of just putting famous jazz musicians on vacant pedestals. Armstrong Circle, in addition to Armstrong Airport and Armstrong Park, would definitely be overkill. New Orleans is a lot more than the home of one famous guy. We should have the courage to acknowledge more of our history than what's safe and cuddly and good for tourism.

Here are my recommendations for what should replace the three existing Confederate monuments. I've also got a suggestion for another monument in a different location that's long overdue.

The big opportunity is Lee Circle—keep the towering column, but let's put someone else up there. Many people have made good suggestions. Almost any figure would be better than Lee, given how tenuous his connections are to New Orleans. It's obvious that he always represented an imposed ideology with very little organic connection to the society of the city. We should replace him with somebody local, but also from the same era.

That said, I think we should resist the temptation to be on the politically safe side and replace all of these monuments to white men with monuments to Black people. The city needs to do more to honor its Black leaders, but that doesn't have to mean a ban on statues of white people.

How about a white New Orleanian of roughly Lee's generation who stood for a more inclusive society than Lee did (when he wore the uniform he wears on the column). Since Lee Circle is in the American Quarter of the city, it would be even better to get somebody with ties to that neighborhood.

The Lee monument was dedicated in 1884, a dark time in New Orleans for local people—white or Black—who envisioned the more inclusive society that had been attempted during Reconstruction. One prominent and nationally successful local writer spoke up: George Washington Cable.

Cable had already written a novel sharply critical of the slaveholding society that the Confederate monument builders were beginning to twist into some fairytale golden age. In 1884, Cable started going around on the lecture circuit—a mass medium of the day—delivering an oration called "The Freedman's Case in Equity." The speech excoriated efforts to erode Black rights that were spreading across the South.

After vituperative attacks in the southern press, followed by death threats, Cable was forced to leave his hometown for good—in the same year New Orleans adorned Lee Circle with its monument to some guy from Virginia who led the war for white supremacy (even though he, too, had later supported Reconstruction).

If we include Armstrong Park, Musical Legends Park, and numerous other locations, how many monuments to musicians do we already have in New Orleans? And how many monuments to writers? A bronze Edgar Allan Poe presides in Baltimore. Shouldn't we celebrate our literary heritage as well as our music?

Through today's sophisticated anti-racist lens, we can see numerous flaws in Cable's literary effort to promote racial equality. Like his buddy Mark Twain, he briefly served in the Confederate military—but so did Afro-Creole writer and activist Armand Lanusse. Subjecting people of the past to contemporary litmus tests about what language they used and what uniform they may have worn, for whatever reason and however briefly, is historical illiteracy.

What we need to do is gauge the courage and vision of the stands people took in their own times. Cable's stand for racial equality got him run out of town. I like the sound of "Cable Circle." Bring the man back home. Put Cable on the column.

I suspect that the Landrieu administration would rather see new monuments that could be better marketed to tourists. Cable Circle would be much more of a head-scratcher than Lee Circle or Armstrong Circle, but it's not a great selfie-op in any case, given how high the column lifts the statue above the street.

My next recommendation would be a tour guide's delight, though she's mistakenly been omitted from the city's official commemoration of great New Orleanians: Marie Laveau, the Voodoo Queen. She should have a statue and it would do double duty for her daughter and namesake. Bayou St. John is the right place for a Laveau statue, since that's where mother and daughter held their St. John's Eve celebrations until they moved them closer to the lake. That makes them the perfect replacement for Beauregard.

The substitution is sure to be a big hit with the tourists, but with locals as well. The elder Laveau was revered by New Orleanians of different races and social classes at the time of her death in 1881. I would depict her seated magisterially, with her daughter Marie, who assumed her mantle, standing behind with a mischievous gleam in her eye—since she was more of a disruptive trickster than her mother. Both should be scaled a bit larger than life, as befits their legends.

My idea about what to do with Jefferson Davis Parkway and the monument to Davis at its Canal Street crossing is influenced by what stands on the parkway neutral ground at Banks Street: a monument to Cuban independence hero, José Martí.

At a time of renewed Hispanic migration into New Orleans, and of renewed ties with Cuba, rededication of this picturesque boulevard provides a unique opportunity to salute our Spanish heritage. I like the series of statues on Basin Street commemorating Latin American revolutionaries, but people have been grousing about wanting to relocate the Simón Bolívar statue for a long time. So why not move it to the parkway? Bolívar could anchor the parkway at Tulane Avenue (where a lesser Confederate now has his bust); and iconic Mexican President Benito Juárez could anchor the other end at the new Lafitte Greenway. The boulevard could be renamed Avenida de las Americas, or something along those lines.

Latinos are abundant in the Mid-City area and deserve an official nod from the city about the contribution of the Spanish colonial period to the city's history. Streets named for the Spanish governors (Miró, Gálvez, etc.) are also close by.

More to the point, remembering the Spanish period is especially useful as a way to distance New Orleans from the South represented by Lee and Davis and Beauregard. One of the most exceptional aspects of New Orleans when it entered the United States in 1803 was the city's high proportion of free Blacks. It was the Spanish who made it so, by allowing numerous avenues to freedom for enslaved people, opportunities that the Americans would quickly block.

Indeed, in 1803, the day after the formal parade celebrating the Louisiana Purchase—a parade that included two militias of free Blacks—General James Wilkinson, an alarmed aide to Governor William Claiborne, sought additional American troops from Washington, warning that the "formidable aspect of the armed Blacks & Malattoes [sic] . . . is painful and perplexing."[1]

The French Quarter features a very prominent monument to Jean Baptiste LeMoyne, Sieur de Bienville, the French founder and four-time colonial-era governor; now it's time to recognize a Spanish-era governor. I propose that the Davis statue be replaced by one honoring Bernardo de Gálvez, the man also remembered in the names of St. Bernard Avenue and St. Bernard Parish. An obscure equestrian statue of Gálvez used to stand in front of the old Trade Mart, but it's since been removed—perhaps it could be pulled out of storage and relocated at the intersection of Canal Street and the new Avenida de las Americas. Among Gálvez's many accomplishments is the capture of the British garrisons at Mobile and Pensacola in support of the American

Revolution. That's right, Gálvez is the only Louisiana governor to have attacked Alabama—and won! That should be reason enough for a monument.

Carl Sandburg's famous poem, "Chicago," celebrates that city of "building, breaking, re-building,"[2] but that's not us. The New Orleans way is not to ignore everything that happened more than five minutes ago, but to agonize over our history in a search for ghosts more amenable to the values we hold dear.

This is not an impossible task. One figure from the past—a figure more deserving of our collective reverence and grief than any other—has been largely ignored to date. Atoning for that neglect provides an opportunity far greater, and also different in kind, from simply swapping a fresh statue for that of a figure who has been disgraced.

We need a memorial to the people who built the city and its wealth, notwithstanding the life of terror forced upon them. We need a memorial to the victims of slavery.

There is John Scott's beautiful "Spirit House" at the corner of Gentilly Boulevard and St. Bernard Avenue, and it should remain there. There is also a "Tomb of the Unknown Slave" in front of St. Augustine Church on Gov. Nicholls Street in Tremé. But a more prominent location should be chosen for a more monumental statement.

The riverfront has an immigrant memorial and a Holocaust memorial, both of which are fine with me—until I reflect on the absence of a memorial to the holocaust of unwilling immigrants. Enslaved Africans were more responsible than anyone else for building the city we now hold dear, and for enriching the jerks who put up the Confederate memorials that we finally have the courage to tear down.

Spanish Plaza, currently in flux, is the perfect place for a more monumental Tomb of the Unknown Slave. People can reflect on it when they buy their outlet mall consumer goods, and it can be a terminus for numerous processionals and political demonstrations. The river is the natural spot for the immigrant memorial, since that's where my Irish ancestors and many others disembarked with a hope and a dream. The memorial to enslaved people needs to be on the old riverfront, too, since that's where they were hustled off in chains to build a great city that would then struggle to forget them—until now. What happens at this newly hallowed public space will be more important than any other public monument in the city, old or new.

Beyoncé, New Orleans, and Afro-Creole Femininity 2016

While we were having Carnival, they had a Super Bowl over in America somewhere. New Orleans was oddly projected into the Americans' festivities by halftime performer Beyoncé, who did the number she had released the day before as a song and video.

"Formation" is a visual essay exploring the meaning of New Orleans in the broader national, and specifically African American, imagination. Most viewers tended to focus on the Hurricane Katrina imagery, but the costumed scenes invoked New Orleans in more historically conscious ways. National critical responses showed how, for most Americans, New Orleans remains an illegible cipher. Symbols of the city trigger strong emotional responses in the viewer, but the reasons why remain unconscious for most.

Social media shares of "Formation" were titled "love song to New Orleans" and "homage to Hurricane Katrina." Many of the video's images were central to New Orleans mythology, not just the flood scenes. If you don't get the New Orleans imagery—both from Katrina and further back in our history—you also don't get why this particular song and video had to be set in New Orleans to achieve its effects.

The loudest critique of "Formation" has been about its arguably exploitative use of Katrina imagery.[1] Some local writers have denounced it as an act of cultural appropriation.[2] The Black voices coming out against the video illustrate what many national (white) viewers don't seem to get: that Black identity is not monolithic, that a universally lauded "celebration of Blackness" is not possible. A secondary realization is that many Black New Orleanians, like their non-Black neighbors, feel their identity at an intersection that includes city as well as race.

It's also obvious that the easy emotional punch of Katrina floodwaters is a fairly cheap shot. It doesn't seem to fit with the other imagery, either, since most of the video celebrates Black power, while the Katrina imagery plays into the age-old cultural habit of casting representations of Black people in

America as disaster voyeurism: a big nasty painful mess. (Where you assign blame neatly sorts you as a liberal or a conservative.)

The intent of the video is clearly not to fetishize Black victimization, though. Its intent is to celebrate Black power in the face of epic obstacles.

While many national critics saw the dancing Black boy in front of a line of cops as a nod to the "Black Lives Matter" movement, the role of Black dancing as resistance is much older than that, especially in New Orleans. Since the video dropped during Carnival, I couldn't help picking up on parade "formation" as one of the title's deliberate connotations. The quick shot of four Edna Karr High School drum majors makes the link more explicit.

The video is framed by Beyoncé on top of a New Orleans police cruiser as it sinks into the floodwaters, and of course New Orleanians know that dancing on top of cars is a frequent feature of second line parades, those mass occupations of public streets that double as a raucous assault on America's precious private property rights.

Ishmael Reed's great 1972 novel *Mumbo Jumbo* imagines an epidemic of funky dancing in 1920s America that threatens to overthrow and Africanize all of western civilization—the epidemic begins, of course, in New Orleans. One hundred and fifty years earlier, the Calinda was a Congo Square song and dance genre that pointedly satirized and challenged white supremacist ideologies. The highly mythologized enslaved rebel Bras Coupé, betrayed and murdered in 1837, was also reputed to be a great dancer, an aspect of his character that is enshrined in the many retellings of his story, including George Washington Cable's in 1880.

But the biggest difference in how New Orleanians and average Americans will view "Formation" is not about dancing or parading as resistance, and not about Beyoncé's unauthorized and arguably unnuanced appropriation of Katrina imagery.

One of the biggest blind spots in the general American thesis that "Formation" is simply and "unapologetically Black"[3] is the typically American failure to note distinctions and conflicts within Black society. New Orleanian Yaba Blay, in her critique of "Formation," has noted the "color-struck" hierarchies and tensions between Black Creoles and non-Creole Blacks in New Orleans,[4] though it's worth remembering that this distinction involves not only shades of color, but Anglo/Latin cultural distinctions as well. Blay cites examples of self-identified Black Creoles in New Orleans who were more proud of their European heritage than of their African roots. She might have added Jelly Roll Morton's answer to Alan Lomax in the Library of Congress interviews recorded in 1938, "All my folks came directly from the shores of . . . France."

But Beyoncé doesn't stop at merely using the term "Creole" to describe herself, she also epitomizes the historical representation of Afro-Creole feminine sexuality. The voluptuous "quadroon" (technically, in early New Orleans, one-quarter African and three-quarters European) is a character type that has lived on in American representations of race long since the term fell out of favor. Beyoncé is just the latest in a long string of Black women who have played on that mythical trope, consciously or otherwise. Her boast that she's always got "hot sauce in (her) bag" is just one example of a self-image that links racial background to her claim of being sexually exquisite.

A celebration of mixed-race feminine sexual capital goes back hundreds of years in New Orleans. The Duke of Saxe-Weimar Eisenach, like many foreign visitors, was entranced by this new breed of femininity. It had already made New Orleans famous by 1825, when he wrote that the city's "quadroon" women resembled "the higher orders of women among the high class Hindoos [*sic*]; lovely countenances, full, dark, liquid eyes, lips of coral, teeth of pearl . . . their beautifully rounded limbs . . . might furnish models for a Venus or a Hebe."[5]

The lyric in "Formation" that Beyoncé could be a Black "Bill Gates" should not distract us from the visual argument that the source of Queen Bey's power is not technological innovation but sexual capital, in particular that of light-skinned Black women, from Lena Horne to Vanessa Williams to Queen Bey herself.

The video's depiction of her in early 1800s finery suggests the *plaçée*, as the free Afro-Creole woman in a *plaçage* relationship was known. Though arguments about historical details persist, the term was intended to refer to the practice of formalized, long-term sexual relationships between free Black women and wealthy white men in early New Orleans. Not all interracial relationships in early New Orleans took place between rich white men and women of color of lesser means, of course. Beyoncé means to invoke not history, but myth, in this case the myth of the quadroon. One way that New Orleans departs from the usual antebellum narrative of interracial sex—as between master and slave—is due to the high number of free people of color. Consent, however tarnished by economic need, lay at the heart of the literary depictions of *plaçage* relationships. The *plaçée*'s free status is essential to understanding her sexuality in a non-victimized way, as Beyoncé intends. The free Afro-Creole courtesan makes the choice to exchange her sexual capital for the highest market value. Alternatively, people fell in love, though, again, mutual romantic love is not what "Formation" is about.

One of the best literary depictions of a *plaçage* kind of relationship comes from Afro-Creole writer Armand Lanusse. His 1843 short story, "Un Mariage de Conscience," shows the role of women elders in establishing younger Afro-Creole women in the best arrangements with white suitors that they could fetch. The young white suitor in the story must seek the blessings of the *plaçée*'s mother before proceeding with their "marriage of conscience."

When Beyoncé sings that she "rock(s) his rock necklaces" or that the "best revenge is your paper"—i.e., money—she is suggesting the shameless marketing of her sexuality as a source of power. Indeed, interracial relationships did lead to significant wealth transfer into the hands of Black women in old New Orleans, usually in the form of real estate. It built economic equity among many Afro-Creoles that other American Blacks did not have access to and is one of the reasons that an economically empowered class of Black leaders was able to shape the South's most racially progressive state constitution during Reconstruction.[6]

Some of the costumed scenes in "Formation" hearken to a later period of Black women's empowerment through sexuality, namely Storyville, the city's iconic red-light district. Several scantily but richly clad Black women in a nineteenth-century parlor are too ribald to conform to the discreet protocols of *plaçage*. They look much more like figures in a scene from Lulu White's Mahogany Hall or Emma Johnson's House of All Nations, brothels that promised a kaleidoscopic range of nominally non-white skin colors for the adventurous white male traveler.

The legendary Storyville madams are also a much better analogy for the role Beyoncé plays in American society, since their every move was documented by the paparazzi of the day and recorded in popular scandal sheets like *The Mascot*. It's essential to note here, too, that these Black women who earned money and a degree of social power through their sexuality did not view themselves as victims. When a new ordinance sought to segregate white and Black brothels in separate districts, Countess Willie Piazza—along with eleven other sex workers of color—sued and won, a rare triumph over legal segregation in the early Jim Crow period.[7]

There's nothing passive about the way Beyoncé displays her sexuality. It may even have a threatening edginess, particularly for white viewers. The clear insinuation is that she intends her sexuality to be a political challenge to white power.

Marie Laveau is history's most famous Afro-Creole woman, and, though she was no *plaçée*, stories about her have often been infused with sexual overtones. She is invariably described as a great beauty, and there were persistent, if unfounded, rumors that she procured young Afro-Creole women for white clients.

In "Formation," Beyoncé picks up on the underworld-crime-boss aspect of the Marie Laveau myth, recently popularized by Angela Bassett's performance in *American Horror Story: Coven*. In his great novel *The Grandissimes*, George Washington Cable described his own fictional voodoo queen, Palmyre la Philosophe, as "a barbaric and magnetic beauty . . . like an unexpected drawing-out of a jeweled sword."[8] Here we see the same complex of beauty, wealth, power, and danger that Beyoncé conveys as she stands on a Spanish-moss flanked porch nodding her head menacingly, middle fingers raised, rows of strong Black men behind her.

It's up to us to choose what to make of Beyoncé's clearly very conscious invocation of the history of New Orleans Black women who have marketed the "hot sauce in [their] bags." But we can't expect that it will or should be without controversy. In a way, she's re-dramatizing the old split between blues people and church people, despite the images of church that she throws into her perhaps toxic floodwater gumbo.

One of the reasons the video is valuable is how it associates with New Orleans—for those who are able to see—a history of Black empowerment rather than the endless and circular narrative of southern Black history as picturesque disaster. On the other hand, the particular form of Black empowerment Beyoncé associates with her own image in the video—women selling sex—is one that is habitually viewed as degradation by puritanical Americans, both white and Black.

As for the charge of Creole exclusivity, we could actually view "Formation" as a repudiation of it. Unlike the mythical *plaçée*, Beyoncé announces, through her preference for a "Negro nose with Jackson 5 nostrils," a commitment to Black men not trying to downplay their Blackness. In the era of Jay-Z, it's no longer necessary to associate wealth and power with white skin. This does nothing to diminish the high sexual valuation of light-skinned Black women, but perhaps Armand Lanusse would be pleased to note that Black men are now as eligible as white men to attain the mythic prize of high-priced Afro-Creole femininity.

Carnival Racism—and Anti-Racism—for Dummies
2017

I remember with pride the Carnival season of 2003. In that year, I was honored as royalty in the Krewe du Jieux, at that time a sub-krewe of Krewe du Vieux. I was dubbed the "King of the Jieuxs" and rode alongside my wife, the "Jieuxish American Princess" for that year. But I have a confession to make, and I would post it on my widely followed Twitter feed if I had one: I am not now and never have been a Jew. I was a Jieux for many years, but never a Jew (my wife is both).

The Krewe du Jieux was the brainchild of photographer and parade impresario L. J. Goldstein. It has since been replaced in the Krewe du Vieux lineup by the very similar Krewe de Mishigas (long story, studded along the way with plentiful opportunities for Jieuxish jokes). Goldstein's idea was to attack anti-Semitism in a distinctively New Orleanian idiom: the idiom of Carnival, whose hallmarks are social inversion and satire.

For years, our krewe's coveted throw was the painted, glittered bagel. Sound familiar? It should, because the Zulu coconut was the inspiration for this throw (and for the Muses high-heeled shoe a few years later). Indeed, the Krewe of Zulu was the inspiration for many aspects of the Krewe du Jieux's masking practice, including the "Big Macher," our version of Zulu's famous "Big Shot."

It's hard to measure the scope of Zulu's influence on what the *Times-Picayune*'s Doug MacCash has called the "new" Mardi Gras,[1] and what I've called the restoration of Carnival, after the dark ages of the white supremacist anti-Carnival ushered in by the Mystick Krewe of Comus in 1857.[2] It's a remarkable testament to the resilience of the ancient Carnival spirit that, in the midst of the white supremacist era, when Comus, Momus, Proteus, and Rex ruled the day, the Zulu king first stepped off a banana boat in the New Basin canal, wearing a lard-can crown.

The year 1909 was a dark one for African Americans all over the country, but the dock workers of the Tramps walking club found a uniquely New Orleans way to express resistance. The city's Black dock workers were also engaged in building a radical biracial labor movement at the time,[3] so their minstrel-esque satire couldn't be mistaken for acquiescence to a racist, capitalist power structure. Indeed, the specifically Black New Orleanian satirical expression embraced by Zulu goes back to the Calinda verses in Congo Square, which raked white bosses over the coals of Black laughter in Afro-Creole French. The same Black Carnival spirit survives today in another practice from the days of the Tramps: the Baby Dolls, who dress like prissy pampered hookers (without fearing that people will call them stooges of patriarchy and racism).

Today, because Zulu riders wear face paint, some of it black, some of it vaguely analogous to what might look like minstrel show face paint from a dead tradition, people with no understanding of Carnival or of New Orleans insist that the city's African Americans recalibrate their aesthetics and iconography to national norms. Black people are not to wear face paint. Ever, for any reason. These unthoughtful critics just don't get that they're shaming traditions far more revolutionary than they're able to comprehend.

Discomfort with Zulu's aesthetic choices has been around since Louis Armstrong was king in 1947, since his participation drew unprecedented national attention. Perturbation and concern arose again in the early 1960s, when restrained dignity was the reigning aesthetic sought by Black leaders at a crucial political juncture. Potential recruits became interested again when the Civil Rights era gave way to the Black Power and Black Arts movements, which prized examples, like Zulu, of uniquely African American vernacular creative genius.

As anyone might have predicted (if they thought about it), Zulu's admission of white riders in the late twentieth century was always a Twitter bomb waiting to happen. We just needed to wait for social media to be invented, so it could take an indigenous New Orleans practice way out of its local context and inspire knee-jerk outrage across America. That's what happened Mardi Gras 2017, when Tales of the Cocktail founder Ann Tuennerman went up on Facebook with a picture of herself in Mardi Gras regalia and who since then, after taking flack, has been agonizing through a multipart act of public contrition.

Tuennerman's sin is to have had the temerity to accept the great honor of riding in the Zulu parade on Mardi Gras morning, wearing the traditional mask of Zulu blackface. I say "Zulu blackface" because the style of blackface worn by Zulu riders is distinct from other forms of blackface that are offensive due to their history as a tool of white supremacist ideology. Zulu riders wear a myriad of different patterns, but one distinctive visual feature of a common Zulu blackface pattern is an enlarged white eye on one side of the face. This one large white eye-frame can be seen in depictions of the Zulu Big Shot, as well as on Tuennerman's face in her much-maligned social media posting. It doesn't look like stereotypical minstrel show blackface to me, and most New Orleanians don't see it as such. But in the world of totalitarian expression—the opposite of Carnivalesque expression—nuances of signification go unnoticed.

A typically clueless (and arrogant) response to Ann Tuennerman's posting came from Chicago's Nikkole Palmatier: "I have a problem with the blackface entirely. As do most people outside of the New Orleans tradition. Just as those who live outside of Cleveland think the Indians logo is racist and the term 'Redskins' is racist."[4]

Yeah. Just let that sink in for a minute. It's hard to conceive of a more egregiously false analogy than this. Are the Cleveland Indians and Washington Redskins actually Native American institutions, founded, owned, and staffed, at all levels, by Native Americans? Palmatier's argument leads us to question whether Zulu's iconography should be practiced by anyone, not just whether Zulu should accept white riders. And that's a whole other can of worms. It calls into question the extent to which Black people should be allowed agency in representing their own experience. It also places limits on how Black people themselves choose to enunciate anti-racist arguments. In the best traditions of Carnivalesque practice, Zulu has expropriated racist representations and inverted them as a form of anti-racist resistance. Those who say people shouldn't try to do that kind of thing just don't get what Carnival is. Maybe because it's not part of their culture. But it is a part of ours.

More knowing observers focused on the fact that Ann Tuennerman is white, and that her wearing of Zulu blackface has a different meaning than a Black rider's exact same mask. The problem with this critique is that it suggests that Zulu should not allow white riders. To Zulu's credit, the krewe has welcomed white members since before the 1992 city council ordinance required parading krewes to include members of different races. (Though the ordinance was later struck down by the courts, it had the salutary effect of removing from our streets the premier white supremacist Carnival club, the Mystick Krewe of Comus).

The suggestion that Zulu should insist on an all-Black membership also strikes at the heart of the radical, anti-totalitarian spirit of carnivalesque expression, which thrives on crossing boundaries and cross-dressing of all kinds. What about the Mardi Gras Indians? Are they racist for parading in stereotypical—though richly embellished—Native American garb? Do drag queens insult femininity by performing it in the way that they do? Some argue yes, but Carnival doesn't give a #$%^.

Yes, I know that the historical reality of white privilege puts white people masking as non-white in a fundamentally different category. Unless, of course, that white person is parading as an honored member of a Black organization.

There was at one time an informal Mardi Gras practice whereby white people masked in blackface, often as mammy stereotypes. That was clearly a racist humiliation ritual, quite the opposite of Zulu's celebration of Blackness. The question about any cultural message is which ideology it serves. But that requires context, something that totalitarian expression eschews. Does the message in question affirm a racist ideology or resist it? Was Ann Tuennerman's blackface on Mardi Gras day part of the nationwide resurgence of white supremacist ideology that Trump has enabled? No one could think such a thing, and no one is claiming it. Instead, critics are saying, "Of course she didn't intend to send a racist message, but . . ."

But what? Some critics have said it was OK for her to wear the prescribed costume, as white riders in Zulu have been doing for decades (at least) but that she shouldn't have shared it to social media because, well, people not from New Orleans wouldn't understand. Sure, but why is that our problem? Why are (white) people who so jealously defend Black authenticity from non-Black interlopers so quick to intrude on a New Orleans culture that they have no knowledge of or respect for?

Still other commenters, not willing to deprive a century-old African American cultural practice of its right to exist, took aim at the caption Paul Tuennerman appended to the "offensive" photo of his wife celebrating Mardi Gras. He quipped, "Throw a little Black Face on and you lose all your Media Skills." One commenter wrote that Tuennerman's statement "suggests that by performing Blackness Ann loses her ability to intelligently and effectively engage media."[5] But this analysis totally ignores the possibility of satirical intent—on Mardi Gras day! It interprets a Carnivalesque message as if it were a message on any other Tuesday in regular old boring America.

I understood Paul Tuennerman's comment as a critique of media, not a critique of Blackness. It suggests his awareness that certain forms of expression are so explosive that they can't be digested at all by national media, with its inability to process the ironies and inversions of Carnival expression. It shows his well-founded fear that the frightened and dishonest world of America's "conversation about race" is likely to cry "racism" whenever it sees an image that might be racist in some other, very different context.

On a broader note, I question how productive it is to second-guess those white people who, in good faith, attempt to publicly embrace Black culture and to celebrate with pride their acceptance in Black circles. Why is this issue so uncomfortable? All this hand-wringing is driven by unproductive white liberal guilt (and envy) on the one hand, and, on the other, by African American guarding of Black cultural capital—which is very understandable given the extent to which Black people have been deprived of other forms of capital. These are reasons why there's always a splashy public argument over which white people deserve their modicum of Black approval and which ones don't. If Zulu has consented to ride with Ann Tuennerman, my assumption is that they are sufficiently able to judge her worthiness for that honor.

It's not like it's hard to find racism in the history and present practice of Mardi Gras. Just tune in to WYES on Mardi Gras night and watch the "public" TV station's obsequious fawning over the king of white supremacy, a.k.a. Comus, in his very white mask, at "The Meeting of the Courts." Get mad about the captains in Ku Klux Klan outfits in all the old-line parades on St. Charles Avenue. Never accept a throw from Proteus. Think twice about attending the Knights of Chaos parade, or Krewe d'Etat and, if you do, bear in mind how closely their satire matches the white supremacist satire of their glory days, when they led the fight to drown Reconstruction in a shower of blood. But if you're looking for racism among the white riders of Zulu, you obviously have no clue what's racist and what's not in the universe of Carnival.

I saw a great sign in the Societé de St. Anne procession on Mardi Gras day this year. It said, "This Parade Fights Fascism." Yes, and it does so by inverting and puncturing the prevailing ideological categories of domination. That's exactly what Zulu is doing by putting Black riders and their white allies together in an inverted version of an aesthetic tool originally intended for racial oppression.

I realize that the vast majority of Americans have no idea what Carnival is, or how to read Carnival messages, and that's OK. But maybe well-meaning liberal observers should take a page from their own playbook and not comment on cultures that they have no exposure to or appreciation for.

Confederates in the Dumpster
2017

When I penned a column about the Confederate monument removal way back in 2015,[1] I barely even considered the various
hypocritical, convoluted, and circular arguments for keeping them in place.
The funniest was about the monuments being "part of history," like what my
Maw Maw had for lunch on a random day in 1938. (No monument has ever
been erected to her excellent chicken and dumplings.)

Back in 2015, the democratically elected representatives of our city, Black
and white, voted, overwhelmingly, to get rid of these memorials to a former
era's tyrants and terrorists. So, I applauded and looked forward immediately
to what we'd replace them with.

But then, just the other day, I read in the *Washington Post* that New
Orleans had "joined the movement to take down symbols of the Confederacy
and the Jim Crow South."[2] Joined? Just now? In April of 2017?

We're not "joining" a movement; we've spearheaded it—and not just
since 2015.

Newsweek trumpeted the news of our Confederate monuments' trip
to the dumpster with this headline: "Racism in America: New Orleans
Confederate Monuments Are Part of City's Long White Power History."[3]
Note the headline in present tense, when "were" would be more grammati-
cally and factually correct. The article teaches readers that, in New Orleans
on the eve of the Civil War, "only white men could vote." Nowhere does the
article remind readers that this was the case pretty much everywhere in the
United States, and certainly in every southern state. Nowhere does it mention the city's strong Civil Rights legacy or that Louisiana's Reconstruction-
era state constitution was the most progressive in the South. Or the 1811
German Coast slave uprising, the largest in US history, or the fact that half
the Black people in New Orleans in 1810 were free and resisted American
efforts to strip them of their freedom with vigor and élan.

Acknowledging a history of struggle is in no way an apologia for the wrongs
of the oppressors. It's quite the opposite: an empowering acknowledgement

of ancestors engaged in struggle for generations. The recognition of continuity in the anti-racist struggle is highly preferable to the paralysis induced by liberal guilt, which allows only for empty and repetitive *mea culpas*, a litany of wrongs with zero recognition of the heroes who have been fighting those wrongs for centuries. National media coverage once again reveals the Americanist bias that frames New Orleans as static and passive, the eternal hapless victim, unable to resist or even recognize racism without help from stronger, smarter, better Americans.

And bear in mind that the occasion for this trite spectacle of media outrage at racism comes with our *removal* of Confederate monuments, not with the erection of them. Every story on the removal of these monuments, even the ones, as in *Newsweek*, that almost forget to mention that we're tearing the statues down, are careful to nudge readers with the reminder that New Orleans is a majority Black city.

This also a microaggression against New Orleanians. The idea of white New Orleanians standing with their Black neighbors is apparently unthinkable. It doesn't mesh with the national media narrative, which has never been able to digest the fact of anti-racist white people in the South. None of these stories mentioned, for example, that a majority of *white* New Orleanians voted against Trump, after voting for Barack Obama twice.

I get mad about constantly being portrayed as a racist just because I live south of the Mason-Dixon line. But then I get slapped in the face by reality: Trump-style (and Trump-supporting) racists still run the state, our beleaguered governor excepted. They surround our city like North Korean artillery batteries trained on Seoul. Congressional Majority Whip Steve Scalise (R-Metairie), Republican state legislator Cameron Henry, US Senator John Kennedy, and Lt. Governor Billy Nungesser, among the most rabidly conservative ideologues in the country, all hail from parishes that border us.

I'd mention ex-Klansman and failed presidential aspirant David Duke, except that his well-preserved mummy is just a distraction from the new generation of white supremacists who are more skillful at euphemism. They continue to celebrate racism in the same way that Trump and company do—i.e., by eschewing the n-word and deploring David Duke's swastika armband, but continuing to rail against "political correctness," their code word for anti-racism.

Evidently emboldened by the renewal of racist rhetoric in Washington, Nungesser threatened to sic Trump on us by declaring New Orleans's Confederate statuary to be "national monuments."[4]

Trump's fluke election may have put white supremacists back in the cat-bird seat in Washington, but not in New Orleans. So instead of getting mad about not getting a pat on the back from national media liberals, we should take a moment to celebrate this beautiful moment in our city's history, just among ourselves.

I agree with Malcolm Suber and Michael "Quess" Moore, of Take 'Em Down NOLA: Dismantling the offensive symbols in the middle of the night is not as satisfying as building a public spectacle to celebrate their removal.[5] I would have greatly preferred a party, parading the disgraced statues through the streets so we could all throw rotten tomatoes at them. But I also understand Mayor Landrieu's caution, given the blood-soaked history of American racism.

It didn't take long before nineteenth-century white supremacists violently crushed the democratically elected coalition of African Americans, Francophone Afro-Creoles, immigrants, transplants from the North, and native-born whites who ran the state during the brief glimpse of racial equality called Reconstruction. During those years, interracial marriage was legalized, integrated public schools started to get a foothold, and the state, governed from New Orleans, embarked on a journey toward racial reconciliation after 150 years of slavery.

On Sept. 14, 1874, a gang of white supremacist thugs—the "Crescent City White League"—murdered thirteen Black and white New Orleans police officers in a ham-fisted coup attempt. It failed, but through further acts of terror, white supremacists eventually succeeded in seizing the state government (as they did in every other former Confederate state).

The lowlifes who shot thirteen New Orleans police officers in the back in 1874 got their monument in 1891. The city took down that abominable obelisk this week—for the second time. (The first was in 1989, but white supremacist pressure on the federal court system brought it back.)

The other monuments slated for removal—Robert E. Lee, P. G. T. Beauregard, and Jefferson Davis—all need to be viewed in the context of the terror inflicted upon the people of New Orleans in 1874. The people who put up those statues are basically the same guys who killed the thirteen police officers. The Confederate regime was itself built on political terror, even more so than the Jim Crow state governments that cheaply used the memory of the most disastrous four years in the history of the South to bolster their morally bankrupt and repressive banana republics.

New Orleans was part of the Confederate States of America for a scant fifteen months. Yet we're told—usually by people who don't live in New

Orleans—that this single year in New Orleans history deserves endless commemoration, at the expense of the other three hundred years and three different national governments that shaped our culture.

Did I say culture? The Confederate misadventure only became "culture"
in works of fantasy masquerading as history, the ones that eulogized the suicide mission of the Civil War as some kind of noble and lovely "lost cause."
To call the novels, poetry, and public sculpture that accomplished this revision of history "culture" is perhaps too dignified. The statues of Kim Il-sung
and Kim Jong-il in Pyongyang are also "culture," I guess, as was the Saddam
Hussein statue toppled by US soldiers as they entered Baghdad in 2003.

Culture and politics intersect, of course, but representationally unimaginative renderings of generals and political leaders are first and foremost political statements, with culture as a transparent delivery system.

The question, then, is what political ideology the statues promote. Some
people actually do argue, hilariously, that racist subjugation is NOT the main
point of statues commemorating men who made war on their own country
rather than even consider limiting the expansion of slavery (slavery of, uh,
Black people, we feel compelled to note).

Louisianans—including a tiny handful of New Orleanians—who oppose
removal of the remaining monuments to racial terror hasten to point out that
Lee and Beauregard supported or at least acquiesced in the Reconstruction
era's commitment to racial equality. But the statues don't show them as elder
statesmen advocating peace and reconciliation.

In their bronze iterations, Lee and Beauregard are in full battle mode,
grimly making war on the United States of America. To use the memories of
these men to support causes they had eschewed is deeply cynical. It's also typical of the Machiavellian genius of white supremacist rhetoric in the bloody
era that crushed Reconstruction under the boot of Jim Crow.

Governor Murphy J. Foster oversaw, in 1898, the legislative counterpart
to the new statues. The Jim Crow laws deprived over 90 percent of African
Americans of their right to vote. They also disenfranchised over half the white
people of Louisiana.[6]

It begs a question that's timely to this day: Why would white Louisianans—
why would anyone?—support a regime that forced them to fight a truly stupid war and then stripped them of so much dignity and power? Why would
white southerners today revere the memory of a wealthy ruling elite who used
them as cannon fodder and then as petty street enforcers but who wouldn't
let them walk in the front door of their mansions? Why would working white
people vote for Donald Trump today, and then stand by him unconditionally

as he works assiduously to expand the gulf between their paltry paychecks and the mushrooming profits of his buddies at Mar-a-Lago?

Of course, racism isn't the sole reason for these perverse trends in American social history. There's also xenophobia, masochism, self-loathing, and sadistic masculine fantasies of power and domination.

Another way of looking at it is much simpler: White working people who revere Confederate leaders and vote for Donald Trump are just ill-informed. While true, this answer doesn't offer a path to changing minds informed by ignorance and idiocy. In the era of Trump, it seems more and more clear that no combination of evidence or reason can sway the hardcore 10 to 15 percent of the US population that clings to racism as a crutch for their own identities. They may have New Orleans surrounded and Washington under siege, but their bumbling incompetence so far has kept them from trashing the whole country.

All little old New Orleans can do is remind America and the world that we are not them, even if it's hard for the world to spot us in the red spill that swamps the region. The task is only harder given the apparent need of too many complacent liberals to put the whole moral burden of racism on the South. It's a handy way of getting past their own vague sense of guilt for the racism they fail to acknowledge in their own cosmopolitan hearts.

Alas, truly racist southerners are quite happy to agree that "real" white southerners share their ideology. Condemned by other white southerners and distrusted by like-minded Americans in other parts of the country, we anti-racist white New Orleanians might seem hopelessly beleaguered. But only if we preference the category of "white" or "southern" over "New Orleanian." What we've been trying to do in New Orleans for decades (longer, if you count Reconstruction) is live as equals—Black, white, and other, side by side. Those white New Orleanians who couldn't handle that prospect decamped for the suburbs decades ago.

Sharing the same space, as equals, hasn't always been easy, but just look at the rest of the United States, where white people will run screaming from a neighborhood when it gets anywhere near half-Black[7] (including, yes, many folks in our own suburbs). Both the conservative racists and the guilt-ridden northern liberals need to see that, in removing the monuments, Black and white New Orleanians have joined together to celebrate the expulsion of white supremacist icons from our city. The Confederates are finally where they always belonged, in the dumpster, and Black and white New Orleanians are tickled pink that we made it happen.

Unlike Reconstruction, removing the monuments to men who led the South to ruin is something we have accomplished all by ourselves, with no help from the feds, and we've done it despite constant bickering and roadblocks from the rest of the state.

They're just statues, I know, just symbols. But their removal signals an end to a long tradition of excusing white supremacy here in New Orleans. It marks the onset of a new era in our history, an era as significant as the sad and sickening one ushered in by the erection of the statues in the first place, over a century ago. Large swaths of our region and country are in the grip of a new dawn of white supremacist authoritarianism. But not us. *L'chaim,* New Orleans! We deserve to love ourselves today.

Hollywood Jazz and the Storyville Complex 2019

In the American imagination, the myth of New Orleans serves as a repository of fears and desires America has about itself, especially concerning race, sexuality, and the possibilities and dangers of the aesthetic life.

The recently released *Bolden*, written and directed by Daniel Pritzker, is an instructive expression of that urge to mythologize New Orleans. It's easy to find fault with the film, but at least it dares to dream, which is to say it dares to probe deep, uncomfortable psychic terrain rich in symbolic imagery. An opposite impulse is the revulsion against the myth of New Orleans in any form, expressed perfectly in a much less ambitious effort, *a Saturday Night Live* skit that aired in January.[1]

While *Bolden* is courageous (again, in spite of its faults), the SNL skit is a classic of middlebrow conformism, an unselfconscious submission to the tyranny of mediocrity. It depicts a couple of tourists just returned from New Orleans who engage in some artful fantasizing about ways in which New Orleans differs from the rest of the United States. They hold forth about the looser attitude toward punctuality, the embrace of sensuality, and a voodoo ritual that appears, upon reflection, to have simply been a mugging.

The guy is wearing a straw hat and, like his partner, feigns a pseudo-drawl intended to make fun of those poor souls who try to perform New Orleanian identity. They are, of course, roundly ridiculed by the other people on stage, including Kenan Thompson, the blandest guy there, who claims he's really from New Orleans and knows that it's no different than the rest of the U.S. The humor is supposed to hit its peak when he assures the dumb tourists that "New Orleans is in America!" It's also significant that the arbiter of American conformity in the skit is African American. SNL cultural policing will allow neither Black people nor New Orleanians the luxury of self-definition.

The mean-spirited little sketch is a shopworn iteration of a puritanical Americanist view: All fantasy, play, or performance is inauthentic fakery. So just try to look like a mid-price fashion catalog and avoid any kind of art or performance at all costs. Never leave Applebee's and you'll be safe. If you do happen to live in New Orleans, you can hang out in the new Marigny Starbucks and no one will call you a poseur.

Unlike the frightened herd animals at SNL, Daniel Pritzker's *Bolden* has the guts to acknowledge and explore the myth of New Orleans in the American unconscious, despite a high risk of combustion. As an origin myth of New Orleans music, *Bolden* has much in common with previous movies purporting to depict the dawn of jazz, such as 1978's *French Quarter*, 1947's *New Orleans*, and 1941's *Birth of the Blues*.

But there's a welcome difference among them. Over the years, the agency of Black people in creating their own culture has steadily grown in these filmic depictions. In *Birth of the Blues*, a white man (Bing Crosby) discovers jazz on a mythical Basin Street. *Bolden* has more in common with *New Orleans*, since both movies feature soundtracks by leading New Orleans jazz musicians of the day—Louis Armstrong in the 1947 film and Wynton Marsalis in 2019.

In *New Orleans*, the musicians are Black, at least at first: Louis Armstrong, Billie Holiday, and several other giants of the first few decades of jazz history. But they aren't allowed to do anything more than play their instruments. The Black characters in the movie are infantilized autistic savants who need white people to manage them, to take the music out of the dives, out of New Orleans, and eventually away from Black people altogether.

The final cringe in a long line of them comes at the end of *New Orleans*, the movie. Jazz finally gets the recognition it deserves, but far away from New Orleans, the city, and with not a single Black person performing. The triumph of jazz on the world stage is represented in the final scene by Woody Herman's big band rendering a safely whitened-up "Do You Know What It Means (to Miss New Orleans)."

Bolden, by contrast, puts Black characters at the center and gives them a Black manager, but perhaps errs too much in the other direction by presenting jazz as something no white musicians even tried to play. And the Black manager is cast as an accomplice to evil, an entrepreneurial parasite who sells out Black people in exchange for a modicum of power conferred by whites.

The extent to which these movies "get it right" factually is a good question, but not the central one. The central question is what psychic process Americans are going through as they tap into that space in the American unconscious called New Orleans.

It goes without saying that the real New Orleans will have to undergo some simplification and misrepresentation as Americans process what it means to them on an emotional level. One result is an inevitable Americanization of the material, to make it something national audiences can understand. We see this Americanization of our social and cultural history at work in every movie set in New Orleans, not just the ones about jazz.

The first step in the process of aesthetic Americanization is bad news for those New Orleanians who like to emphasize how the city has distinguished itself from the broader region. In myriad ways, New Orleans's history in the American mind is flattened into southern history. New Orleans society is almost always presented as not significantly different from Mississippi, Alabama, South Carolina, etc. One way this is accomplished is by erasing the French presence. We saw it in *American Horror Story: Coven*, when Kathy Bates's French-speaking Madame LaLaurie was depicted speaking English with a standard Hollywood version of a southern accent.

The language and cultural divides of Creole New Orleans are especially confusing to Americans as they relate to Black people. Though French-speaking *gens de couleur libres* of antebellum New Orleans were a subject of fascination to nineteenth-century writers, Hollywood has been unable to acknowledge their existence in any antebellum costume drama set in the city, no matter if it's the white supremacist Hollywood of William Wyler's *Jezebel* (1938) or the ostensibly anti-racist statement of Richard Fleischer's *Mandingo* (1975). In *Bolden*, the Afro-Creole/African American divide is vaguely alluded to but reduced to simple colorism. The film refers to Afro-Creoles as "blue-eyed n-----s" and "light-skinned n-----s" but never as "French" Blacks or, dare we suggest, "Creoles." They even anglicize the pronunciation of Afro-Creole clarinetist George Baquet's name, calling him "Backette."

The reduction of New Orleans's historic linguistic and ethnic complexity into the generically "southern" white/Black dichotomy is common to almost all movies set in the city, but origin myths of New Orleans music have their own special mythical calculus, dating from early twentieth-century social conditions and American fears and desires stemming from them. I call that bundle of anxieties and yearnings the "Storyville Complex." It hinges on a fairly simple equation: race + sex = crime + music.

Historian Shannon Lee Dawdy has written about how the earliest myths of New Orleans were rooted in fears of social disorder. The Storyville Complex is no exception. Dawdy lists several definitions of disorder from an eighteenth century French dictionary, including a "disarray of rank or organization," "moral" disorder, and, finally, "*un beau désordre*"—beautiful disorder, disorder as an aesthetic category.[2]

Though Dawdy was writing about colonial New Orleans, the different registers of the meaning of "disorder" also basically explain the Storyville Complex. Race + sex (interracial sex) is a "disarray" of social rank, a disruption of the racial order, and can be seen as the original sin of America's original "Sin City." The perception of interracial sex as an unforgivable sin has not changed, though nineteenth-century white supremacist Americans and latter-day anti-racist Americans deplore it for ostensibly different reasons. The onus has shifted from the unscrupulous octoroon temptresses described by Grace King in *New Orleans: The Place and the People* (1895) to the white supremacist prerogative of owning and violating Black women's bodies. But puritanical Americans continue to struggle inordinately with the notion of consensual interracial sex.

As several well-researched studies have shown, notably Alecia P. Long's, interracial sex was the crux of both the attraction and opprobrium of the vice district known as Storyville in the first decades of twentieth-century New Orleans, an era that coincides with the formation of early jazz. But most films about the era have had great difficulty with the race + sex side of the equation. Dennis Kane's 1978 *French Quarter*, for example, gives a prominent role to Countess Willie Piazza—but makes her white.

Just as free people of color remain invisible in the popular American imagination of the antebellum era, the iconic Black madams of Storyville—Willie Piazza, Lulu White, Emma Johnson—have proven too explosive for Hollywood in any era.

Likewise, *Bolden* touches on the race + sex angle only peripherally, if we limit the equation to explicit reference to sex between white and Black. Its richly symbolic imagery does invoke, however, the trope of the "octoroon cyprien," to borrow one of Lafcadio Hearn's descriptions of a mixed-race New Orleans temptress.[3] *Bolden* features an unnamed, unscripted, beautiful Afro-Creole woman who fulfills her usual symbolic function: Afro-Creole femininity as a prize that white and Black men fight over.[4]

In earlier scenes, we see Buddy Bolden longing for her as some kind of unattainable goddess, playing a cello, an instrument associated more with European classical than with African American vernacular music forms. His longing for her coincides with the beginnings of his demise. Thus, however unconsciously, the movie does invoke the classic trope of the mixed-race Afro-Creole woman as disrupter of the social order, in this case as a siren for Black men rather than white.

In a wordless later scene, we see the same actress by the side of the white devil of the movie, a judge named "Leander Perry," an obvious reference to the white supremacist political boss of Plaquemines and St. Bernard parishes, Leander Perez, who died in 1969. The Anglicization of Perez's name reflects the filmmakers' fear that American audiences would not know how to process a white supremacist character with a Hispanic name, despite New Orleans racial history's deep connections with the Latin world.

It eventually becomes clear that this mysterious, beautiful woman is Buddy Bolden's muse. After the white devil destroys Bolden's only recording, we see her naked, mutilated body on the floor. That image crystallizes the way the movie plays on the Storyville Complex, even while dodging the uncomfortable issue of interracial sex. Black sexuality in the movie is as much a visual subject as Black musicianship is—scenes of Black people having sex are as common as scenes of Black people playing music. Thus, a linkage is made between Black sexuality, Black music, and the hopelessly corrupt world the story takes place in, the crucible of moral disorder that gives rise to the beautiful disorder that strikes the ears of the early jazz listener.

The term "crime" in the Storyville Complex equation needs to be understood more broadly as corruption on three levels: political (including police), spiritual (moral), and also physical. The high incidence of disease in nineteenth-century New Orleans was the perfect sign to puritanical America that race mixing, a moral crime in their eyes, resulted in physical corruption as well.

As advances in medicine and public health curbed the raging outbreaks of yellow fever, cholera, and other killers, drug addiction took their place in America's imagination of New Orleans as a cancer on the national morality. *Bolden* dutifully fulfills that expectation and adds to it the post-Civil Rights era understanding of the primal source of the corruption infecting every aspect of life in mythical New Orleans: Not African savagery, the bogeyman of the white supremacist era (when voodoo was routinely described as "devil worship"), but the savagery of white supremacy itself. The Prince of Darkness in *Bolden* is the white judge, and he's the one who passes on to his Black lesser demon (Bolden's manager) an unnamed white powder that begins to lay waste to the Black community.

Locating the source of New Orleans evil in white supremacy rather than in race mixing or in people of African descent is an improvement over earlier iterations of the myth of New Orleans corruption, to be sure, but it poses a new set of problems. The most glaring of these is that New Orleans—when presented as the paragon of southern racial injustice—serves as a scapegoat for a failing that afflicts the entire nation. When white northern liberals like Pritzker, director of *Bolden*, or Richard Fleischer, director of *Mandingo*, or Arthur Lubin, director of *New Orleans*, project white America's fears and fantasies about race onto New Orleans, their films flirt with implying that the rest of the country is somehow absolved.

Of course, it also hurts my feelings that every white New Orleanian in *Bolden* is an n-word spewing cracker stereotype with a Mississippi accent. On the other hand, we can't pretend that Bolden's New Orleans was not a viciously racist society, and it's probably OK if the hordes of white early jazz fans, like the crowd at Jazzfest's Economy Hall Tent, experience a little racial discomfort from time to time.

A deeper problem for New Orleans mythology is suggested by the most insightful line of the movie, though it seems discredited by the ethos of the speaker, the white devil, Judge Perry: "Hate your oppressors and you'll be enslaved forever by your memories." This points to an intractable paradox identified a hundred years ago by W. E. B. DuBois in *The Souls of Black Folk*, the psychic impossibility of an identity defined as a social "problem." If your whole existence is a problem, nothing is untainted. Can the "beautiful disorder" of inspired art ever be separated from its roots in barbarism and appreciated for its own sake? Should we even try?

Such questions lead to an impossible further question: If New Orleans is to be the repository of America's darkest fears and guilt about race, how can it ever be anything other than a nightmare? Perhaps *Bolden*'s accomplishment is that it presents the dawn of jazz as a nightmare that is somehow, inexplicably, also beautiful.

EPILOGUE
Katrina Playlist: A Jeremiad

2015

Dr. John, "Goin' Back to New Orleans"[1]

1985, 1999, 2005, 2010. These are the years I've gone back to New Orleans to stay. If you're driving down from the north, it's best to cue up Dr. John's "Goin' Back to New Orleans" (cassette, CD, or iTunes, depending on your era) right when I-55 comes to an end and merges into I-10 over the swamps edging Lake Ponchartrain. There's a swooping flyover that rises high and then curves down onto twin bridges pointed straight east, at the city you feel before you see.

Goin' back home, too-na-nay, to the land of the beautiful queen

I was in Glencoe, Illinois, at my in-laws, on the night of September 23, 2005. I was happy, ecstatic. According to the TV news I'd been pacing in front of the past three weeks, New Orleans was destroyed. Big deal, I was going back. Had my ticket in my hand. If there was one floating rooftop on the sea over what used to be New Orleans, I was going back to lie on it until I died. I cued "Goin' Back to New Orleans" and shut the door to my wife's childhood bedroom. I closed the blinds on the leafy cool suburban pastoral outside. I pictured a New Orleans street and me dancing in it and I rocked my parade dance, an arm-chugging high-stepping march. I never was much into dancing, except in association with New Orleans. Like I couldn't separate the basic concept of dancing from the specific place of New Orleans, where we do it in the street. I lived in Chicago for years, and the way they do it, in dark low-ceilinged pits, always struck me as uncivilized. Europeans do it that way, too. "Clubs" everybody calls them. The French term is best: *boite de nuit*, a night-box. Who wants to dance in a box? I'd rather dance on water.

Verdi, *Requiem: Dies Irae*

Like New Orleans parades and music acts, New Orleans history is a spectacle. We offer real-life drama, shit that other people can't believe happens in America, and we just keep on dishing out the hits. Voodoo, Yellow Fever, sex parties, sex crimes, corruption, axe murders, violent storms. New Orleans is always already pre-apocalyptic or post-apocalyptic. We do the end of the world and then get up and do it again for the generation that hasn't had the chance yet.

Verdi's *Dies Irae* starts with four full orchestral blasts on the downbeat, followed by tortured cries of *"Dies irae!"* as the strings tumble in descending scales like everything on earth tipping into the chasm. Then the systematic punches return, this time with bass drum left hooks on the upbeat. It's a vision of fire and flood and the vicious spirit of the universe that wallops us in the face until we have no choice but to call it beautiful. Fuck you. But I love you. Fuck you. We're masochists for weeping at the beauty of destruction, it makes us pathetic, it's an abandonment of our freedom and will. Divine vengeance has its way with us. "As flies to wanton boys are we to th' gods," says Gloucester in *King Lear*.

Dies irae, dies illa

I was feeling it after a slow drive on my first day back home. Only major routes had been cleared. Like out Elysian Fields from my house in Faubourg Marigny to the University of New Orleans campus. The shit-stripe (waterline) started around Claiborne Avenue, a few feet off the ground, along the houses and businesses on either side. It got higher and higher, then disappeared above the roofline. Roofs with jagged holes hacked out from within by people fighting for their lives. What caused the sticky brown residue slapped across every structure in a straight horizontal line? Shit. Oil. Chemicals. Dead animals and dead people. Fifteen hundred dead people. Fuck you. And your mother. And you can't do shit about it, so shut up.

Neville Brothers, "Can't Stop the Funk"

But I went out there again, just driving around. My house is on the higher ground in the old part of the city, the "sliver by the river," and it was very much intact. But it had no electricity, gas, or water, so the car was a more comfortable place to be. I had decided that the city needed me to drive around it—especially in the miles and miles of total desolation—jamming a New Orleans funk anthem. I rolled down the windows and maxed out the volume.

We're here, in here
Can't stop the funk

It was mostly big trucks, city vehicles, and military on the streets. And men with cellphones scribbling on pads. The 82nd Airborne was stationed a couple blocks from my house. I heard the national anthem blaring every morning early, on a tinny loudspeaker, from their temporary barracks in a coffee warehouse. They did a foot patrol every evening around sundown. Two columns walking at a steady pace past my stoop. M-16s ready but casual, pointed down. One time, they came by when I was sitting in my car charging devices and rocking "Can't Stop the Funk." They all glanced over at me as they marched by. A couple of smiles, but mostly they stayed stoic, professional. Their commander, cigar-chomping Afro-Creole general Russell Honoré, was the latest military savior of the beset colony on the necessary river. The latest Andy Jackson, the latest Bernardo de Gálvez.

We're ready, as Freddie
Can't stop the funk

One afternoon, I drove through the French Quarter and saw and smelled the insurance write-offs of a legion of restaurants. My first job, at fifteen, was at a gay neighborhood restaurant in the Quarter called the Quarter Scene, on Dumaine and Dauphine. It was the first place I got funky, though I was musically not so compatible then. It was my job on Mondays to take out the garbage from the weekend, Sunday being the one day with no garbage pick-up in the Quarter. We didn't have an alley and were barred from storing garbage on the sidewalk, so we stored the two-day-old food waste in a small dark airless closet. It was actually a long cupboard-like space, since you had to duck to fit into it. In the summer, a greasy reddish film would form outside the bags. There was no light in the little enclosure, so I'd shine a flashlight and poke the rats off with a broom. It was a crash course in getting over cockroach phobia, too. Then, the bags needed to be hauled through the dining room to get to the sidewalk. The manager always fussed about why I was doing it at a particular time, rather than a mythical thirty minutes before or later. When the garbage truck pulled up, I ran out with a ten and a five, neatly folded, to hand to the garbage man—since we, like every French Quarter restaurant, were always over the weight limit.

In late September 2005, every restaurant in the Quarter put out their month-old food waste at the same time. The whole place smelled like the rat cupboard at the Quarter Scene on a Monday morning in August. A reminder of how the old city—all old cities—probably always used to smell. Like death. But food is the source of life, and pleasure, so how can it smell like death? If you find out what stuff smells like when you're dead, come back and let me know. Thomas Mann's *The Magic Mountain* taught me years ago that rot and decay are simply the flipside of living. That living is, in fact, a process of decay, going down slow and reveling in the sensation. No sense has the power to make us feel more viscerally alive than smell.

The rats came out of the woodwork after Katrina. A plague of rats. They'd flocked to the higher ground in the old city, and a few shacked up with us. We put out rat traps. They squeal when they can't unstick themselves and then you put on boots and take them out to the sidewalk and smash their heads in. The streets were dotted with rat carcasses, smashed under the big trucks driving debris everywhere. They also had their distinctive smell.

Katrina means cleansing, they said. Yes, the cleansing away of all the obfuscatory bullshit of rhetoric and reason, enabling a stark-naked apprehension of living. A mud massage, full body and to completion. For those of us, that is, who'd managed to cheat death one more time.

Richard Strauss, "*Im Abendrot*"

When I was in high school, I was a classical music freak. My friends wanted to get down and party with the Clash or Tom Petty or the B-52s or Cameo, but I wanted to drop acid and rock out on Mahler, Stravinsky, Bartók. I blame the Old World look of my neighborhood. I pretended then that life was a movie, something I sadly am less able to do as I get older, though I appreciated Katrina for bringing back a sense of dramatic cinematic intensity. I realized at a young age that my neighborhood—the French Quarter and Marigny—looked like a movie set, and then we saw them filming *Cat People* in 1982, and I started to think I might as well approach life like it was a movie. It was a gothic movie, so the music of the late Romantics was perfect. It was the Sony Walkman era. I blew all the money that didn't go to drugs at a big music store Uptown called the Metronome. They had a separate little classical music cottage across Octavia Street from the main store, which was always crowded with people looking for everything but classical. What I couldn't afford, I shoplifted. I figured it was their own fault for assuming punk and funk were the security threats. My preferred route home was by bike down Coliseum Street through the Garden District, right past the old mansion where Anne Rice sat writing about vampires. I always hoped for gray skies and a light rain, and thunderstorms were always worth the thrill.

I scheduled music according to time of day, occasion, mood. The summer before I went off to college, I prepared to leave, I thought, forever. The perfect music was Richard Strauss's *Four Last Songs*. The camera was behind me, watching me get smaller as I coasted down Chartres Street in the Lower Quarter, past the Ursuline Convent, where the praying nuns turned back the great fire of 1788. In the dimming twilight, to the slow high woodwind trills and long slow descending whole notes in the lower strings, my form melted into the hazy middle distance. I think I knew then that I was just rehearsing my actual death, when I will hear the same song on the same street.

Zwei Lerchen nur noch steigen,
nachträumend in den Duft[2]

Aaron Neville, "*La Vie Dansante*"

I was quite the scenester during my Chicago years, from the final notes of "*Im Abendrot,*" when I thought I'd laid New Orleans to rest, consigned it to dream, to the day I cued up "Goin' Back to New Orleans" in the moving van in 1999. I figured out fast that being from New Orleans was valuable cultural capital—as long as you're not in New Orleans. Everywhere I've gone, Chicago, Berlin, Dakar, people's eyes light up when they hear I'm from New Orleans. (Except for the few brief years after Katrina, when their eyes darkened.) A lot of the guys I went to school with—most notably Harry Connick—have parlayed their NOLA capital to international stardom. For me it's just gotten me dates and jobs. My first job out of college was at Chicago's Heartland Café. I remember sitting at the bar as the owner read over my app. "Oh, you're from New Orleans," he beamed. "Of course you got the job!" It turns out he and his co-owner had got the idea to open their now iconic "rebel café" while tripping under a Live Oak in Audubon Park.

Thus, New Orleans makes dreamers of us all.

That's why I wander, and follow la vie dansante

Aaron's "*La Vie Dansante*" makes me weepy with bliss. The soft strummed string-band arrangement, the mandolin solo, Linda Ronstandt's back-up vocals. The tune lilts. It's about the irrepressibility of "the dancing life," wistful and joyous at the same time. A young night bathed in a Gulf Breeze, or the memory of one. A New Orleans specialty: breathless abandon. "Surrender," the crooner advises. So easy for the young, a true art form for the aging.

I felt older before Katrina than I did after it.

My last job in Chicago was at the Artful Dodger in Bucktown. It featured dancing, but it wan't *la vie dansante* to me, since no breeze could make it into the box, pit, whatever, where people shook it under the neon. One of Chicago's best known Mardi Gras parties took place there every year, and I worked every one. But New Orleanian breathless abandon needs to happen outdoors. There's nothing Mardi Gras about paying a cover to stand in a hermetically sealed drinking box. The year 1999 rolled around and I had to get back. Remember the rumors about a big breakdown of the power grid and civilization at the dawn of the new millennium? Of course I had to be in New Orleans for the end of the world.

Dr. John, "*Litanie des Saints*"

Katrina is a loa, a voodoo deity—or *loi*, as they say in French, which also means "law." Zora Neale Hurston wrote on the origins of new loas: "Some unknown natural phenomenon occurs, which cannot be explained, and a new local demigod is named."[3] It's a no-brainer that Katrina has entered our souls to stay and insinuated herself into the fabric of our structures and our lives. Why shouldn't she? She proved herself with her power. People who pooh-pooh the magnitude of Katrina are disrespecting the spirits.

Dr. John gets it. His "*Litanie des Saints*" is a tone poem depicting the transformational essence of New Orleans, how new loas are added, layered over older ones who also never go away. Yellow fever, crime, storms, but always love in the ruins. The invisible machinations of charmed or offended deities.

Dr. John begins with a theme of Louis Moreau Gottschalk, who rose, flared, and crashed between the years 1829 and 1869. America's first international concert pianist was also a New Orleanian. He used to live on the corner of Royal and Esplanade, and he used to stroll over to Congo Square, like many curious white Creoles, to witness the dances. His "*Danse des Negres*" mimics what he heard, and Dr. John rephrases it again. Then the Neville Brothers chant the names of loas: Mama Oshun, Shango, Santa Maria, Papa Legba, Mam'sell Erzulie, Saint Cecilia. To cap off, Dr. John riffs on Gottschalk in twentieth-century New Orleans style, a mild, elegant boogie. It keeps changing, nothing ever stands still, but nothing goes away.

Katrina is here to stay. She must be paid her due.

Neville Brothers, "By the Waters of Babylon"

But the wicked, who carried us away in captivity, required from us a song

I'd always loved being a New Orleanian away from New Orleans. But Katrina took that away from me. I became a refugee, a problem, cause for guilt, pity, anger, or resentment from other Americans. The performance of New Orleanian authenticity, once a kick, now became a test, an audition to merit continued existence, in front of a skeptical audience. The city became a diaspora, scattered. Many reported how much they liked the places they ended up. Others stewed and plotted their return.

By the rivers of Babylon, where we sat down
And there we wept, when we remembered Zion

The last week of September 2005 was the only time I was in New Orleans illegally. I had to be ready with a story and a Doctor Who Pass for all the checkpoints (I used my UNO ID; said I was a "researcher"). New Orleans resident was not a sufficient qualification. One had to be an "expert," animal rescuer, or, of course, commercial property owner. No one was authorized to remain in the city at night, when I hid in my house with a candle and wondered about the safety of opening the back door for a breeze.

By the end of the month, Mayor Ray Nagin did the best thing he ever did: end the quarantine and let everybody come back legally (those who could afford it). Feds and national "observers" cried out in protest, deeming the city not safe for human habitation. But C. Ray said fuck them, come on back. Thus, were we restored to the bosom of New Orleans (those who could afford it) and who were driven beyond reason to hurry back.

Some hurried, some trickled. My three-year-old son and pregnant wife returned in mid-October. The boy was a spectacle. People crossed streets to look at him, slowed down their cars, and rolled down their windows, sometimes even saying, "Thank you, thank you!" because they knew a city without children isn't a city.

I was advised to not even open my refrigerator, just to tape it shut and get it out to the sidewalk. That's what I did. I put cardboard under it so it wouldn't scrape up the wood floors as I manhandled it out of there. It took off a chunk of door frame on the way out. After a month had passed, it had company. More people had come back and now refrigerators lined the street. A plague of flies buzzed all around them for blocks and blocks. One day a truck with a crane came by and hoisted them all up and into the back. People stood on their stoops and cheered.

One day I was driving around the deserted streets and I heard a brass band. I pulled over and they passed. A trad parade combo with snare, bass drum, trumpet, trombone, a few folks straggling behind. I smiled gleefully and gave them the thumbs-up, before I realized it was a funeral.

Soul Rebels, "NO-LA, NO-LA, Big City of Dreams"
(They haven't done this, but they should: A New Orleans version of the Grandmaster Flash classic, "New York, New York")
Too much, too many people, too much
We worried if anyone would ever come back, besides a tiny faithful core. But now there are too many people. Or maybe just too many cars. The streets are clogged with them, and the drivers are pissed. Struggling to get to work so they can pay their exorbitant rent. American normalcy has returned. We feared ten years ago that New Orleans would no longer be a city; now people fret about the city no longer being New Orleans. In the fall of 2005, the moving trucks were all heading away, but people came to replace the ones

who left. The city is still 100,000 people smaller than before the storm, but so many more cars. The new people have more money. Many of them are tired of hearing about Katrina because they weren't here for it. They're also tired of hearing about themselves, especially when people call them "gentrifiers." One worried older neighbor assured me that the newcomers would split after the first Katrina-level event—which is always on the way. But they're New Orleanians now, another layer on top of the older layers. One day they may experience their own apocalypse, a storm or a bullet to the face. Verdi's *Dies Irae* or Strauss's last song on Chartres Street. Then we'll know they are us. Everyone who dies in New Orleans is a New Orleanian. Their spirits stay here forever.

New Orleans is hot again, a destination, New Orleans is "back." But I'll always remember the miles of blocks of empty houses, the dark silent powerless nights, the plague of rats, the plague of flies, the empty ruin with no one in it except the handful who couldn't bear to be away.

ACKNOWLEDGMENTS

Besides family and friends, I want to thank first and foremost the editors who helped me to shape the essays in this collection. None played a greater role than Jed Horne, my editor at *The Lens*, where most of these first appeared. He offered me a space with unique possibilities, an opportunity to contribute essays of two-thousand words rather than the very constraining typical newspaper column of only around six hundred words. He also engaged with every draft in challenging ways that made me hone my thought as well as language.

I'm also thankful to the other editors, at other journals and newspapers, who helped shape this work, including Annette Sisco, Michael Sartisky, David Johnson, Gina Frangello, Zoe Zolbrod, and Martha Bayne. Finally, I also want to thank at least some of the many interlocuters whom I've enjoyed talking New Orleans with over the past few years: Nancy Dixon, Lydia Y. Nichols, David Beriss, Maurice Ruffin, Doug MacCash, L. J. Goldstein, Jarret Lofstead, Christine Horn, Drew Bourn, Christina Schoux Casey, David and Daniel Hammer, Aurélie Godet, Rosary O'Neill, Jessica Kinnison, and my dear old family friends, the Rogans—Ama, Davis, Sims, Alcena, and the late beloved Patrick.

ENDNOTES

Introduction

1. Tyler Bridges, "Study: N.O. Economy to Take Pummeling," *New Orleans Advocate/Times-Picayune*, March 19, 2020.

2. Most comprehensively in Thomas Jessen Adams and Matt Sakakeeny, eds. *Remaking New Orleans: Beyond Exceptionalism and Authenticity.* Durham, NC: Duke University Press, 2019. For a more detailed critique of their conclusions, see C.W. Cannon, "The Myth of New Orleans at Year 301," *New Orleans Review*, February 28, 2020.

3. Friedrich Nietzsche, *Jenseits von Gut und Böse* (Berlin: Hofenberg Digital 2016), 156. Translation by the author.

4. Caryn Cossé Bell, *Revolution, Romanticism, and the Afro-Creole Protest Tradition in Louisiana, 1718–1868* (Baton Rouge: LSU Press, 1997).

5. Kate Chopin, *The Awakening* (1899; repr., New York: Avon Books, 1972), 106.

6. See Theodor Adorno, *Aesthetic Theory*, trans. R. Hullot-Kentor (London: Athlone Press, 1999), 311.

7. Quoted in Mike Scott, "Popular Protests Back in 1895 Saved the Cabildo and Presbytere from the Wrecking Ball," *Times-Picayune/*New Orleans *Advocate*, November 24, 2020. https://www.nola.com/entertainment_life/home_garden/article_1a75e8f2-2d11-11eb-bf3b-c7e831dbd9cc.html.

8. See Rien Fertel, *Imagining the Creole City: The Rise of Literary Culture in Nineteenth-Century New Orleans* (Baton Rouge: LSU Press, 2014), 52–53.

9. Lafcadio Hearn, *Inventing New Orleans: Writings of Lafcadio Hearn*, ed. S. Frederick Starr (Jackson: University Press of Mississippi, 2001), xii, 159–61.

10. Robert Azzarello, *Three-Hundred Years of Decadence: New Orleans Literature and the Transatlantic World* (Baton Rouge: LSU Press, 2019), 9.

11. Raymond Williams, *Marxism and Literature* (Oxford: Oxford University Press, 1977), 195–96.

12. Quoted in Azzarello, *Three Hundred Years*, 7.

13. See Michael Silk, "Nietzsche, Decadence, and the Greeks," *New Literary History* 35, no. 4 (Autumn 2004): 587–606.

14. Raymond Williams, "Base and Superstructure in Marxist Cultural Theory," *New Left Review* I/82 (November-December 1973): 459.

15. Leon Trotsky, *Literature and Revolution*, trans. Rose Strunsky (New York: International Publishers, 1925), 188.

16. Bill Lavender, *Q* (New Orleans: Trembling Pillow Press, 2013).

17. Everette Maddox, *I Hope It's Not Over, And Good-by: Selected Poems of Everette Maddox*, ed. Ralph Adamo (New Orleans: UNO Press, 2009), 152.

18. Ishmael Reed, *Mumbo Jumbo* (New York: Atheneum, 1972), 6.

19. Brenda Marie Osbey, *All Saints: New and Selected Poems* (Baton Rouge: LSU Press, 1997).

Chapter 1: Pretty Lively for a Dying City

This essay was originally published in the *Times-Picayune*, December 28, 2007.

1. Brenda Marie Osbey, *All Saints: New and Selected Poems* (Baton Rouge: LSU Press, 1997), 25.

2. Ben C. Toledano, "New Orleans—An Autopsy," *Commentary*, July 2007.

Chapter 2: A Living Carnival Takes All Comers

This essay was originally published in the *Times-Picayune*, February 12, 2012.

1. In 2011, Krewe of Rex threatened Krewe of 'tit Rex with a lawsuit if it didn't change its name. 'Tit Rex eventually resolved situation by changing the "e" in their Rex to an upside-down lowercase "e" (or "ə"), also called a "shwa." For more, see Doug MacCash, "Rex Demands that Krewe of 'Tit Rex Change its Name," NOLA.com, September 12, 2011. https://www.nola.com/entertainment_life/arts/article_9bcf427f-f91c-5e48-a4af-df57813b251e.html.

Chapter 3: Is NOLA Hip and Is That Cool?

This essay was originally published as "The New Orleans Dilemma: Is It Hip to Be So Very, Very 'Hip?'" in *The Lens*, June 25, 2012.

1. Katrina Brown Hunt, "The Fifteen Best Cities for Hipsters," *Travel + Leisure*, November 18, 2013. https://www.travelandleisure.com/culture-design/americas-best-cities-for-hipsters-2013.

2. Jay Walljasper and Daniel Kraker, "The Fifteen Hippest Places to Live: The Coolest Neighborhoods in America and Canada," *Utne Reader*, November–December 1997.

3. Norman Mailer, "The White Negro: Superficial Reflections on the Hipster," *Dissent*, Fall 1957.

4. Curtis Wilkie, "Bohemia's Last Frontier," *Nation*, September 15, 2005. https://www.thenation.com/article/archive/bohemias-last-frontier/.

5. Thomas Frank, *The Conquest of Cool: Business Culture, Counterculture, and the Rise of Hip Consumerism* (Chicago: University of Chicago Press, 1997).

6. Mezz Mezzrow and Bernard Wolfe, *Really the Blues* (1946; New York: Citadel Underground, 1990).

7. Herbert Marcuse, *One-dimensional Man: Studies in the Ideology of Advanced Industrial Society* (Boston: Beacon Press, 1964).

8. LeRoi Jones (later known as Amiri Baraka), *Blues People: Negro Music in White America* (New York: William Morrow, 1963; 1999), 213.

9. Raymond Williams, "Base and Superstructure in Marxist Cultural Theory," *New Left Review* I/82 (Nov–Dec 1973): 459.

10. As I re-read this years later, I feel constrained to point out the obvious: that white "affinity" for Black culture has resulted in pervasive white appropriation of Black culture. The history of culture is a constant process of assimilation and incorporation, and unequal power relations impact cultural history as they do every other aspect of history.

Chapter 4: Go-Cups, Roosters, and NOLA Identity

This essay was originally published as "Identity Politics: Gentry Cling to Go-Cups While Kids and Roosters Face Extinction," in *The Lens*, September 6, 2013.

1. Alex Rawls, "Delicate Balance: Neighborhood Peace vs. the City's Greatest Treasure—Its Music," *Lens*, April 17, 2013. https://thelensnola.org/2013/04/17/a-delicate-balance-neighborhood-serenity-vs-the-citys-greatest-treasure-its-music/.

2. C.W. Cannon, "Curfew: Stripping Kids' Access to the Cultural Heart of New Orleans," *Lens*, January 18, 2012. https://thelensnola.org/2012/01/18/debating-new-orleans-curfew-proposal/.

3. Casey Ferrand, "New Orleans Parents Find Bar Ad Inappropriate for Children," WDSU News, August 8, 2013. https://www.wdsu.com/article/parents-find-bar-ad-inappropriate-for-children-1/3364915.

4. Marta Jewson, "Urban Roosters No Longer Welcome Pets in New Orleans," *Gambit Weekly*, July 30, 2013.

Chapter 5: Faking Relevance at the French Market

This essay was originally published as "Garbage In, Garbage Out: 'Grand Vision' for French Market Junks Tradition," in *The Lens*, November 5, 2013.

1. Richard A. Webster, "French Market Corp. Hires Jon Smith as Executive Director after First Pick Declines Job over Salary Dispute," NOLA.com/ *Times-Picayune,* September 25, 2013. https://www.nola.com/news/politics/article_b5d3d722-527f-56d6-aa89-8e80f063c5cd.html.

2. Richard A. Webster, "French Market Vendors Clash with Ideas of New Executive Director," NOLA.com/ *Times-Picayune,* October 11, 2013. https://www.nola.com/news/politics/article_829562b4-4e9c-5ebd-a84e-4ec9e6735352.html.

3. Lafcadio Hearn, *Inventing New Orleans; Writings of Lafcadio Hearn,* ed. S. Frederick Starr (Jackson, MS: University Press of Mississippi, 2002), 22–30.

4. Webster, "French Market Corp."

Chapter 6: Why NOLA Hates Starbucks

This essay was originally published as "Hipsters Take Note: Still Not Crazy About Starbucks After All These Years," in *The Lens*, December 19, 2013.

1. Richard A. Webster, "French Quarter Residents Threaten to Sue if Habana Outpost Approved," NOLA.com/ *Times-Picayune,* May 21, 2013. https://www. nola.com/news/politics/article_7babab34-89a1-53aa-8375-018249637e67.html.

2. George Washington Cable, *The Grandissimes: A Story of Creole Life* (1880; New York: Penguin Classics, 1988), 167.

3. Chopin, *The Awakening* (Chicago: Herbert S. Stone & Co., 1899; New York: Avon Books, 1972), 175.

4. Tennessee Williams, *A Streetcar Named Desire* (1947; repr., New York: New Directions, 2004), 3.

5. Bruce Rutledge, ed., *Do You Know What It Means to Miss New Orleans?* (Seattle, WA: Chin Music Press, 2006), x.

6. Karl Marx, Capital Vol. 1; Chap.1, section 4, "The Fetishism of Commodities and the Secret Thereof." First English edition (1887), translated by Samuel Moore and Edward Aveling. E-edition at Marxists. org, https://www.marxists.org/archive/marx/works/1867-c1/ch01.htm#S4. Accessed December 20, 2020.

7. Sara Ruffin Costello, "The Intoxicating, Tradition-steeped Charm of New Orleans," *New York Times Style Magazine* Blogs/Travel Diary, October 3, 2013. https://tmagazine. blogs.nytimes.com/2013/10/03/travel-diary-the-intoxicating-tradition-steeped-charm-of-new-orleans/.

8. "We Want Starbucks in Mid-City," Neighborland.com. https://neighborland. com/ideas/nola-mid-city-starbucks.

9. Pierre Bourdieu, *Distinction: A Social Critique of the Judgement of Taste*, translated by Richard Nice (Cambridge, MA: Harvard University Press, 1984).

10. See "A Death in Bohemia—Starbucks Comes to Faubourg Marigny,"114.

Chapter 7: The Golden Age of Carnival Is Now

This essay was originally published as "When Was Carnival's Golden Age? Take a Look Around—You're Living in It," in *The Lens*, February 14, 2014.

1. M. M. Bakhtin, *Rabelais and His World*, translated by Helene Iswolsky (Bloomington: Indiana University Press, 1984), 7–19.

2. Rachel Wulff, "City Council Unanimously Passes Mardi Gras Ordinances," WDSU News, January 23, 2014. https://www.wdsu.com/article/new-orleans-city-council-unanimously-passes-mardi-gras-ordinances/3368501.

3. Howard Reich, "Why New Orleans Matters," *Chicago Tribune*, September 18, 2005.

Chapter 8: Frenchmen Street and the Nouvelle New Orleans

This essay was originally published as "Is Frenchmen Still Cool—Or Just a Bourbon Street for Hipsters?" in *The Lens*, May 23, 2014.

1. See Alecia P. Long, *Great Southern Babylon: Sex, Race, and Respectability in New Orleans, 1865–1920* (Baton Rouge: LSU Press, 2004), 181.

Chapter 9: I Miss My Schwegmann's—and I Got a Right To

This essay was originally published as "Call Me a Sentimental Old Fool, But I Miss My Schwegmann's—And I Got a Right To" in *The Lens*, August 20, 2014.

Chapter 10: A Chic Makeover for a Shabby Economy

This essay was originally published as "Shabby Chic Gives Way to Merely Chic: How Come? It's the Economy, Stupid" in *The Lens*, April 7, 2015.

1. See Peter Moskowitz, "How New Orleans Is in Danger of Losing Its Identity," *Vice,* February 27, 2015.

2. Alice Walker, *You Can't Keep a Good Woman Down*, UK ed. (London: The Women's Press, 1982), 17.

3. As I recall, only the Fischer Projects (William J. Fischer Housing Development) on the Westbank were done in the modernist style common in many Midwestern projects, probably because it was built in the mid-1960s. The 1996 federal Hope VI grant covered Fischer's demolition too.

Chapter 11: Got the Airbnb Blues? Get Hip to Creative Disruption!

This essay was originally published as "Whole-House Rentals Got You Down? Get Hip to 'Creative Disruption'!" in *The Lens*, October 30, 2016.

1. See Dana Eness, "Short-term Rental Vote Deals a Blow to Neighborhoods—and Citizen Engagement," *The Lens*, October 25, 2016. https://thelensnola.org/2016/10/25/str-vote-deals-a-blow-to-neighborhoods-and-citizen-engagement/. Regulation of short-term rentals in New Orleans has since been tightened.

Chapter 12: Restless Super-Natives: New Orleans and the Anxiety of Authenticity

This essay was originally published as "Anxiety and Authenticity: Are 'Super-Natives' loving New Orleans to Death?" in *The Lens*, June 1, 2018.

1. See "Bobos Go Native: Gentrification and New Orleans Exceptionalism," 59.

2. Hannibal Burris, "A Love Letter to New Orleans," YouTube, November 11, 2016. https://www.youtube.com/watch?v=R34UjzJvJeQ.

3. New Orleans Airbnb Tracker, *The Lens*, May 2018. https://thelensnola.org/new-orleans-airbnb-tracker/.

4. Peter Horjus, "Short-Term Rentals Create a Long-Term Problem: Soaring Taxes for the Rest of Us," *The Lens*, August 25, 2017. https://thelensnola.org/2017/08/25/short-term-rentals-create-a-long-term-problem-soaring-taxes-for-the-rest-of-us/.

5. Missy Wilkinson, "'Southern Charm' Is Bravo's Newest Reality T.V. Show Set in New Orleans, But How Real Is It?," *New Orleans Advocate*, April 8, 2018. https://www.nola.com/entertainment_life/movies_tv/article_1f8e268b-d923-5b14-b67b-81f456d04fb5.html.

6. Richard Florida, "Bohemia and Economic Geography," *Journal of Economic Geography* (2002): 55–71.

7. See Jeff Adelson, "New Orleans Greenlights Taller Developments on Riverfront, Nixes Incentives for Affordable Housing," *New Orleans Advocate*, February 22, 2018. https://www.nola.com/news/article_de7600bb-f856-5d85-a74f-5d43773bb07b.html.

8. Bruce Eggler, "New Orleans City Council Poised to Move Up Curfew for Young People in French Quarter," NOLA.com/*Times-Picayune*, January 5, 2012. See also C.W. Cannon, "Curfew: Stripping Kids' Access to Cultural Heart of the City," *The Lens*, January 18, 2012.

9. See Charles Maldonado, "New Orleans City Council to Consider Ban on Most Whole-House Short-term Rentals in Historic Neighborhoods," *The Lens*, May 21, 2018. https://thelensnola.org/2018/05/21/new-orleans-city-council-to-consider-ban-on-most-whole-home-short-term-rentals-in-historic-neighborhoods/.

10. Emily Peck and Charles Maldonado, "How Airbnb Is Pushing Locals out of New Orleans' Coolest Neighborhoods," *The Lens*, October 30, 2017.

Chapter 13: New Orleans in the Age of Social Distancing

This essay was originally published in *The Lens*, March 24, 2020, and "Us and Them in the Spring of COVID-19" in *The Lens*, May 18, 2020.

1. Holly Rockwell-Celerier, "Mayor Deflects Blame from Self to Tourists," Your Opinions, *Times-Picayune/New Orleans Advocate*, March 20, 2020. https://www.theadvocate.com/baton_rouge/opinion/letters/article_98171822-6880-11ea-bc24-ef12afd25e7f.html.

2. Terry Gross, "What the 1918 Flu Pandemic Can Tell Us About the COVID-19 Crisis," Interview with John Barry, *Fresh Air*, National Public Radio, May 14, 2020. https://www.npr.org/2020/05/14/855986938/what-the-1918-flu-pandemic-can-tell-us-about-the-covid-19-crisis.

3. Sanjana Karanth, "Gov. Whitmer Creates Coronavirus Task Force to Address Effect on Black Americans," *Huffington Post*, April 20, 2020. https://www.huffpost.com/entry/michigan-coronavirus-task-force-disproportionate-impact-black-americans_n_5e9e3fe3c5b6a486d07e21a2.

4. Faimon Roberts III, "Jefferson Chamber President to New Orleans Mayor: 'Risky' Cancellations Will Likely Set Region Back," *Times-Picayune/New Orleans Advocate*, April 17, 2020. https://www.nola.com/news/coronavirus/article_288ec40e-80fa-11ea-8a97-8b2ceb597feb.html.

5. Bryn Stole, "Latoya Cantrell's 'Demagogue Approach' and 'Adversarial' Stephen Perry: Tense Re-Opening Debate in New Orleans," *Times-Picayune/New Orleans Advocate*, May 9, 2020. https://www.nola.com/news/politics/article_cca47c22-918b-11ea-b091-67712fc9d65a.html.

6. Franco Valobra, Robert Lupo, David Monteleone, and Jay Batt, advertisement, *Times-Picayune*, April 19, 2020.

7. Doug MacCash, "Carnival Krewe Delivers Chicken to Tense ER during Coronavirus Crisis: 'It Feels Good,'" *Times-Picayune/ New Orleans Advocate*, March 19, 2020. https://www.nola.com/news/coronavirus/article_66caf016-6945-11ea-85b2-4f4d4b1b3711.html.

8. In the year and a half since this piece first appeared, New Orleans has continued to lead the nation in fighting the virus, though still without much national recognition. We were the third city in the country, after New York and San Francisco, to require proof of vaccine or negative test to enter places of public accommodation (effective August 16, 2021), and the first in the country to announce plans to require proof of vaccination or negative test also for children five years of age or older (effective February 1, 2022).

Chapter 14: Bobos Go Native: Gentrification and New Orleans Exceptionalism

This essay was originally published as "Gentrification Flap Rooted in Older Debate Over New Orleans Exceptionalism," in *The Lens*, April 9, 2013.

1. Richard Campanella, "Gentrification and Its Discontents: Notes from New Orleans," New Geography February 28, 2013. https://www.newgeography.com/content/003526-gentrification-and-its-discontents-notes-new-orleans.

2. Pierre Bourdieu, *Distinction: A Social Critique of the Judgement of Taste,* trans. Richard Nice (Cambridge, MA: Harvard University Press, 1984), 333.

3. Brett Will Taylor, "Love NOLA: A Fool's Journey," ViaNolaVie, March 1, 2012. https://www.vianolavie.org/2012/03/01/love-nola-a-fools-journey-43643/.

4. Christine Horn, "Reading the White Teapot," Nolafugeespress.com, March 2013 (site discontinued).

Chapter 15: Music and Murder: A New Orleans Story

This essay was originally published as "Second-Lining's Silver Lining: Mainstream Embrace of Our Cultural Exotica," in *The Lens*, May 16, 2013.

1. Tom Dent, "Ritual Murder," *N.O. Lit: 200 Years of New Orleans Literature*, ed. Nancy Dixon (New Orleans: Lavender Ink, 2013), 458.

2. Quoted in Herbert Asbury, *French Quarter: An Informal History of the New Orleans Underworld* (New York: Alfred A. Knopf, 1936; Basic Books, 2003), 317.

3. Deborah Cotton "New Orleans Must Hold Leaders Accountable for Violence Prevention Programs" *Lens,* June 14, 2013. https://thelensnola.org/2013/06/14/

new-orleans-must-hold-its-leaders-accountable-for-their-violence-prevention-pro-grams/. In 2017, Cotton died as a result of injuries sustained during the shooting.

4. Jan V. Ramsey, "Follow Your NOLA, New Orleans Visitors Targeted," *Offbeat*, May 15, 2013.

5. Andrew Vanacore, "Fox News Hosts Draw Ire of New Orleans Civic Groups After Calling City a 'Vast Urban Wasteland,'" NOLA.com/ *Times Picayune,* April 9, 2013. https://www.nola.com/news/politics/article_e827879c-11b6-577b-b415-0c1a33635ca4.html.

6. Sonja Steptoe, "The City Tourists Never Knew," *Time*, May 10, 2006. http://content.time.com/time/subscriber/article/0,33009,1101568-1,00.html.

Chapter 16: An American Vegetable in Magical New Orleans

This essay was originally published as "A Kale of Two Cities: The Magical New Orleans and the Americanist Version" in *The Lens*, March 14, 2014.

1. Lizzy Goodman, "Experiencing New Orleans with Fresh Eyes and Ears," *New York Times,* March 3, 2014. https://www.nytimes.com/2014/03/09/travel/experiencing-new-orleans-with-fresh-eyes-and-ears.html.

2. Jarvis DeBerry, "What the Kale?: NYT Says That Green's Not Available in New Orleans" NOLA.com/ *Times-Picayune,* March 7, 2014. https://www.nola.com/opinions/article_b30e59f2-dc36-516f-a7c4-345416d66ac3.html.

3. Dave Thier, "Sorry, Louisiana Is Not Actually Made of Magic," *Esquire,* March 11, 2014. https://www.esquire.com/entertainment/tv/a27742/louisiana-is-not-magic/.

4. Charles Gayarré, *History of Louisiana: The French Domination*, Vol. I (New Orleans: F. F. Hansell & Bro., 1903), 9.

5. Tennessee Williams, *A Streetcar Named Desire* (1947; repr., New York: New Directions, 2004), 145.

6. Sigmund Freud, *Civilization and Its Discontents*, trans. James Strachey (New York: W. W. Norton, 1961), 11–12.

Chapter 17: Waving the Trashy Shirt: Class War in the French Quarter

This essay was originally published as "The French Quarter's a treasure—so should those trashy T-shirt shops be banned?" in *The Lens*, April 11, 2014.

1. Karen Gadbois, "Crackdown on French Quarter T-shirt Shops Yields Some Compliance, Some Delays," *Lens*, November 8, 2013. https://thelensnola.org/2013/11/08/crackdown-on-french-quarter-t-shirt-shops-yields-some-compliance-some-delays/.

2. Richard A. Webster, "New Orleans City Council Demands Crackdown on Illegal T-shirt Shops," NOLA.com/*Times-Picayune*, September 17, 2013. https://www.nola.com/news/politics/article_854c52e7-9f95-577c-88d1-f36cffce8dd6.html.

3. Sadiq H. Khan, BRIEF SUMMARY OF FACTS AND POLICY CONSIDERATIONS TO THE BOARD OF ZONING ADJUSTMENTS RE: BZA 017-14, BZA 022-14, BZA 021-14, November 2013.

4. Scott Gold, "Things You Have to Explain to Out-of-Towners About New Orleans," Thrillist, March 21, 2014. https://www.thrillist.com/entertainment/new-orleans/things-you-have-to-explain-to-out-of-towners-about-new-orleans-thrillist-new-orleans.

5. City of New Orleans Comprehensive Zoning Ordinance, Article 2, Section 168.

6. Kevin Fox Gotham, *Authentic New Orleans: Race, Culture, and Tourism in the Big Easy* (New York: New York University Press, 2007), 20.

7. "Yat" is a common New Orleans term for white ethnic working class, based on the frequent greeting, "Where Y'at?"

8. Alan Richman, "Yes, We're Open," *GQ*, November 2, 2006. https://www.gq.com/story/katrina-new-orleans-food.

Chapter 18: New South Quackery: The Cultural Politics of *Duck Dynasty*

Originally published in *The Lens*, June 27, 2014.

1. Rachel Maresca, "'Duck Dynasty' Star Jase Robertson Kicked Out of NYC Hotel after Being Confused for Homeless Man," *New York Daily News*, August 16, 2013.

2. Drew Magary, "What the Duck?" *GQ* December 18, 2013.

3. Richard Hofstadter, "The Paranoid Style in American Politics," *Harper's Magazine*, November 1964.

4. Billy Hallowell, "We're Up Against Evil: 'Duck Dynasty' Star Phil Robertson Blasts White House, Tells G.O.P. to 'Get Godly,'" Blaze.com, May 30, 2014. https://www.theblaze.com/news/2014/05/30/were-up-against-evil-duck-dynasty-star-blasts-white-house-tells-gop-to-get-godly.

5. Jose Delreal, "Jindal Hits 'Duck Dynasty' Backlash," *Politico*, December 19, 2013. https://www.politico.com/story/2013/12/bobby-jindal-duck-dynasty-101330.

6. Creator unknown, http://twitpic.com/dqskeq, retrieved June 20, 2014.

7. Christian Bonoan, "Senate Candidate Blames Hip-Hop for Gun Violence, Studies Show Different," *XXL Magazine*, January 7, 2014. https://www.xxlmag.com/senate-candidate-blames-hip-hop-for-gun-violence-studies-show-different/.

8. "Tea Party Targets GOP Veteran in Mississippi Senate Race," NBC News, March 25, 2014. https://www.nbcnews.com/politics/elections/tea-party-targets-gop-veteran-mississippi-senate-race-n60981.

9. Mark Ballard, "Duck Commander Kin Enters Fifth District Race," *Advocate*, June 17, 2014. https://www.theadvocate.com/baton_rouge/news/politics/elections/article_d4d42166-3933-51a3-a086-dba95a4e5765.html.

Chapter 19: New Orleans as Subject and Object

This essay was originally published as "Is Debunking Our Obsession with What's Hip About New Orleans Just the Latest Way to Seem Hip?" in *The Lens*, October, 21, 2014.

1. W. E. B. DuBois, *The Souls of Black Folk* (Chicago: A. C. McClurg & Co., 1903; repr. Mineola, NY: Dover Thrift Edition, 1994), 1–3.

2. Charles Gayarré, *History of Louisiana: The French Domination*, Vol. I (New Orleans: F. F. Hansell & Bro., 1903), 9.

3. Katy Reckdahl, "Experts Ask if New Orleans' 'Exceptionalism' Masks Grimmer Reality," *New Orleans Advocate*, September 23, 2014. https://www.nola.com/news/article_2cf01dd4-fe7f-549f-b340-034901c0bc51.html.

4. See "Waving the Trashy Shirt—Class War in the French Quarter," 72.

5. Stuart Hall, "Notes on Deconstructing the Popular," in *Cultural Resistance Reader*, ed. Stephen Duncombe (London: Verso, 2002), 185–92.

6. See "Bobos Go Native: Gentrification and New Orleans Exceptionalism," 59.

Chapter 20: I Want Magic—A Defense of New Orleans Exceptionalism

This essay was originally published in *Louisiana Cultural Vistas*, February 10, 2015.

1. Richard Campanella, "The Seduction of Exceptionalism," *Louisiana Cultural Vistas,* Summer 2014, 24.

2. Thomas Adams and Matt Sakakeeny "New Orleans as Subject: Beyond Exceptionalism and Authenticity," conference introduction, Tulane University, September 19, 2014.

3. Charles E. O'Neill, S. J., foreword to *Our People and Our History: Fifty Creole Portraits*, by Rodolphe Lucien Desdunes, trans. Sister Dorothea Olga McCants (Baton Rouge: LSU Press, 1973), ix–xx.

4. Kenneth Frampton, "Towards a Critical Regionalism: Six Points for an Architecture of Resistance," in *The Anti-Aesthetic: Essays on Postmodern Culture*, ed. Hal Foster (New York: New Press, 1998).

5. Ludwig von Reizenstein, *The Mysteries of New Orleans,* trans. Steven Rowan (Baltimore, MD: Johns Hopkins University Press, 2002), 189.

6. Quoted in Orville Prescott, "Books of the Times," *New York Times*, January 23, 1950. Scrapbooks 1950, Box 3: 5H, Robert Tallant Papers, Manuscripts Collection, Louisiana Division, New Orleans Public Library.

7. Friedrich Nietzsche, *Beyond Good and Evil*, trans. R. J. Hollingdale (London: Penguin, 1984), 83.

Chapter 21: Adieu, Vieux Carré

This essay was originally published as "Bidding Adieu to the Vieux Carré as We Once Knew and Loved It" in *The Lens*, November 5, 2015.

1. Daniel Wolff, "'Reinventing the Crescent' Reconsidered: Mere Gentrification or Good for Us All?," *Lens*, August 8, 2013. https://thelensnola.org/2013/08/15/reinventing-the-crescent-reconsidered-mere-gentrification-or-good-for-us-all/.

2. See Danny Monteverde, "Musician Says Troopers Roughed Him Up during Stop," *New Orleans Advocate*, July 31, 2014. https://www.nola.com/news/article_30949c9c-e5e6-5e38-a337-9645380e6774.html.

3. As of 2020, this has not yet happened. It is today the site of Homer Plessy Community School, a public school very much in the spirit of the McDonogh 15 of my childhood.

4. Greg LaRose, "$20 Million French Quarter Project Turning Civil War Widows Home into High-End Housing," NOLA.com/ *Times Picayune*, November 3, 2015. https://www.nola.com/news/business/article_ee12c993-2eba-5304-89f4-cf-6b710ce642.html.

5. Charles Gayarré, *History of Louisiana: The French Domination*, Vol. I (New Orleans: F. F. Hansell & Bro., 1903), 9.

Chapter 22: A Slap-Down for Old Hickory

This essay was originally published as "Old Hickory Axed from $20 Bill; So Is It Time to Rename Jackson Square?" in *The Lens*, May 2, 2016.

1. Matthew Rosza, "Why Andrew Jackson Never Should Have Been on the $20 to Begin With," Salon, April 21, 2016. https://www.salon.com/2016/04/21/why_andrew_jackson_never_should_have_been_on_the_20_to_begin_with/.

2. Nick Gass, "Trump on Harriet Tubman $20: 'Pure Political Correctness,'" Politico, April 21, 2016. https://www.politico.com/blogs/2016-gop-primary-live-updates-and-results/2016/04/trump-20-harriet-tubman-222256.

3. Gina Kolata, "Death Rates Rising for Middle-Aged White Americans, Study Finds," *New York Times*, November 2, 2015. https://www.nytimes.com/2015/11/03/health/death-rates-rising-for-middle-aged-white-americans-study-finds.html.

4. Gass, "Trump."

5. Amanda Marcotte and Moe Tkacik, "Hillary Clinton Thinks Breaking Up the Big Banks Won't End Racism and Sexism: Is She Right?" *In These Times* / AlterNet, March 27, 2016. https://www.alternet.org/2016/03/hillary-clinton-thinks-breaking-big-banks-wont-end-racism-and-sexism-she-right/.

6. Caryn Cossé Bell, *Revolution, Romanticism, and the Afro-Creole Protest Tradition in Louisiana, 1718–1868* (Baton Rouge: LSU Press, 1997), 54.

7. Quoted in Rodolphe Lucien Desdunes, *Nos hommes et notre histoire* (Montreal: Arbour & Dupont, 1911; repr. Oxford: Livres Generaux, 2010), 4. Translated by author.

8. "The Best and Worst US Cities for Living Comfortably on an Average Paycheck," SFGATE, April 21, 2016. https://www.sfgate.com/personal-finance/article/The-best-and-worst-US-cities-for-living-7269314.php.

Chapter 23: Why Hipster Haters Are Worse than Hipsters

This essay was originally published as "Trumpistas, Brexitistas, and Hipsters: Shared Anxiety about Class Identity" in *The Lens*, July 8, 2016.

1. See Frank Langfitt, "Britain's 'Brexit' Vote Has Echoes of the U.S. Presidential Race," NPR, June 22, 2016. https://www.npr.org/sections/ parallels/2016/06/22/483111789/ britains-brexit-vote-has-echoes -of-the-u-s-presidential-race.

2. Janet Hook and Stu Woo, "Donald Trump Hails U.K.'s 'Brexit' Vote," *Wall Street Journal*, June 24, 2016. https://www.wsj.com/articles/ donald-trump-hails-u-k-s-brexit-vote-1466777977.

3. Tom Peck, "Nigel Farage's Triumphalist Brexit Speech Crossed the Borders of Decency," *Independent* (UK), June 24, 2016. https://www.independent.co.uk/news/uk/ politics/brexit-recession-economy-what-happens-nigel-farage-speech-a7099301.html.

4. Nigel Farage, "This Will Be a Victory for Real People," Campaign Speech, June 23, 2016. https://www.theguardian.com/politics/video/2016/jun/24/ nigel-farage-eu-referendum-this-victory-for-real-people-video.

5. See "Bobos Go Native: Gentrification and New Orleans Exceptionalism," 59.

6. Pierre Bourdieu, *Distinction: A Social Critique of the Judgement of Taste,* trans. Richard Nice (Cambridge, MA: Harvard University Press, 1984), 338.

7. Jason DeParle, "Harder for Americans to Rise from Lower Rungs," *New York Times*, January 5, 2012. https://www.nytimes.com/2012/01/05/us/harder-for-americans-to-rise-from-lower-rungs.html.

8. Ashley Lopez, "Kentucky's New Governor Could Roll Back Medicaid, Even as State Benefits," NPR, December 8, 2015. https://www.npr.org/2015/12/08/458887771/ plans-to-roll-back-medicaid-expansion-doesn-t-seem-to-worry-rural-kentuckians.

9. Janell Ross, "Donald Trump's Surge Is All about Less Educated Americans," *Washington Post*, July 27, 2015. https://www.washingtonpost.com/news/the-fix/ wp/2015/07/27/donald-trumps-surge-is-heavily-reliant-on-less-educated-americans-heres-why/.

Chapter 24: Donald Trump, Andrew Jackson, and *The Walking Dead*

This essay was originally published as "Something in Common? Trump, Jackson Square, and 'The Walking Dead'" in *The Lens*, October 16, 2016.1. See Leslie Savan, "Whose Side Is the 'Walking Dead' On?" *Nation*, April 5, 2013. https://www.thenation.com/article/archive/whose-side-walking-dead/.

2. Dawn Keetley, "'The Walking Dead' and the Rise of Donald Trump," Popmatters, March 16, 2016. https://www.popmatters.com/the-walking-dead-and-the-rise-of-donald-trump-2495444431.html.

3. Steve Inskeep and Arezou Rezvani, "Divided States: Georgia Auto Mechanic Ties Racial Tension to Obama," *National Public Radio*, September 26, 2016. https://www.npr.org/2016/09/26/495435828/divided-states-of-america-georgia-auto-mechanic.

4. Inskeep and Rezvani, "Divided States."

5. Alexandra Berzon, "Donald Trump's Business Plan Left a Trail of Unpaid Bills," *Wall Street Journal*, June 9, 2016. https://www.wsj.com/articles/donald-trumps-business-plan-left-a-trail-of-unpaid-bills-1465504454.

6. Max Ehrenfreund, "A Massive New Study Debunks a Widespread Theory for Donald Trump's Success," *Washington Post*, August 12, 2016. https://www.washingtonpost.com/news/wonk/wp/2016/08/12/a-massive-new-study-debunks-a-widespread-theory-for-donald-trumps-success/.

7. J. D. Vance interview with Judy Woodruff, "The Struggling, Rural, White Communities That Feel Like No One Cares," *PBS Newshour*, September 27, 2016. https://www.pbs.org/newshour/show/struggling-rural-white-communities-feel-like-nobody-one-cares.

Chapter 25: A Death in Bohemia—Starbucks Comes to Faubourg Marigny

This essay was originally published as "Starbucks in Faubourg Marigny? There goes the Neighborhood . . ." in *The Lens*, October 12, 2018.

1. Timothy Boone, "Starbucks, Animal Hospital Coming to Robert Fresh Market Shopping Center in New Orleans," NOLA.com, September 25, 2018. https://www.nola.com/news/business/article_b2c8eb0a-570b-5686-ab54-7088b042c19f.html.

2. See "Why NOLA Hates Starbucks," 17.

3. Alex Kennon, "Change Is Brewing: Loyola Replaces CC's Coffee Kiosk with New Starbucks," *Maroon (Loyola University)*, August 21, 2014. https://loyolamaroon.com/566/life-times/change-is-brewing/.

4. Alana Davis, "Opinion: Freret Starbucks Falls Short," *Maroon* (Loyola University), February 24, 2018. https://loyolamaroon.com/10016532/showcase/opinion-freret-starbucks-falls-short/.

5. *Nextdoor Marigny*, October 5, 2018. The post has since been removed.

6. Theodor Adorno and Max Horkheimer, *Dialectic of Enlightenment,* trans. John Cumming (New York City: Continuum, 1997), 148.

7. John Kennedy Toole, *A Confederacy of Dunces* (New York City: Grove Press, 1980), 306.

8. See Emily Gaudette, "Starbucks Continues So-Called 'War on Christmas' with Lesbian Positive Ad," *Newsweek*, November 21, 2017. https://www.newsweek.com/starbucks-lesbian-holiday-cups-conservatives-719063.

Chapter 26: Wine from Sour Grapes in Whodat Nation

This essay was originally published as "Botched Refereeing Rekindles a Familiar Whodat Nation Vibe: Paranoia" in *The Lens*, January 25, 2019.

1. Randy Newman, "Louisiana 1927," on *Good Old Boys*, Reprise, 1974.

2. Shannon Lee Dawdy, *Building the Devil's Empire: French Colonial New Orleans* (Chicago: University of Chicago Press, 2008), 26.

3. Sonja Steptoe, "The City Tourists Never Knew," *Time,* May 10, 2006. http://content.time.com/time/subscriber/article/0,33009,1101568,00.html.

4. Karen Armstrong, *A Short History of Myth* (Edinburgh, UK: Canongate, 2005), 11.

5. See John Simerman, "For Saints Fans, Stages of Grief Muddled by Conspiracy Theories over 'Sickening' Referee Lapse," *New Orleans Advocate*, January 21, 2019. https://www.nola.com/sports/article_1c5838fd-79af-584d-be74-86bad60f88ec.html.

6. See David Hammer, "New Orleans Saints Fans Agree, the NFL's Punishment for the Bounty Scandal Is Too 'Harsh.'" *Times-Picayune*, March 22, 2012. https://www.nola.com/sports/saints/article_0db460b8-c793-5c1b-a340-1b3d2719ce69.html.

7. Laurel Walmsley, "Angry with NFL After No-Call, Saints Fans Resort to Lawsuits, Billboards," National Public Radio, January 22, 2019. https://www.npr.org/2019/01/22/687540716/angry-with-nfl-after-no-call-saints-fans-resort-to-lawsuits-billboards.

Chapter 27: American Horror in New Orleans

This essay was originally published in the *Rumpus*, June 29, 2014.

1. The Musée Conti Wax Museum closed in 2015. See "Adieu, Vieux Carré," 94.

2. James Franco, "Fassy-B Heats up 'Twelve Years a Slave,'" Vice, November 8, 2013. https://www.vice.com/en/article/5gkpnk/fassy-b-heats-up-twelve-years-a-slave. Emphasis in original.

3. Walter Benjamin, *Illuminations: Essays and Reflections,* ed. Hannah Arendt, trans. Harry Zohn (New York: Schocken Books, 1969), 256.

Chapter 28: South of the South?

This essay was originally published as "If Jindal's Anti-Gay Order Reflects Southern 'Values,' New Orleans Has Seceded from the Region" in *The Lens*, May 29, 2015.

1. Emily Lane, "Gov. Bobby Jindal's Religious Freedom Executive Order: What Does It Actually Do?," NOLA.com/ *Times-Picayune*, May 23, 2015. https://www. nola.com/news/politics/article_a1eaa66e-9a72-586d-af3b-79e840171a05.html.

2. John Kennedy Toole, *A Confederacy of Dunces* (New York: Grove Press, 1988), 311.

3. Dominique Mosbergen, "Customers at New Orleans Restaurant Given Receipt with Racial Slur: 'N----r: 100% Dislike," *Huffington Post,* May 22, 2015. https:// www.huffpost.com/entry/racist-receipt-new-orleans_n_7419344.

4. See "New South Quackery: The Cultural Politics of *Duck Dynasty*," 77.

Chapter 29: From *Passé Blanc* to *Passé Noir*

This essay was originally published as "Politics of Passing: Rachel Dolezal Would Have Had an Easier Time of It in Old New Orleans" in *The Lens*, June 18, 2015.

1. See Kareem Abdul-Jabbar, "Let Rachel Dolezal Be as Black as She Wants to Be" *Time*, June 15, 2015. https://time.com/3921404/ rachel-dolezal-naacp-race-kareem-abdul-jabbar/.

2. Michael T. Jeffries, "Rachel Dolezal Story a Lesson on How Racism Works," *Boston Globe,* June 13, 2015.

3. Lafcadio Hearn, *Inventing New Orleans; Writings of Lafcadio Hearn,* ed. S. Frederick Starr (Jackson: University Press of Mississippi 2002), 22.

4. George Washington Cable, *The Grandissimes* (1880; repr. London: Penguin Classics, 1988), 107.

5. It can be found today in Alice Dunbar-Nelson, *The Works of Alice Dunbar-Nelson*, vol. 3, ed. Gloria T. Hull (Oxford: Oxford University Press, 1988.

6. Alice Dunbar-Nelson, *The Works of Alice Dunbar-Nelson*, vol. 3, ed. Gloria T. Hull (Oxford: Oxford University Press, 1988), 52.

7. Dunbar-Nelson, *Works*, 64.

8. Alcée Fortier, ed., *Louisiana Folk-Tales: In French Dialect and English Translation, Vol. 2* (London: Houghton, Mifflin and Co., 1895), 45.

9. Martha Ward, *Voodoo Queen: The Spirited Lives of Marie Laveau* (Jackson: University Press of Mississippi, 2004), 45.

Chapter 30: Monumental Decision:
Who Should Be Honored in Place of the Confederates?

This essay was originally published in *The Lens*, July 21, 2015.

1. Caryn Cossé Bell, *Revolution, Romanticism, and the Afro-Creole Protest Tradition in Louisiana, 1718–1868* (Baton Rouge: LSU Press, 1997), 29.

2. Carl Sandburg, "Chicago," in *The Norton Anthology of Modern Poetry*, 2nd ed., eds. Richard Ellmann and Robert O'Clair (New York: W. W. Norton, 1988).

Chapter 31: Beyoncé, New Orleans, and Afro-Creole Femininity

This essay was originally published as "New Orleans Is the Prime Ingredient in Beyoncé's Viral Video 'Hot Sauce'" in *The Lens*, February 19, 2016.

1. See Shantrelle Lewis, "'Formation' Exploits New Orleans' Trauma," Slate, February 10, 2016. https://slate.com/human-interest/2016/02/beyonces-formation-exploits-new-orleans-trauma.html.

2. See Maris Jones, "Dear Beyoncé, Katrina Is Not Your Story," BDG Blog, February 10, 2016. https://www.bgdblog.org/2016/02/dear-beyonce-katrina-is-not-your-story/.

3. Lilly Workneh, "Beyoncé Is Back and Unapologetically Black in New Music Video," *Huffington Post*, February 6, 2016. https://www.huffpost.com/entry/beyonce-formation-video_n_56b67a09e4b08069c7a789e6.

4. Yaba Blay, "On 'Jackson Five Nostrils,' Creole vs. 'Negro' and Beefing Over Beyoncé's 'Formation,'" *Color Lines*, February 8, 2016. https://www.colorlines.com/articles/jackson-five-nostrils-creole-vs-negro-and-beefing-over-beyonces-formation.

5. Quoted in Herbert Asbury, *French Quarter: An Informal History of the New Orleans Underworld* (New York: Alfred A. Knopf, 1936; repr. 2003), 133.

6. See Mary Gehman, *The Free People of Color of New Orleans: An Introduction* (Donaldsonville, LA: Margaret Media, 1994).

7. See Alecia P. Long, *The Great Southern Babylon: Sex, Race, and Respectability in New Orleans, 1865–1920* (Baton Rouge: LSU Press, 2004), 214–24.

8. George Washington Cable, *The Grandissimes: A Story of Creole Life* (1880; repr., London: Penguin Classics, 1988), 60.

Chapter 32: Carnival Racism—and Anti-Racism—for Dummies

This essay was originally published as "Behind the Zulu Blackface Flap: Liberal Guilt, Clueless Outsiders" in *The Lens*, March 10, 2017.

1. Doug MacCash, "The New Mardi Gras: Is There Really Such a Thing?" NOLA.com/*Times-Picayune*, February 22, 2017. http://www.mardigras.com/news/2017/02/mardi_gras_2017_new_red_beans.html.

2. See "The Golden Age of Carnival Is Now," 21.

3. See Eric Arnesen, *Waterfront Workers of New Orleans: Race, Class, and Politics, 1863-1923*. University of Illinois Press, 1991.

4. Todd A. Price, "Zulu Ride Leads to Apology and a Resignation at Tales of the Cocktail," NOLA.com/*Times-Picayune*, March 5, 2017. https://www.nola.com/archive/article_085f494b-fdde-5fcc-abcb-cf0e3908886e.html.

5. Price, "Zulu Ride."

Chapter 33: Confederates in the Dumpster

1. This essay was originally published as "Memo to Liberal Media: New Orleans Hasn't Just 'Joined' Movement Against White Supremacy" in *The Lens*, May 7, 2017.

See "Monumental Decision: Who Should Be Honored in Place of the Confederates?," 143.

2. Jesse J. Holland and Gerald Herbert (AP), "New Orleans Takes Down Confederate Monument," *Washington Post*, April 24, 2017.

3. Cristina Silva, "Racism in America: New Orleans Confederate Monuments Are Part of City's Long White Power History," *Newsweek*, April 24, 2017. https://www.newsweek.com/racism-america-confederate-statues-new-orleans-are-part-long-history-racial-588989.

4. Kevin Litten, "Nungesser Wants Trump's Help Keeping Confederate Monuments: Report," NOLA.com/*Times-Picayune*, April 10, 2017. https://www.nola.com/news/politics/article_023d8c49-d8a0-5aac-b730-d26971c029a9.html.

5. See Danielle Dreilinger, "Confederate Monument Removal Party Proposed by Take 'Em Down NOLA," NOLA.com/*Times-Picayune*, April 17, 2017. https://www.nola.com/news/politics/article_1210901c-d9e1-52a9-92ec-d403191347b5.html.

6. J. Morgan Kousser, *The Shaping of Southern Politics: Suffrage Restriction and the Establishment of the One-Party South, 1880–1910* (New Haven, CT: Yale University Press, 1974), 163.

7. David R. Harris, "'Property Values Drop When Blacks Move in, Because . . .': Racial and Socioeconomic Determinants of Neighborhood Desirability," *American Sociological Review* 64, no. 3 (1999): 462–63.

Chapter 34: Hollywood Jazz and the Storyville Complex

This essay was originally published as "Less to Cringe About: 'Bolden' Updates Hollywood's Evolving Riff on Jazz and Race" in *The Lens*, May 28, 2019.

1. Saturday Night Live, "New Orleans Vacation," YouTube, January 26, 2019. https://www.youtube.com/watch?v=l1vFZ6Wal3g.

2. Shannon Lee Dawdy, *Building the Devil's Empire: French Colonial New Orleans* (Chicago: University of Chicago Press, 2008), 28.

3. Lafcadio Hearn, *Inventing New Orleans: Writings of Lafcadio Hearn*, ed. S. Frederick Starr (Jackson: University Press of Mississippi, 2001), 144.

4. See "Beyoncé, New Orleans, and Afro-Creole Femininity," 148.

Epilogue: Katrina Playlist, a Jeremiad

1. This playlist was originally published in the *Rumpus*, August 23, 2015. Playlist at https://open.spotify.com/playlist/2NDgGCz2cJtsyK7GY6lqig?_php=1.

2. Just two larks still climb, still dreaming in the scented air (translated by the author).

3. Quoted in Ishmael Reed, *Mumbo Jumbo* (New York: Atheneum, 1972), 11.

SELECTED BIBLIOGRAPHY

Adorno, Theodor and Max Horkheimer. *Dialectic of Enlightenment.* Translated by John Cumming. London: Verso, 1997.

Asbury, Herbert. *French Quarter: An Informal History of the New Orleans Underworld.* 1936. Reprint, New York: Alfred A. Knopf, 2003.

Azzarello, Robert. *Three-Hundred Years of Decadence: New Orleans Literature and the Transatlantic World.* Baton Rouge: LSU Press, 2019.

Bakhtin, M. M. *Rabelais and His World.* Translated by Helene Iswolsky. Bloomington: Indiana University Press, 1984.

Bell, Caryn Cossé. *Revolution, Romanticism, and the Afro-Creole Protest Tradition in Louisiana, 1718–1868.* Baton Rouge: LSU Press, 1997.

Bourdieu, Pierre. *Distinction: A Social Critique of the Judgment of Taste.* Translated by Richard Nice. Cambridge, MA: Harvard University Press, 1984.

Cable, George Washington. *The Grandissimes.* 1880. Reprint, London: Penguin Classics, 1988.

Chopin, Kate. *The Awakening.* 1899. Reprint, New York: Avon, 1972.

Dawdy, Shannon Lee. *Building the Devil's Empire: French Colonial New Orleans.* Chicago: University of Chicago Press, 2008.

Desdunes, Rodolphe Lucien. *Nos hommes et notre histoire.* 1911. Edition Livres Généraux, 2010.

Dixon, Nancy, ed. *N.O. Lit: 200 Years of New Orleans Literature.* New Orleans: Lavender Ink, 2013.

Dunbar Nelson, Alice. *The Works of Alice Dunbar-Nelson, Vol. 3.* Edited by Gloria T. Hull. Oxford: Oxford University Press, 1988.

Emerson, Ralph Waldo. "Self-Reliance," *Essays.* Columbus, OH: Charles E. Merrill Co. 1907. Gutenberg e-book edition.

Florida, Richard. "Bohemia and Economic Geography." *Journal of Economic Geography* 2, no. 1 (January 2002): 55–71.

Frampton, Kenneth. "Towards a Critical Regionalism: Six Points for an Architecture of Resistance." In *The Anti-Aesthetic: Essays on Postmodern Culture,* edited by Hal Foster. New York: New Press, 1998.

Gayarré, Charles. *History of Louisiana, Vol. 1*. New Orleans: F.F. Hansell & Bro., 1903.

Gehman, Mary. *The Free People of Color of New Orleans: An Introduction*. Donaldsonville, LA: Margaret Media, 1994.

Gotham, Kevin Fox. *Authentic New Orleans: Race, Culture, and Tourism in the Big Easy*. New York: NYU Press, 2007.

Hearn, Lafcadio. *Inventing New Orleans; Writings of Lafcadio Hearn*. Edited by S. Frederick Starr. Jackson: University Press of Mississippi, 2002.

Jameson, Frederic. *The Political Unconscious: Narrative as a Socially Symbolic Act*. Ithaca, NY: Cornell University Press, 1981.

Jones, LeRoi (Amiri Baraka). *Blues People: Negro Music in White America*. 1963. Reprint, New York: William Morrow, 1999.

Kousser, J. Morgan. *The Shaping of Southern Politics: Suffrage Restriction and the Establishment of the One-Party South, 1880–1910*. New Haven, CT: Yale University Press, 1974.

Long, Alecia P. *The Great Southern Babylon: Sex, Race, and Respectability in New Orleans, 1865–1920*. Baton Rouge: LSU Press, 2004.

Marx, Karl. *Capital: A Critique of Political Economy, Volume 1*. Edited by Frederick Engels, translated by Samuel Moore and Edward Aveling. Moscow, USSR: Progress Publishers, 1887. Online edition at marxists.org.

Nietzsche, Friedrich. *Beyond Good and Evil*. Translated by R. J. Hollingdale. London: Penguin Classics, 1984.

Osbey, Brenda Marie. *All Saints: New and Selected Poems*. Baton Rouge: LSU Press, 1997.

Reed, Ishmael. *Mumbo Jumbo*. New York: Atheneum, 1972.

von Reizenstein, Ludwig. *The Mysteries of New Orleans*. Translated by Steven Rowan. Baltimore, MD: Johns Hopkins University Press, 2002.

Silk, Michael. "Nietzsche, Decadence, and the Greeks." *New Literary History* 35, no. 4 (Autumn 2004): 587–606.

Toole, John Kennedy. *A Confederacy of Dunces*. New York: Grove Press, 1988.

Trotsky, Leon. *Literature and Revolution*. Translated by Rose Strunsky. New York: International Publishers, 1925.

Williams, Raymond. "Base and Superstructure in Marxist Cultural Theory." *New Left Review* I/82 (November–December 1973).

——. *Marxism and Literature*. Oxford: Oxford University Press, 1977.

Williams, Tennessee. *A Streetcar Named Desire*. 1947. Reprint, New York: New Directions Publishing, 2004.